Cape Verde

Other Places
Cape Verde
Callie Flood

Published by
OTHER PLACES PUBLISHING

First edition
Published June 2010

Cape Verde
Other Places Travel Guide
Written by: Callie Flood
Cover designed by: Carla Zetina-Yglesias
Published by:
Other Places Publishing
www.otherplacespublishing.com

ISBN 978-0-9822619-2-7

The Author

Callie Flood

After receiving her degree in Literature at the University of Massachusetts, Callie packed her suitcases filled with ideals and began a two year adventure in the archipelago of Cape Verde. The rich experience provided her the opportunity to return independently to merge her understanding of the culture and "down-to-Earth" realities of life in Cape Verde with her passion for writing. Through this book, Callie hopes to offer the reader an informed and personal guide to the fascinating diversity of this island nation.

Contributing Writer: Brittany Kuhn

Brittany Kuhn served as a Peace Corps volunteer on the island of Fogo from 2006-2008. During her service she taught English, worked on community development projects, and sought funding grants for those seeking medical assistance in the town of Ponta Verde. Brittany has also worked in Brazil and with USAID in Mozambique. Currently she is pursuing her Master's degree in International Human Rights as a Fellow at the University of Denver, Colorado.

Acknowledgements

The writing of this book would not have been possible without the help of many people and organizations. First, Peace Corps Cape Verde and its staff introduced me to the country while offering a life changing experience. Thanks to Jacob, Vanda and Kelly (and Ná) from Language Link Lda. for all the help and support, the short lived EU hiking crew—Ana, Klara, Enrico, Konstantin, and various others along with the many friends I made along the way. There are many fellow volunteers from Cape Verde who contributed in large and small ways—from responding to incessant emails and offering incredible insight to letting me crash on a couch, spare bed or floor for a couple of days. Some are acknowledged in the book, but thanks to (in no particular order) (Santiago) Emily L., Alex A., Tina R., Rob S., Brian N., Andrew H., Dacia D., Jessica S., Dannielle T., Courtney P., Joe D., Sarah M., Scott J., Anthony Justin B., Mike M., Andrew V., Adeyemi A. (Fogo) Andrea G., Lauren D., Dave T., Sean W., Judy D., Andrew B., Sarah R., Jonny M. (Brava) Ana (Maio) Rachelle F., Julia K., Stephanie L. (Boa Vista) Leland S., Rhonda, SHON! (Sal) Jacky L., Kyle C., Caryn S., Leah T. (Sao Nicolau) Ross G., Nate L., Nelson, Brett, Brett, Chase (Sao Vicente) Lindsay W., Cathryn D., Andrew K., ASANGA, JOÃO C. (Santo Antao) Christina W., Dove & Josh R., Tiffani M., Daron C., Nadia F., Lauren K., Laurie H., Leanna D., Phil D... and I am sure that I am missing some names. Lastly, I need to thank my family for their love and support and Fraser for unending patience, advice and so much more.

Quick Reference

Official Name: The Republic of Cape Verde (*Republica de Cabo Verde*)

Barlavento ("windward" islands): Santo Antão, São Vicente, Santa Luzia (uninhabited), São Nicolau, Sal, Boa Vista

Sotavento ("leeward" islands): Maio, Santiago, Fogo, Brava

Official language: Portuguese; Recognized regional dialect: Kriolu, also known as Creole

Location: Atlantic Ocean, approximately 604 km (375 miles) off the coast of West Africa

Country size: The islands have a combined size of just over 4,000 square kilometers (1,557 square miles). Santiago is the largest island (990 sq km) and Santa Luzia is the smallest (35 sq km).

Coordinates: 16 00 N, 24 00 W

Total area: 4,033 sq km (slightly larger than Rhode Island)

Climate: Temperate; warm, dry summer; precipitation meager and very erratic

Terrain: Steep, rugged, rocky, volcanic

Lowest point: Atlantic Ocean 0 m

Highest point: Mt. Pico do Fogo 2,829 m (volcano on Fogo)

Population: 429,474 (2009 estimate)

Ethnic groups: Creole (mulatto) 71%, African 28%, European 1%

Government: Republic; Major political parties: African Party for Independence of Cape Verde (PAICV) and Movement for Democracy (MPD)

President: Pedro Pires (PAICV); Prime Minister: José Maria Neves (PAICV)

Flag: Blue with white and red horizontal stripes, a circle of ten yellow stars

GDP (gross domestic product): $1.762 billion

Per capita: US$3,498 (2008 estimate)

Currency: Cape Verdean Escudo (CVE)

Religion: Roman Catholic (mixed with indigenous beliefs); Protestant

Life expectancy: 71.6 years (2009 estimate)

International telephone code: +238

Time zone: GMT -1 (Cape Verde does not adjust time for daylight savings)

Electricity supply: Voltage = 220 V, Frequency = 50 Hz, Plug= C&F, Round two-pin attachment plugs and Schuko plugs

Quick Reference

General business hours: Business hours are generally split into two periods with a two-hour lunch break. Schedules vary by business, but are usually between 8:00-12:30 and 14:30-18:00, Monday to Friday. In cities and larger towns, most stores are open for an extended period on Saturday mornings, but on Sundays many businesses, even restaurants, close their doors.

Metric System: Cape Verde's measurements are based on the traditional metric system.

Public holidays (2010): Jan. 1 (New Year's Day), Jan. 20 (National Heroes' Day), Feb.16 (*Carnaval*), Feb. 17 (Ash Wednesday), May 1 (Labor Day), May 19 (Municipal Day), June 1 (Children's Day), July 5 (Independence Day), Aug. 15 (*Nossa Senhora da Graça* – Assumption/Our Lady of Grace Day), Sept. 12 (Nationality Day), Nov. 1 (All Saints' Day), Dec. 25 (Christmas Day) *For island specific holidays, please refer to the relevant island section.*

Pricing Key

Accomodations:
This scale roughly encompasses the cost of one night's stay. Actual prices of rooms may vary slightly depending on specifics of the room (A/C, balcony, etc.). Please check description to see if breakfast is included.

$ = 1000$ - 2500$
$$ = 2500$ - 5000$
$$$ = 5000$ - 7500$
$$$$ = 7500$ - 12500$
$$$$$ = 12500$ - 20000$
$$$$$$ = 20000$ +

Dining Out:
This scale roughly encompasses the cost of one entrée. Drinks and appetizers are an additional price. Price varies greatly depending on the dish chosen (chicken +/- 500$, lobster +/- 1200$).

$ = 100$ – 500$
$$ = 500$ - 800$
$$$ = 800$ - 1200$
$$$$ = 1200$ +

Prices are in Cape Verdean Escudo unless otherwise noted. Exchage rates at time of publication (June 2010):

100 CVE = 1.35 U.S. Dollars (USD)
100 CVE =.85 Pound Sterline (GBP)
100 CVE = 1 Euro (EUR)

Book Icons

Author recommended accommodation or eatery

Accommodations

Airport

Bank/ATM

Bar/nightclub

Beach

Bus Station/Stop

Capital

Church

City/Village

Clinic

Ferry Dock

Hospital

Information Office

Landmark

Mountain

Pharmacy

Point of Interest

Police

Post Office

Restaurant/eatery

Contents

Introduction

By Brittany Kuhn

Preconceived notions of Cape Verde can be disappointing. Those expecting the African "bush" experience will find themselves sulking in their safari gear. And similarly, those prepped for a perfectly functioning tropical paradise of pina coladas and cabanas should pack up their hula instructional guides and head straight for Hawaii. Cape Verde is an experience all its own.

Yet for those who can get past the stereotypes, pre-conceived notions, and erroneous expectations, Cape Verde's raw, gritty beauty offers much more than the typical vacation. Those with an open mind will find that it's stark contrasts of colorful clothing and dusty paths, of white sand beaches and rural villages, its energetic dancing and mournful ballads, will enchant you, enthrall you, and become part of you. Indeed, the departing nostalgia of its rich music and inviting people are what become the traveler's most valued souvenirs.

A disclaimer to those taking on this forgotten land: first impressions of the nation will only take one so far. Cape Verde is a constant contradiction, and travelers will find that every island, street corner, or inquisitive step can lead one into a different world. For this reason, it is unlikely for you to come away from this book with a singular and distinct definition of what Cape Verde is. And though you will now be able to point it out on a map, there is no way to accurately pinpoint the country itself. In the end, ultimately, Cape Verde will be what you make it.

Traveling in this country has its frustrations and its struggles. Yet above all, Cape Verde is about relationships. It is about finding yourself in a place completely foreign to you, perhaps a place you could not have imagined or didn't know existed, and watching in amazement as the people there make you feel like it's home.

THE ISLANDS

In the spirit of the national dish *cachupa*, a corn-based stew that requires the inclusion of any and all ingredients, the country of Cape Verde is a mix. It is a seasoning of Portugal, a dash of Brazil, a pinch of the Caribbean, a hint of America and a slice of Africa. These multi-national flavors are manifested in the clothing that people wear, the multiplicity of languages and cultures encountered in urban areas, and the hodge-podge collection of imported foods that line the shelves of even the smallest shops. Although Cape Verde is considered part of Africa, upon visiting, it is unmistakable that the islands have a recipe all their own.

For the tireless traveler, the varying terrain of Cape Verde's distinctive islands serves up a unique beauty that will appeal to any taste. The archipelago consists of ten islands that offer everything from isolated windswept beaches, mountainous misty forests, giant salt flats and black volcanic lava flows. During the dry season (November through June), the desert effect of drought is inescapable, but the brief rainy season (intermittent showers from July through October) breathes a vibrant, green life into the rocky slopes of the more mountainous islands, turning them into a lush paradise. What makes this place worth visiting is the beauty, from subtle to striking, and the contagious candor of its people.

The best way to enjoy Cape Verde is to come with patience and flexibility, as each island has a different dialect of Kriolu, traditional dishes, and unique cultural customs that define the region. There are top-of-the-line luxury hotels with the latest technology as well as small-town pensions (*pensões*) in remote villages of times past. Such diversity offers something for everyone. Yet the most inviting and predictable aspect of the country is its *morabeza*—the charm, candor and genuine hospitality of its people—and the vibrant, rich diversity of its land. These are the steadfast staples of Cape Verde.

They may be known as the Forgotten Islands, but they are anything but forgettable.

Santo Antão

Santo Antão is just a 50-minute ferry ride from Mindelo and is famous for its spectacular heights and staggering beauty. This, the second largest of the islands, is notorious for steep ridges lined with stone terraces and the perpetually green northeast where people live entirely off the fruits of their agricultural labor and the near constant production of grogue, a strong sugar cane-based rum. Visit for stunning hikes and breathtaking views, the festival of São João (June 23-25), a glimpse of agricultural life at its fullest and a taste of grogue and goat cheese.

São Vicente

Home of the "northern capital" of Mindelo, São Vicente is the second most populous island with both sandy beaches and rocky terrain. Visit for the celebration of Carnaval, the music festival Baía das Gatas, New Years, the rich culture of music and arts and the open, welcoming culture that makes Mindelo famous.

Santa Luzia

Santa Luzia is the smallest island of Cape Verde. Once home to a small agricultural community, this island was abandoned due to desertification in the 18th century and has been uninhabited ever since. It currently houses a meteorology station and groups of fishermen on week-long trips from Salamansa, São Vicente. Curious travelers can visit Santa Luzia as a day trip from São Vicente.

São Nicolau

São Nicolau is likely the first island to be noticed on a map for its strange shape, but is often overlooked by visitors. Much of the island and expanse of coastline is barren and uninhabited, but there are hidden verdant pockets and a population that takes pride in the beauty and tranquility that exist here. Visit for the feeling of true isolation, endless exploration and the grit and humility of residents.

Sal

Sal boasts 350 days of sunshine a year and has the most developed tourism industry. Visitors will find an array of resorts and restaurants unlike anywhere else in the archipelago. Visit for the water sports, all-inclusive resorts and the massive saltpans of Salinas/Pedra de Lume.

Boa Vista

Boa Vista (Portuguese for "good view") is known for its marine turtles, traditional music and sand dunes. It is also proclaimed as one of the best spots in the world for kite surfing and windsurfing; the World Windsurfing Championships have been held in the bay of Sal Rei drawing water sports devotees from around the world. Visit for the water sports; wind surf-ing/kite surfing, diving, snorkeling; resorts and intimate pensões, turtle tracking (August/September) and miles of untouched beaches.

Barlavento
Islands

Porto Novo

Mindelo

Vila de
Ribeira Brava

Espargos

Sal Rei

Maio

Maio has miles of stunning, pristine beaches that are almost untouched by developments. The island offers the beauty of Sal and Boa Vista, yet is complemented by a distinct peacefulness. Visit for a leisurely paced exploration and the savoring of time on isolated beaches.

Santiago

Santiago is the largest, most populous, most ethnically diverse and historically richest of the islands. Praia, the nation's capital, is home to almost one quarter of the population. Upon leaving the city, it is possible to experience a little of everything – long hikes through verdant mountains, sandy beaches, hidden coves and small, lonely villages reminiscent of the historical origins. Visit for the past, the present and everything in between.

Fogo

Fogo is an archetypal volcanic island. The land and people possess an enchantment unique to the lava-strewn slopes. With its visible volcanic scars, tf is island has a dramatic beauty amidst the somewhat strange environment. Visit to climb the highest peak in Cape Verde, pass the festival of N nô São Filipe (April 28-May1) and drink wine from grapes grown in the fertile black soil.

Brava

Brava is also likely to be overlooked by tourists, as it is difficult to get to (and to get off of). Those that make the trip are delighted by the perpetually flowering Vila Nova Sntra, endless walks, and the hidden gem of Fajã de Água. It is difficult to overlook the staggering peak of Fogo off in the distant horizon. Visit for the peace found only in the most obscure places in the world, long meandering and sometimes challenging walks.

Vila do Maio

☆ Praia

● São Filipe

Vila Nova
Sintra ●

N

Cape Verde

20 km

*Sotavento
Islands*

The Forgotten Islands

History

PORTUGUESE COLONIALISM

Cape Verde is a nation that has endured a long history of mystique, exploitation, and tragedy. Centuries ago it was shrouded in baffling tales of overseas exploration, as weary voyagers who journeyed across the seas were known to disappear south of the Canary Islands, never to be seen again. Divers who have recently investigated the archipelago's reefs estimate that over 600 boats have been shipwrecked amidst Cape Verde's reefs, as a result of intense and unreliable coastal winds. Due to these erratic wind patterns, the islands sat undiscovered and uninhabited until the Portuguese settlers, through the improvement of nautical techniques, stumbled upon their shores between 1455 and 1461 under the reign of Prince Henry "the Navigator."

Though countless have laid claim to discovery of the islands, official credit goes to explorers Antonio de Noli and Diogo Gomes. Upon arrival, it is rumored that the islands were originally named Cape Verde not after the archipelago's own verdant greenery (in fact, the islands often suffer from frequent drought), but rather due to the vibrant coast of neighboring Senegal, nearly 300 miles to the east.

The Portuguese officially began colonization of Cape Verde in 1462, after recognizing strategic potential in the islands' ideal locale amidst the Atlantic Ocean's trade routes. As a result, small communities began to develop, comprised of Portuguese and Spanish settlers, many of whom were encouraged to live there through incentives such as lucrative trading rites along the Western African coast. Initially, colonists intended to establish the region for agricultural production, where they employed slaves to work within the dried-out riverbed valleys in an effort to yield what little they could from the meager natural resources of the islands.

Cape Verde's soil, however, simply could not provide enough produce to enable any tangible profit, and the severity of a harsh, arid climate and persistent droughts quickly led settlers to abandon such aspirations.

Over time, Portuguese leaders began to write off the anticipated economic potential of Cape Verde as a useless venture, and the myth of forgotten islands almost came to pass—until the emergence of the transatlantic slave trade. During the peak years of mass human trafficking from the African content to the Americas, the islands (particularly Santiago, where the capital now resides) served a fundamental role for Portuguese colonialists as a vital port and trading center for ships carrying cargoes of human slaves.

By the time ships of slaves had reached the islands, those who had survived the brutal journey were considered extremely desirable and of particular advantage to slave traders. They had often learned Portuguese words (and could therefore understand orders) and had often been baptized. Clearly, conditions for slaves were horrendous. Journeys from countries such as Mali, Guinea-Bissau, and Senegal were brutal, and those who made it to the archipelago had endured months of confinement at sea surrounded by illness, intolerable conditions, and uncertainty.

Yet slavery was not the only way in which Cape Verde's location served a crucial role for the Portuguese. As the islands were positioned along the great trade routes from Europe and Africa to the New World, they also provided harbors for ships to refuel. Cape Verde became an important coaling and resupply stop for whaling and transatlantic shipping. Throughout the 1500s, Cape Verde became well known as a place to restock on essential basic needs such as food and water before journeying across the treacherous Atlantic Ocean. Maize, beans, abundant salt from the island of *Sal*, and dried meat were sold at inflated prices, along with livestock, animals, and hides.

The slave trade allowed for the trade of goods from along the African coast as well, including items such as ivory, wax, honey, and gold. Wealthy Africans bought European treasures such as beads, silver, and coral. Untold items were exchanged during this time, as language, information, plants, disease, and many other transactions were bartered in the import-export epicenter that was Cape Verde. When the Portuguese colony reached its peak in the 1600-1700s, its prominence as a trade post was booming. So much so that nearly three-quarters of Portuguese national revenues were garnered as a result of profits received through the slave trade in Cape Verde.

It was not to last, however. Increasingly competitive international actors began their quests as rival nations, intent on conquering key slave posts and securing wealth for themselves. At this time, there was also stirring discontent among Cape Verdean inhabitants who had watched Portugal profit so substantially from their personal efforts. Resentment toward the colonizing nation that continued to treat the islands simply as a "storehouse" for slaves grew, and people who lived in Cape Verde started to create their own cultural identities, developing a way of life that was utterly separate from distant Portugal.

Those who had settled and created lives among the islands (consisting mainly of Portuguese and European men) increasingly began to form relationships with female slaves on the islands, resulting in emerging generations that were ethnically and culturally mixed. As there was no prior indigenous population on the islands, the descendants of interracial families began to create their own unique identities—and to see themselves as utterly distinct from the colonizers who sought to maintain increasingly tight control over the population. After all, those in Cape Verde were subject to heavy restrictions; they were prohibited from doing business with any non-Portuguese traders and coerced into contracts that enabled unfair monopoly margins. Those who did not comply with Portuguese stipulations experienced severe punishment and death threats for disobeying trading laws, which further exacerbated high-running tensions between Cape Verdeans and the Portuguese. By 1700, those within Cape Verde seemed past the breaking point.

During this time of widespread territorial expansion, several factors contributed to a shift in Cape Verde's future. Portugal was being drawn into the War of the Spanish Succession, which quickly became a top national priority. The eventual demise of the slave trade in 1876 led to a decline in Portuguese use of the islands. Soon Cape Verde became nothing more than a convenient place to deport felons, prisoners and society's outcasts. According to historians, nearly 2,500 of these *degrados* were dumped into the Cape Verdean population in the 1800s.

Portugal had officially relaxed its grip upon the archipelago, as well as its interest, and inhabitants were more or less left to fend for themselves. Meanwhile, periods of intense drought and the subsequent failure of crops during the second half of the 20th century resulted in devastating famines that ravaged the nation over recent centuries and prompted the deaths of thousands of Cape Verdeans. In a period of three years (from 1773-1776), almost half the population had died. The myth of the Forgotten Islands appeared to have prevailed—Cape Verde was left abandoned, unequipped to protect itself, and forgotten at sea.

Over time, drought continued to plague the nation and the islands became increasingly unstable, impoverished, and riddled by starvation. In 1945 alone an estimated 30,000 perished amid a drought-stricken crop season that failed to yield. By the 1900s, due to the lack of resources and high unemployment rates, many Cape Verdeans were forced to emigrate. They began to escape by the thousands to neighboring islands and countries, which has continued throughout the decades. Currently, the amount of Cape Verdeans living throughout the world is far greater than the population of those living within the islands themselves. One is likely to encounter pockets of Cape Verdeans in most of Europe—Portugal, France, Holland, Luxemburg, and Spain to name a few. In the United States, large communities have been established along the east coast from Boston to Providence, due to years of migration through the whaling trade. Ships would stop to rest and refuel on Brava and Fogo, often taking in additional crew members from the eager and knowledgeable seafaring population who sought escape, adventure, or a means of better providing for families who were left behind.

Today, it is nearly impossible to find a resident of either Fogo or Brava islands who cannot boast some family in the United States. These emigrants now serve as fundamental sources in the island-nation's economy; they send generous remittances to families back home and therefore assist in supporting much-needed national income that makes up close to 20 percent of the country's overall GDP.

REVOLUTION AND INDEPENDENCE

Cape Verde endured a painful history of slavery, colonialism, and famine. The 20th century, however, brought an era of revolution. A nation that had been exploited and then left to survive on its own had fostered a race of people who were resilient, strong, and accustomed to fighting for survival. As a Portuguese-African nation, Cape Verdeans were able to lean upon opportunistic qualities such as higher levels of education, which spurred a revolutionary movement that spread throughout other African nations and ultimately became key to successfully triumphing over the fascist dictatorship of Portugal's supreme reign.

The most crucial contributing element that led to Cape Verdean independence was actually made possible by the colonizers themselves. Since the Portuguese identified the mixed heritage of the Cape Verdean population as closer to their own identities than other African nationalities, Cape Verdeans were granted an "honorary" form of Portuguese citizenship and the archipelago became well-known as the educational hub of all Portuguese colonies in Africa. As such, a group of lighter-skinned Cape Verdeans emerged that were educated, employed, and somewhat respected by the Portuguese. This sense of Portuguese commonality provided select Cape Verdeans with upward social mobility and

Historical Timeline of Cape Verde

1456   First European settlers arrived in Cape Verde.

1495   Cape Verde became a Portuguese colony.

1956   Cape Verdean-born Amilcar Cabral founded the African Party for Independence of Guinea and Cape Verde (PAIGC) in Guinea-Bissau.

1960   PAIGC-led liberation war against Portuguese rule in Cape Verde and Guinea-Bissau.

1975   Cape Verde became independent and adopted a constitution of unity with Guinea-Bissau.

1980   Cape Verde opted for independence after a coup in Guinea-Bissau.

1981   African Party for the Independence of Cape Verde (PAICV) replaced the PAIGC and became the country's single party.

1991   Antonio Mascarenhas Monteiro became president in Cape Verde's first free election.

1992   A new constitution was formed which introduced a multi-party system.

1996   Mascarenhas Monteiro was re-elected and his party, the Movement for Democracy (MPD), won the majority vote during parliamentary elections.

2001   (January) The government accepted defeat in parliamentary elections, which led the former ruling PAICV party back to power.

2001   (March) Pedro Pires (PAICV) was elected president after beating his rival, Carlos Veiga (MPD).

2005   The Millennium Challenge Corporation (MCC) signed a five-year, US$110 million contract with the Government of Cape Verde aimed at contributing to the transformation of their economy from aid-dependency to sustainable, private-sector led growth.

2006   (January-February) Pedro Pires was re-elected in closely-contested presidential polls.

2006   (June) Approximately 7,000 NATO troops participated in war games on São Vicente Island, the organization's first major deployment in Africa.

2007   (December) Cape Verde became the 153rd country to join the World Trade Organization (WTO), as well as the first African nation to succeed in entering the organization as a member since its creation in 1995.

increased status in a way that enabled motivation for literacy advancement and progressive thinking. Utilizing such opportunities, this select group began to thoughtfully cultivate the essence of *Kabuverdianidade* ("Cape Veredanness") through art, music, poetry, and journalism; defining their own distinct culture.

As a strong self-identity of culture began to take root in Cape Verdeans' attitudes about themselves and their entitlements, the more they became outraged by the history of famine and abuse by their colonizers. These became the early embers that sparked and then fanned into flames a willingness to risk the belief that independence was the only future that would allow the islands to emerge as a viable home to its inhabitants.

One of the leading educated and enduring figures to ignite this movement was Amilcar Cabral, revered even today as "Cape Verde's only national hero." He was born on September 12, 1924 in Bafata, Portuguese Guinea and was the son of a Guinean mother and Cape Verdean father who is claimed to have fathered 62 children. Cabral was educated at a *liçéu* (school) in Cape Verde where he was strongly influenced by first-hand exposure to the great famines of the early 1900s. Cabral soon distinguished himself as a leader through his ability to inspire Africans with self-identity and inherent pride for nationalism. His revolutionary beliefs flourished as a student in Lisbon, where he founded student movements dedicated to African liberation, and fostered ideas of liberalism that spread throughout the colonies.

Cabral was clearly instrumental in forming a number of independence movements on the African continent. In 1956 he formed a small movement group that he called PAIGC (Party for the Independence of Guinea and Cape Verde or *Partido Africano da Independência da Guiné e Cabo Verde*), which was later followed by the MPLA (The Popular Movement for the Liberation of Angola or *Movimento Popular Libertação de Angola*). Through these actions, Cabral sought to shake up the typically accepting nature of Africans who had become accustomed to their plight and therefore were generally apathetic toward ideas of independence. His original peaceful approach to seeking improved conditions for Africans, however, led to a series of empowered strikes and protests, some of which led to massacres and death.

Back in Cape Verde, unsuccessful rebellions were being suppressed by the arrests of various rebel groups. Despite his many efforts against the persecution of Portuguese colonial rule, Cabral soon became aware that his safety was at stake among his own comrades. He is known to have said: "If anybody is going to hurt me, it will be someone who is among us. Nobody else can destroy the PAIGC, except ourselves." Indeed, on January 20, 1973 Amilcar Cabral was assassinated in Conakry by leaders of the PAIGC who had turned against him. What he did for the liberation movement in Cape Verde, however, elevated Cabral to the status of national hero, and he is often credited as the driving force behind the movement for independence against the colonial rule of oppression.

Following the 1974 coup/revolution in Portugal, and shortly after the European nation decided to abandon its colonial empire, the islands were granted independence on July 5, 1975. PAIGC became an active political party in Cape Verde. In December 1974, the PAIGC and Portugal signed an agreement calling for a transitional government composed of both Portuguese and Cape Verdean citizens. On June 30, 1975, an official National Assembly was elected, which received an acknowledgment of independence from Portugal on July 5, 1975. Even after independence, the harsh climate of the islands made life extremely difficult for inhabitants, as frequent droughts and famines continued to plague the archipelago. Thus, a large diaspora of Cape Verdeans are now found around the globe.

Government

The Republic of Cape Verde is a sovereign country that is considered a representative and stable democratic republic that serves and functions as a parliamentary system. There are three branches of government—the executive, legislative, and judicial. The executive branch is led by the head of state, President Pedro Pires, who was elected by popular vote for a five-year term. The head of government is the prime minister, José Maria Neves, who is nominated by the National Assembly, appointed by the president, and is responsible for the appointment of ministers and secretaries of the state. The executive branch consists of the Cabinet of Cape Verde, the legislative branch is comprised of the National Assembly, and the judicial branch consists of the Supreme Court. Members of the National Assembly are elected by popular vote for 5-year terms, like the president. Three parties currently hold seats—PAICV with 40, MPD with 30, and the Cape Verdean Independent Democratic Union (UCID) with 2.

Local governance among the islands is organized by *conselhos*, also known as counties or councils, depending upon the context. Each island is divided into these *conselhos* and for each *conselho* there is a local governing body known as a *Câmara Municipal*, or Municipal Chamber. Each *Câmara* has a council, composed of representatives from a variety of organizations within the *conselho* who serve as a consultative body. This building of local governance can be likened to a city hall, where a president oversees the council in its services to the community.

The local government ideally exists to promote and enhance the quality of life for those living within the community by providing a range of services and financial opportunities, such as fostering various civic and cultural activities like art shows, stage performances, exhibits and festivals. There are 22 different *conselhos* within the nation of Cape Verde.

Economy

Cape Verde's economy, in comparison to many of its African neighbors, has come a long way. What were once known as Forgotten Islands have now emerged as "Africa's Jewel of the Atlantic" and one of just a few small island developing states to show economic promise. In 2007, it managed to successfully graduate from the United Nation's list of least-developed countries to a nation of developing status; a feat that only one other African nation has proven able to achieve. Given the significant challenges due to small size, insularity and geographic make-up, it is remarkable that the nation has defied its many economic barriers for growth. The Cape Verdean economy has steadily progressed since the late 1990s and has demonstrated relatively strong performance in recent years, considering its many shortcomings. GDP is estimated to have increased by 6.1 percent in 2008 alone and it passed a fifth review of the International Monetary Fund's Policy Support Instrument (PSI) in December 2008.

Additionally, the World Bank named Cape Verde the "Best Managed African Economy of the Year," and according to the United Nations Development Program Report in 2007-2008, Cape Verde has one of the highest life expectancies (68 years for men and 74 for women) and adult literacy rates (81.2 percent) in Africa. It has enjoyed a stable democratic system and on July 4, 2005 became the third country to sign a contract with the U.S. Government-funded Millennium Challenge Corporation (MCC); the five-year assistance package is worth over $110 million, which will be devoted to addressing rural economic expansion and infrastructure development.

However, these proclamations of economic stability may be premature as Cape Verde's graduation into developing world status poses more challenges than immediate benefits to society members. According to a 2008 report from the Organization for Economic Cooperation and Development (OECD), Cape Verde has needed one of the highest levels of overseas assistance per person in Africa. Due to few economic resources, poor rainfall and limited access to fresh water, about 90 percent of food that is consumed in the nation is imported from abroad, many of it in the form of aid. Another

20 percent of the country's GDP is comprised of remittances from other Cape Verdeans who are living in developed countries such as the United States or Portugal, where there are more opportunities for work and education.

The country manages to export only a small quantity of goods, and has yet to find ways to properly utilize untapped markets. Over 70 percent of the Cape Verdean population is living in rural areas, but agricultural goods constitute only nine percent of the overall GDP. Massive reduction in access to official development assistance, particularly in rural areas where infrastructure is lacking and community members rely on aid programs to survive, has the potential to increase poverty in areas where development is needed most.

Cape Verde has very few natural resources and limited rainfall, which attributes to low agricultural production, making the economy of Cape Verde heavily reliant upon crop yields. Approximately a third of the Cape Verdean population engage in agriculture and live off the land producing the main staple of corn as well as bananas, sugarcane, coffee, fruits, and vegetables. Four of the ten islands—Santiago, Brava, Fogo and Santo Antão—have environments conducive to farming, and therefore their products normally support a significant amount of the nation's produce. For the moment, any hope of increasing agriculture relies on the ability to improve water sources through irrigation techniques. In order to make up for the inability to provide for more than ten percent of the population, however, over ninety percent of goods that are consumed in Cape Verde are imported from abroad and rural Cape Verdeans in particular rely heavily upon international aid and family remittances from abroad to make ends meet.

As a result, Cape Verde's economy is service-oriented. Commerce, transport, and public services make up more than seventy percent of the overall GDP. Since 1991, the government has maintained market-oriented economic policies that welcome foreign investors and have opened the door for an extensive privatization program. The country's top official priorities are to pursue market economy and private sector projects, particularly through the promotion of tourism and fisheries.

In many ways, it appears that Cape Verdean officials are seeking to replace their previously substantial reliance on foreign aid and remittances with free-market policies that attract foreign investors in aims of privatization. The nation's growing construction industry is a result of the tourism boom and further encouraged by the construction of second homes for the strong presence of ex-patriots and elites in the country. Large-scale projects and development has been flowing forth at a high rate. In October of 2008, the largest hotel complex in the nation opened up on the sandy island of Boa Vista. That same year, work began on the US$1 billion Cesaria resort in São Vicente, named after the country's most popular singer. A number of current projects, however, are currently being stalled due to credit constraints. On the tiny island of Sal alone, five resort projects have been postponed.

Even with the benefit of external aid, there has arguably been inadequate attention focused on improving investment in agriculture and productivity on some islands. Fishing provides the best potential for utilizing the nation's resources. Although it is severely underdeveloped, it still accounted for nearly 10 percent of Cape Verde's total export value in 2007. Once capacity and investment increased, the nation saw a surge in fish exports, growing by 62 percent in 2008. Though the country has a large amount of shellfish, only small quantities are currently exported. Utilizing these resources could be a prime solution to the nation's goals of advancement.

Cape Verde's strategic harbor locations along the mid-Atlantic air and sea routes has aided the country and resulted in significant improvements, particularly in Mindelo and Sal. There was approximately $407 million in foreign investments made, with 58 percent allocated to tourism, 17 percent to industry, 4 percent for infrastructure and 21 percent for fisheries and similar services. Chinese and Spanish investors seem to have recognized this potential more quickly than Cape Verdean officials. Both countries have endeavored to renovate shipyards and cold-storage plants on the islands through private investment projects.

Despite the small-town feel of rural communities amidst these enchanting islands, one can't help but acknowledge that the growing economy of Cape Verde is in a constant state of flux, particularly in urban areas and tourism destinations. New buildings and businesses continue to pile upon one another in a push toward socioeconomic progress in an effort to combat poverty. Business ownerships and locations change here with the cyclical nature of the sun, and the nation is particularly vulnerable to fluctuations in international economic markets. Considering the fragility of this environment, this guide makes every effort to promote domestically owned and operated ventures in a way that supports sustainable local tourism and development projects that enable local community members.

Geography

The ten-island archipelago located 375 miles off the Western coast of Senegal is an area that comparatively is only slightly larger than Rhode Island, the state that many Cape Verdean-Americans call home. The islands themselves are split into two groups. The *Barlavento* (windward—the point from which the wind blows), or northern islands, consist of Santo Antão, São Vicente, Santa Luzia, São Nicolau, Sal and Boa Vista and the *Sotavento* (leeward—the point to which the wind blows), or southern islands, consist of Brava, Fogo, Santiago and Maio.

The southernmost archipelago of the Macaronesian Island groups, Cape Verde's origin is similar to that of its northern neighbors, the Azores and Canaries, and other famous hotspot island chains including the Hawaiian, Samoan and the Galapagos archipelagos. These islands are thought to have developed as a result of geologic hotspots that force lava to swell up from a fissure, or mantle plume, in the tectonic plate. As the plate shifts, the flow of lava continues creating islands separate from one another. Cape Verde is a part of the African Plate and is considered by geologists as active due to the eruption of Fogo in 1995.

To the tourist arriving at the international airport in Sal, the nearly flat and barren landscape may not fit the typical volcanic description, but its origin is undeniable when gazing up at the magnificent peak of Fogo, the youngest of the islands, dating back only 100,000 years. The variation in terrain makes the islands unique from one another, but also marks their difference in age. Unlike the Hawaiian archipelago that is a fury of growth and development, Cape Verde has taken a leisurely path, coming into existence with an age range between the oldest island, Sal, and the youngest, Fogo and Brava, formed an upwards of 15 million years.

Climate

Located in the Atlantic at approximately 604 km (375 miles) west of the western-most point of Senegal, the islands are affected by their proximity to the continent. Droughts that have increasingly devastated the Saharan desert belt have made their mark on this tiny land mass out at sea, causing periods of drought and famine spanning more than a decade. The Sahel and trade winds that blow through the winter months from December to the middle of March/April fill the air with a fine dust (*bruhma seca*) that often makes it impossible to look out to sea, never mind admire the nearest visible island. During these months, the temperature drops to the 20s (Celsius) or 60s (Fahrenheit) and the islands experience persistently strong winds. The effects are easily noted on Maio, Sal and Boa Vista which have been eroded from their original volcanic form to nearly flat, windblown dusty landscapes.

Between July and October the temperature rises to an average of 27°C/80°F and the islands receive erratic and often negligible rainfall. Characteristically, rain either falls lightly in the early morning hours or arrives with intensity, pouring down for anywhere from 20 minutes to 24 hours. The more mountainous islands tend to attract moisture by capturing passing clouds and are able to maintain a greener landscape throughout the year. Average rainfall is below 10 inches (24cm).

Culture *Kabuverdianidade*

Cape Verde is an anomaly. The people who live here are mixed descendants of another era, when exiled Portuguese criminals and aristocrats blended with African slaves who were trafficked from the continent on their way to the Americas through the thriving transatlantic trade. What resulted was a nation of people who were either ripped from their homes or driven from them, and who suffered through waves of brutal famines, exposed to the elements amidst uninhabitable rocks of land engulfed in an unrelenting sea. Over the centuries, Cape Verdeans have endured year after year of extensive droughts followed by periods of intense rainfall, touch-and-go colonialism, and a remoteness that stems from geographic isolation.

Out of this despair arose a subtle strength, reliance upon one another in the face of crises, and an indisputable determination to survive. Despite its bleak past and count-

---

Txuba! (Rain)

Now that the rains have started, Santiago is quickly turning greener than I thought it could in such a short time. Tiny tufts of green creep out of every crack and crevice, and the hillsides are starting to look more and more like fertile Latin America and less and less like arid Africa. The best part about the rains is how excited Cape Verdeans get. They're constantly in a good mood in the house when it rains, so much so that you might believe the rain brings some sort of magical powers with it. And I'm starting to think it does, because not two days after the first rain, plants are growing like crazy everywhere you look. Families immediately head for the hills to start planting corn, beans, and peanuts and things started sprouting right away, like the flag had been waved for some sort of secret race that began among the plots of land.

It's really just a good time to be in Cape Verde—it's more beautiful, people are happy, the air is fresher (though more humid), and resources are in greater quantity (though not necessarily in abundance). *Txuba* (rain) comes up in most conversations, in which you're expected to be as ecstatic as they are, since of course rain is the most glorious thing that can occur on this earth. And here, it's kind of true; it's so much more necessary for survival than we're used to with all of our many ways of securing water sources, so usually I am just as ecstatic. In Cape Verde the rain can't be depressing - everyone's too happy for the promise it contains, and their energy is so contagious, you can't help but share in their joy and catch yourself yelling "*Txuba*!!" all over the place. Additionally the rain usually causes a giant Willy Wonka-style chocolate river that runs rapidly through the back of town. Makes you want to jump in...until you remember that it's mud.

- Courtney Phelps

less hurdles, a resilient culture was born. The people of Cape Verde have emerged into a nation that is known for its *morabeza* (hospitality), its world-renowned *musica Kabuverdiana*, and an admirable willingness to thrive. It is a nation whose cultural fabric has been woven intricately, with colors and shapes that range from one island to the next, in a myriad quilt of diversity.

All of these factors combine to create the culture visitors will encounter in Cape Verde today: *Kabuverdianidade* (Cape Verdeanity). Each of the ten islands of Cape Verde has its own identity and way of life. The northern islands, also known as *Barlavento*, pride themselves on a distinctly European influence—as opposed to the southern islands of *Sotavento*, which tend to have stronger cultural ties to the continent. In line with the nature of the country's various traits, Cape Verdeans are ethnically mixed; their physical appearances range from dark features of African ancestry, to light characteristics that suggest a European descent.

The country is also undergoing an intense period of change in an ever-increasingly global community. In the capital of Praia on the main island of Santiago, where approximately one quarter of the Cape Verdean population resides, the city is increasingly advanced, international and expanding. At the same time, residents of rural areas live arguably more traditional lives and often lack basic resources such as electricity and running water. It is for these reasons that most inhabitants of rural communities and neighboring islands flock to Praia and abroad in an effort to find work and a more reliable income. Urban areas boast supermarkets teeming with international luxuries, while residents of rural islands often rely upon dried corn from the annual harvest and meager social services and resources.

As one of the most rewarding gifts of travel is the ability to expand cultural knowledge abroad, the most engaging promise that Cape Verde offers is its cultural vibrancy and the hospitality of its people that can be found everywhere, but which is particularly strong in smaller communities. This concept of *morabeza*, and the welcoming spirit the word embodies, is unmistakable in rural areas where tradition is thoroughly ingrained in people's lives. Even those with very little will readily invite you into their home to *txiga* (arrive/visit) and serve up a traditional dish or *lanche* (snack). Instead of touristy trinkets, often the most valuable gifts visitors take home with them are the memories of those met along the way.

The significance of Cape Verdeanity can be expressed through the unique ways in which the culture is celebrated - most notably, through the arts, music, dance, religion, festivals and cultural norms that make *Kabuverdianidade* authentic and truly unique. If you visit Cape Verde, take the time to fully respect and appreciate its unique culture - this is the essence of Cape Verde.

Religious Beliefs

As houses are often far apart and dispersed throughout rural communities, often the only existing communal structure is the church. Religious events play an enormous role in the realm of community participation throughout the archipelago. Cape Verde, a former Portuguese colony, is predominantly Catholic—with small percentages of Jehovah's Witnesses, the Church of Latter Day Saints, Lutheran, and Jewish presence.

Religious events are sometimes the primary opportunity for women and children to leave the domestic duties of the home and back-breaking work of the fields. Church is an excuse to get together, make community announcements, and gossip (it is less common for men to attend). Prayers that are recited at length before *festas* are invariably conducted either out of habit or through genuine religious fervor, depending upon the individuals involved. Virtually every cause for celebration—flag days, saint's days, and festivals—is related to religion, or a celebration of birth or death. Many musical genres that have sprung from the archipelago are inspired by such festivities. Historically, such events provided a small taste of liberation for those enslaved and an opportunity to combine the compulsory practice of Catholicism with familiar traditions that had originated in continental Africa.

Those in more remote areas have been known to uphold generational beliefs that take root in African animism, which upholds a variety of superstitions and "old wives' tales." Clothless babies are often seen wearing a string of black and white beads around their stomachs called *contra bruscha*, which means "against the witch," in an effort to provide protection against evil spirits. A variety of other more African-based beliefs contradict yet nonetheless continue to coexist with the colonial-based religion, resulting in an interesting hybrid of beliefs and convictions.

Music and Dance

Music is one of the most important aspects of Cape Verdean culture, as well as its most memorable. Those who have heard of Cape Verde often know it for its poignant melodies, which are internationally acclaimed for their ability to inspire richness, meaning, joy, anguish, and haunting beauty.

The most recognized of the varying Cape Verdean genres of music is *morna*, a type of folk music that is sung in the local dialect of Kriolu, accompanied by instruments like the clarinet, violin and guitar. It originates from the English

introduction

saying, "to mourn" and embodies a romantic quality, complemented by a ballroom-type dance that is slow and dramatic. The popularity of *morna* has produced some of the culture's most beloved artists such as Eugénio Tavares, Cesária Évora, Ildo Lobo, and Celina Pereira. The lyrics of this genre often relate to themes of love, longing, connection to the land, and of course, mourning.

In the 1930s, however, a more upbeat version of *morna* emerged called **coladeira**, which is light-hearted, often humorous, and yet thoroughly sensual. It possibly stems from **tabanca**, the musical and processional celebration of recognized Saint's Days. During the time of slavery, the observed holidays allowed the slaves a day free of work—both a physical and mental escape from hardship. *Tabanca* processions often included a mass service and the transportation of particular saint statues to a special alter (visible on hillsides throughout Cape Verde). During the procession, horns and drums were used to keep the beat as slaves sung in celebration, but also in criticism and mockery of their masters.

Similarly birthed from the islands is the fun and lively **funaná**, an accordion-based style of music that originated on Santiago and features a varied, upbeat tempo. The lyrics are often metaphoric and in the form of poetry, requiring that the audience is well-versed in both the language as well as the cultural meaning. As with many forms of Cape Verdean music during the colonial period, the Portuguese scorned *funaná* for being "too African." Since independence, however, there has been a revival, and Cape Verdeans see such forms of music as an integral part of their identity and culture of resilience. Groups such as Bulimundo and Ferro Gaita have reignited pride for the genre, added pop influences and incorporating elements of *coladeira* that has resulted in a melodical hybrid called *funacola*.

Batuque is considered the oldest genre of Cape Verdean

Funaná lyrics from the song "Sema Lopi":

Lyrics in Kriolu	Literal English translation	True meaning
Ódju mó' lua,	Eyes like the moon,	Open wide eyes,
Pistána sí'ma árcu-dâ-bédja	Eyebrows like the rainbow	Completely arched eyebrows
Bóca sí'ma câ tâ cúme nada	Mouth like doesn't eat anything	Mouth that starves
Ôi, Séma Lópi, côrpu dí tchõ, álma dí Crístu	Oh, Sema Lopi, body of ground, soul of Christ	Oh, Sema Lopi, everybody steps on you, but you forgive everyone

music, but it is also a traditional type of dance. With its drum beats, strong lyrics, and exotic hip-shaking flicks, this dance was once forbidden in rural areas for its messages of women empowerment, overt sexuality, and freedom of expression. Though it was once an outlet to express group exaltation or anguish, it is now regularly performed for entertainment value. In the past, *batuque* had a specific social meaning, as it was performed on holy days during ceremonies, feasts, and weddings. Similar to *tabanca*, it allowed the slaves to express their frustrations and difficulties in a way that was hidden to their masters. Many speculate that the movement of dance has a sexual meaning, indicating that the goal may be to promote fertility.

Those who perform the dance are mainly women who are called **batukaderas**. They gather in a circle, play a low beat and the dancer begins to sway almost apathetically to the music. In unison, those who are chanting and singing pick up the tempo. As the drums quicken, so do the movements of dance—so much so that the song builds velocity and the fervor of the group accelerates until the dancer is flicking her hips in a furious rhythm of shaking, her skirt whipping back and forth for the increasingly motivated crowd. Her upper body remains almost motionless while her hips begin swinging and swaying in an almost unnatural gyration. The performance reaches its peak in a strong crescendo of movement, drum beats and voices, and the immediate silence leaves the beat echoing delightfully across stone walls and pounding within the ears.

Food and Drink

Food, like music, plays a tremendous role in Cape Verdean culture. The traditional *festas* that occur on Saint's Days are considered essential breaks from the monotony of work to the community members who celebrate them. As with most cultures around the world, food, as well as its preparation, is

Major Music Festivals

Specific musical events are available throughout the book. Live performances are prevalent on Praia, Mindelo, Sal, and Boa Vista. Check nightlife descriptions in each island chapter for details.

São Vicente: Creole Carnival, February 16; *Baia das Gatas* Festival, held in August during the full moon

Boa Vista: Santa Isabel (Municipality Day) July 4

Sal: Nossa *Sra. De Piedade* (Our Lady of Pity) August 15; Santa Maria Festival (Municipality Day) September 15.

Santiago: Gamboa Festival, May 17-19; Tabanka, June/July.

central to such celebrations. Women will spend days pounding corn for the *cachupa* and *xerem*, cleaning and cutting vegetables, and preparing meat. Men generally are responsible for the killing of animals, a ceremonial occasion that often draws large crowds who assist or simply gather to watch.

TRADITIONAL DISHES

Cape Verde's tendency to experience prolonged periods of drought, as well as its history of Portuguese colonialism and slavery, has greatly influenced the traditional cooking practices of those who live there. Africans who arrived in Cape Verde through the transatlantic slave trade brought their knowledge of growing tropical crops and cooking techniques while Portuguese settlers introduced European goods to the archipelago.

Since Cape Verde was mainly utilized as a port for refueling sailing and whaling ships, it also became a place for sailors to refuel and restock their ships with food to sustain themselves throughout the long journey across the Atlantic, making it an experimental station for growing foods from newly discovered lands—such as corn, hot peppers, pumpkins, and cassava. Cape Verdeans also experimented by planting sugar, bananas, mangos, papayas, and other crops from Asia.

Regardless of the variety of crops, however, the uncontested food preference is corn—the staple crop throughout the country. When in season, everyone raves about *midju verde* (fresh corn on the cob), and in any rural area people will be sure to proudly offer more of it than you could ever possibly eat. Once the crop is harvested, the prized corn is dried and stored throughout the winter, then stewed either as whole kernels or pounded in a large mortar and pestle (*cutxi*) to various degrees of fineness so that it may be used as corn meal or flour.

Cachupa, a slow boiled stew of corn, beans, spices, onions, potatoes, and chicken (or other meat like tuna or beef), is the national dish of the Cape Verde Islands. There is a noticeable difference between *cachupa rica* (rich man's *cachupa*) and *cachupa pobre* (poor man's *cachupa*). *Cachupa rica* consists of a variety of ingredients while *cachupa pobre* is less fancy, comprised simply of corn, beans, onion and chicken stock. *Cachupa refogado* (refried *cachupa*) is a popular breakfast and is served in almost every restaurant. It is accompanied by a fried egg, bread, goat cheese, and a banana.

These dishes vary from island to island and from household to household. In restaurants, *cachupa* costs around 350/600$, but is best enjoyed in the company of someone's home.

In addition to *cachupa*, dried corn is used to make *xerem*, a traditional dish for weddings and festivals. In order to make this dish, the dried corn is pounded in a large mortar and pestle until it becomes the consistency of rice. *Djigacida* is finely ground corn steamed over a pot of boiling beans, pork and vegetables. *Kuskus* is made from corn that is finely-ground into flour and is then steamed in a ceramic pot. Much like cornbread, it is served hot with butter and milk (*kuskus ku leite*) or honey (*kuskus ku mel*).

Local Sweets

Typical desserts consist of fresh goat's cheese accompanied by local *doces* (specialty jams) like guava paste. *Açucrinha*, slow-boiled brown sugar bars, are popular, as well as *freskinhas*, popsicle-like juice frozen in baggies. Be sure that the water used for such local treats was properly treated before consumption.

EATING OUT

At times, items listed on the menu are not actually available, so it is best to ask what is available or prepare a few alternative preferences. When you order an item from the menu, it is generally not prepared ahead of time. The positive side is that the food that arrives in front of you is fresh to order; the downside is that it often takes a long time to be served.

Many restaurants offer a *prato de dia* (plate of the day) during normal hours of lunch or dinner service (more or less from 12:00–2:30 and 19:00–22:00). This daily option will generally be less expensive and more immediately available. It is always the best option for a quick lunch and is likely the closest thing you will get to "fast food" in the country.

Vegetarians will find it very difficult to eat out (you may find yourself living off of french fries). More upscale restau-

---

Food and Water Safety

Visitors should remain aware of the condition of their food, as most stomach problems and dysentery can be caused by dirty food or water. Caution should be taken when drinking water and when eating shellfish, uncooked food, or unpeeled fruits and vegetables. Meat dishes should not be undercooked and drinking tap water is not advised.

Always be sure to:
- Drink water from water bottles that have an unbroken seal.
- Boil tap water to sterilize, or use water purification tablets.
- Eat fresh, thoroughly cooked food.

Avoid:
- Food that has been left out for long periods of time.
- Ice in drinks.
- Uncooked fruits and vegetables.
- Ice cream or popsicles prepared in a home.
- Milk, cheese and dairy products that are not sealed or refrigerated.
- Undercooked seafood or meat.

rants may have a vegetable soup and some pasta dishes, but most sauces include some sort of meat. When you try to order a dish without the meat, prepare for some strange looks, as it is not culturally typically to receive such requests. Vegetarian-friendly restaurants have been noted in the restaurant descriptions within each section.

Fish and Seafood

Fish is a popular dish that is fresh, easy to find, and relatively inexpensive. Grilled lobster is one of the main dishes for tourists (prices start at around 1,200$). It is possible to find women on the streets of the city grilling fish for 150$ - 200$ a plate. Both throughout rural areas and near the sea ports, travelers will find vendors selling the catch of the day. Often, sellers will blow on a conch shell to indicate to the community that the fish has arrived. Many restaurants will list all available fish and shellfish items, but are often limited by what has come in for the day. In port towns it is possible to purchase fish fresh off the boat. Tuna is a particularly popular fish, and its high-quality meat is canned and available within country.

Market Food

Supermarkets, markets and bakeries are a good source for cheap, on-the-go lunches, and bottled water is widely available in any ordinary shop for less than hotel prices. It is not unusual to find imported goods from Portugal, and if travelers are lucky enough to find a Shell gas station, the store often contains a wide variety of rare international treats and popular name brand items. Homemade sweets and popcorn are the most common food sold on the streets by vendors. Sometimes women will have trays full of *pasteis* (fish pastries) and fried *moreia* (moray eel). Visitors should be able to find restaurants offering a variety of European cuisine throughout more touristy areas (in places like Praia there are Chinese and Italian options) but the local food is highly valued, unique, and not to be missed for those interested in an authentic experience.

LOCAL BEVERAGES

There are three main beers in Cape Verde: *Strela*, the household brand (around 100$), and the slightly more expensive *Superbock* and *Sagres*, imported from Portugal (sold for around 250$).

Wine is mainly imported from Portugal, yet travelers should be sure to taste the rich locally-produced wine that was grown within the volcanic crater of Chã das Caldeiras on the island of Fogo (see pg 218) and sold readily throughout the islands.

Cape Verde's most famous beverage is *grogue*, a strong local rum that is produced from distilled sugar cane on the islands of Santo Antão and Santiago. This drink is such an important part of Cape Verdean culture that its process of production has proven to be a rich source of inspiration for its well-known music. In addition to pure *grogue*, people drink *ponche* (punch), which is *grogue* that has been sweetened with sugarcane molasses and condensed milk.

Tourists can experience the *grogue* production process by running the old-fashioned press known as a *trapiche* in the town of Paul on Santo Antão or Cidade Velha on the main island of Santiago. In some tourist locations, visitors can request Brazil's national drink, *caiparinhas*, which can be made with the local Cape Verdean *grogue*. The refreshing beverage blends the flavors of both nations.

Some *grogue* brand names include: *Pelourinho, Fortaleza* and *Convento*.

See Cidade Velha on pg 183 for more information on how to learn more about and participate in *grogue* production.

Cultural Norms

In urban areas of Cape Verde, there is diversity, independence, development and employment that are not afforded in other areas. As such, the culture of cities differs in many significant ways from culture in more remote agricultural communities. The *fora*, otherwise known as the countryside (or literally, "outside of the city") contains a richness of tradition and culture that is unique to Cape Verde. As such, this section is dedicated to the cultural components of the *fora*.

Some men have multiple wives, and there is an emphasis on the permanence of relationships, no matter how strained.

COLLECTIVISM

Cape Verdeans in remote areas often treat everyone in their village as though they are family—because, often, they are. Rural areas are composed of a highly collectivist culture, and values rest upon communal living and collaboration. Women often make large cauldrons of the traditional dishes of corn-based meal to share with those who will inevitably drop by. It is considered extremely rude for people to eat in public in rural villages, and one is not allowed to do so unless they have brought enough food for everyone else to share. Cape Verdeans attitudes about sharing extend to the way they treat ownership of land, and community members are often free to borrow and lend personal possessions.

Collectivism is essential to survival in many areas of Cape Verde. Children often take part in communal tasks and are expected to do their share of duties within the household and agriculture, as women can have as many as 15 children per household. Children are thus expected to be highly self-sustaining, and toddlers can often be seen in groups working in the fields on their own, running errands, or playing without supervision. If a child wishes to sleep at someone else's home, they may do so. They will be welcomed into the house and expected to take care of themselves, no matter how young (or taken care of by older children). Beds and food are seen as communal property and it is typical for people in the *fora* to open their home to anyone, no matter how little they have. People often sleep together, and the youngest child in a household is referred to as *pe di cama*, which means "foot of the bed." An additional strange phenomenon is to observe that most children do not fight over toys or objects with their siblings or other children, and often offer their possessions to others.

MACHISMO & NEGATIVE ATTENTION

In Cape Verde, discrimination against women is arguably an issue. *Machismo* is often in full-swing—although some urban areas work to provide support and services for women, polygamy and domestic abuse are not unheard of in some areas. On certain islands, a man is defined by how many women and children he has. The first woman a man claims is called his *mudjer* (woman) and the other are referred to as *pequenas* (girlfriends). Young women are often enticed by the opportunity of freedom from familial duties and are can be "pulled from the house" (*tra di casa*) by older men, only to find the responsibilities of motherhood and domestic duties awaiting them.

Foreign women travelling alone or in the company of other women will possibly encounter *machismo* on a regular basis, whether while dining out or walking around crowded areas. Men are extremely forward and can at times cross what Western cultures have defined as a line of propriety. Unwanted attention and physical contact could almost be considered a norm, and is not uncommon. Men will often whistle, hiss, speak directly in a woman's face, hold tightly to her hand and not let go, or insist that she be near him.

Though it varies from island to island (i.e. in touristy areas where Cape Verdean men are more accustomed to interacting with foreign women, they may be less vocal) on some islands, taking offense to unwanted male attention by yelling or attempting to pull away can sometimes make a man laugh and insist further. It is important to observe local women and how they respond to unwelcome pursuits. Sometimes the only culturally appropriate way to make a man go away is to ignore him or look right through him, as though he does not exist. By not making eye contact, the woman signals that she refuses to acknowledge the come-on, as eye contact is often perceived as an invitation for interaction. At the same time, it is important to feel out the situation, and to clearly be sure to get help in the case of harassment or an emergency.

ATTITUDES TOWARD SPACE

Cape Verdeans often have a distinct desire to be close to others. Especially as a foreigner, in rural villages it may be hard to find privacy. People's desire to be near one another is so accepted that in areas where there are no people and someone sits along the path, another person walking by will come and sit right next to the other, even if they do not know one another well. *Hiaces* (public cars), tend to be packed with people, goats, chickens, and buckets of produce and fish. However, when people get out and leave an entire row empty, no one will move, and they will continue the bumpy ride, crammed up against one another without comment or complaint.

Common Characterics in the *Fora*

- Strong ties to the land – cultural identity centered on *nha terra* (my land)
- Open, welcoming, and exuberant culture, a quality known as m*orabeza*
- Cape Verde is a high-context society, where cultural notions are communicated "below the surface" through behavior, assumption, and physical gestures
- Racial stigmas: Generally speaking, the lighter a person's skin is, the higher their social status
- Politeness to foreigners—people tend to tell foreigners what they want to hear (reluctance to say no)
- "*Spera un bokadinho*" ("Wait a little while") is a common phrase (island-time mentality) that often leads to long periods of waiting
- Religion is predominantly a mix of Catholicism and African beliefs/superstitions
- There is a high level of gender-based tasks in more remote areas
- Community-based society—being alone or individual isolation can appear to signify depression or loneliness
- Meetings are often formalized and long—a direct influence from the Portuguese
- Main form of communication is with the eyes—staring is common and not rude
- Few social stigmas against mental illness, physical disabilities, etc.
- Ostracizing is not typical, and overt alcoholism, confrontation, and volume of voice is often not considered cause for alarm, but is rather silently accepted and overwhelmingly ignored.
- Elders are extremely respected, and those who are younger are supposed to raise their hand to the air in the direction of an elder to accept a blessing by saying, *Da'm bensum* "Give me a blessing," to which an elder will take the person's hand and put it to their forehead saying, *Bensum di deus, pa eal fazi bu bon mudjer/homem*, which means "A blessing from god, that he makes you a good woman/man."
- High level of acceptance and toleration
- Community and collective cohesion is valued above the individual and are the most highly regarded values in rural villages

As many as ten people can sleep together on a bed, and students in remote schools can sometimes sit two to a chair for lack of space. There is no stigma for men to walk hand in hand with other men, or whisper into each others' ears, or even to dance close with one another. Women form extremely intimate bonds, and female friends often sit on each others' laps, interlace hands, and walk arm in arm together along the road.

ATTITUDES TOWARD TIME

Spera un bokadinho. Inda sta cedo. "Wait just a little while. It's still early."

Time in Cape Verde is an oxymoron. People around the world are familiar with the term "island time," and Cape Verde is no exception. As such, there is a saying, *spera un bokadinho,* which is seen as a humorous way to respond to someone's inquiry about when something is going to happen with "eventually...maybe." This attitude toward treating time impartially is perhaps the greatest challenge for travelers to overcome during their time in Cape Verde. For visitors who have an itinerary and time frame for which to complete a certain amount of excursions, be aware that transportation is notorious for being cancelled or delayed. Itineraries are often changed, and patience mixed with good humor is a part of life here.

Visitors or internationals working in Cape Verde often complain of enduring countless months of frustration waiting for people to meet deadlines, fulfill promises, or arrive for meetings, only to be confronted with the saying *inda sta cedo* (it is still early). Apparently, it is always early, especially in areas where there is no infrastructural change to encourage or promote promptness. Again, flexibility during travel is an essential component for those wishing to visit Cape Verde. Things do not run on time—that's the bad news. The good news is that for those who are willing to go with the flow, Cape Verde will become a land of welcome surprises, quiet relaxation, rich cultural exchanges and an unforgettable trip—one that will forever stand apart from your typical "go-go-go" vacations.

LANGUAGE: KRIOLU ANTIGO

Communication is a "mix" as well. Whereas the official language is Portuguese, the more widely practiced regional dialect of Kriolu, a pidgin dialect that combines Portuguese and African phrases, varying from island to island. Learning how to speak Kriolu is only a part of the process in learning to communicate in Cape Verde. More importantly, one who wants to interact should learn to communicate through gestures, facial expressions, and with the eyes. Cape Verdeans who are deaf and unable to speak have been known to communicate effectively, even without being taught sign language. Go to any local *festa* and look around closely at the life going on around you—it is evident that Cape Verdeans say much without words.

GREETINGS

No matter how rushed someone is on the street, it is essential that rural community members go through a lengthy greeting ritual with each person they pass, even if they have already seen that person earlier in the day. People shake one another's hands while kissing on both cheeks. They then ask a series of questions. The following are just a few examples:

Modi ki bu maesche? Maesche bom?
How did you wake up? Did you wake up well?

Bu corpu, modi ki ael sta hoje?
Your body, how is it today?

Familia sta tudu dreto?
Is your family doing well?

Kuze ki bu sa ta fazi gosi?
What are you doing right now?

Fika contenti pa'm odja-bu. Deus bai ku bo.
I am happy to have seen you. God be with you.

A survival dictionary is at the end of the book, but a Portuguese/English dictionary may be a valuable investment.

Popular Cape Verdean Sayings

Ma ora ki mi odja abo ta parsi mas es mundo de mi ku bo.
When I look at you, it appears that all that exists in the world is me with you.

Kenha ki subi mas alto mas baixo el ta kai.
Whoever goes further up has further down to fall.

Entre spinho ta nasi um rosa.
Within the bone is born a rose.

Quel ki bu fazi de noite pal manha ta monstra.
What you do at night in the morning will come to light.

Conberso na hora e sabi na boka.
Conversation at the right time is good in the mouth.

Kenha ki ka ta obi ka ta odja.
Those who do not hear will not see.

Nhos e neba detado.
You are the fog laying down. (It is a way of saying that people are really close, good friends, or always together.)

Bu e kor de rosa na mare de tarde.
You are the pink color of the beach in the afternoon.

Nos coracao papia de nos ku lingua ki ta ultra passa tal como misterio da vida ki ta oferece.
Our hearts speak in a language that passes all with a mystery only life offers.

Ta bai e triste, bem e maguadu.
To go is sad, to come (return) is painful yet.

- Compiled by Alicia Casali

The Basics

When to Go

In general, Cape Verde boasts sunny and warm weather that is enjoyable year-round. Even the short-lived rainy season from August to October can have weeks without a downpour. Proximity to the cool ocean breezes and offshore winds offer travelers to Cape Verde one of the lowest temperatures in the West African region. Moderate weather is typical during February, ranging from the mid to high 60s (Fahrenheit) at night and to the mid eighties from May to November.

Summer temperatures, especially in the northern islands, can be cooler than in Europe, though the southern islands, especially Fogo, can get hot and sticky. From December to March you may need a sweater in the evenings, especially at higher altitudes. Winter months are·also marked by gusty winds, which blow in dust all the way from the Sahara, and are called *bruhma seca*.

For those interested in windsurfing, January and February are the best months to visit. The calmest waters for divers and swimmers are from June to December. Those who want to enjoy the beach without winds may want to avoid the winter months. Marlin fishing is big from May to October and tuna fishing is at its best in August. Hiking is most beautiful both during and after the rainy summer months. Partygoers interested in *festas* will want to visit São Vicente or São Nicolau in February to be a part of Carnaval. In August São Vicente has a music festival, and beginning on May 1 there is a three-day Festival de São Filipe on the island of Fogo which features local Cape Verdean artists and sometimes international ones (particularly from Brazil) as well.

Those who are strapped for cash will want to visit the Cape Verde islands from April to June or in the month of October, when hotel rates are not as high as they are during the high season of *Carnaval* and Christmas.

What to Pack

As always, what to pack will depend on where you want to go and what you want to do. Though dress on the islands is typically casual, Cape Verdeans take public appearances seriously and it is customary to be clean and neat as a sign of respect. Warmer clothing is necessary if you plan on visiting during the cooler seasons, especially in higher altitude areas such as Rui Vaz on Santiago, or the crater of Chã das Caldeiras on Fogo. If you plan to go hiking in the mountainous or rocky regions of Santiago, Fogo or Santo Antão, hiking boots and proper foot apparel are a must.

To make the logistics of packing both efficient and fun, try the online Universal Packing List at http://upl.codeq.info

Sunscreen and bug spray are two items that are not as easy to find that the traveler may want to pack prior to the trip. Flip flops and beach gear are great for the sandy beaches of Maio, Sal, or Boa Vista. Those planning on going out to some nice restaurants will want to bring dressier clothing for going out.

Just about every *pensão* or hotel provides sheets and towels, toilet paper, and soap. Those staying at a home stay or someone's house in a rural community may want to bring sheets, towels, a sleeping bag, and possibly flip flops to bathe in. The main towns of Santa Maria, Praia, and Mindelo usually sell the basic necessities such as tampons, shampoo and conditioner, razors, film, and pain medication.

CLOTHING

Keep in mind as you are packing that there is an 80-pound weight restriction on baggage.

It is important to remember that there are often no washing machines in areas of Cape Verde that you may be visiting. The traditional scrub-board washing that is typically used will likely wear out your clothing at a fast rate, so do not pack delicate or fade-sensitive fabrics. The climate is hot, dry and windy, so basic cotton clothing is probably the best choice while packing.

- Light and casual but presentable (preferably "wash and wear" clothing)
- Baggy and raggedy jeans are not acceptable for official or formal events
- Shoes: comfortable and durable sneakers, hiking boots (if needed) and sturdy flip-flops. Note that cobblestone, dirt, and rocky roads are tough on shoes in Cape Verde.
- A sweatshirt or sweater for cool evenings—particularly during the winter months and early spring (also in high altitudes, year-round)
- A bathing suit
- Bandanas/ handkerchiefs (good for dusty road trips)
- Hats and sunglasses
- Small easy-to-carry umbrella to guard from the sun and occasional bursts of rain

PERSONAL ITEMS

The most essential items can be found in Cape Verde, yet it is important to remember that they are more expensive and of lesser quality. You can get shampoo, conditioner, toothpaste and brush, deodorant, and lotion, but you may not find your favorite brands, and the prices are high. Some personal items may not be possible to find such as insect repellent, alcohol-based hand cleaner, and aerosol cans.

ELECTRONICS

Cape Verde struggles with its electricity supply. While many hotels have generators, many do not. It may be useful to bring a flashlight for power outages. It is important to note that most electronics items are at higher risk to break because of Cape Verdean's landscape (rust/corrosion, dust, sand, and/or proximity to sea) and climate (heat and/or humidity). It is advised that travelers conceal electronic items in public, as it greatly increases the likelihood of theft.

- Shortwave radio: good for news; travelers can tune in to the BBC
- MP3 player for bus rides and ferry trips
- Plug adapters (voltage = 220 V, frequency = 50 Hz, plug= C&F, round two-pin attachment plugs and Schuko plugs)

MISCELLANEOUS ITEMS

- Extra batteries (rechargeable ones are best)
- Backpack for day trips
- Pocket-size Portuguese dictionary
- Pictures of home, family, or friends to show new Cape Verdean friends (great conversation-starter)
- Money belt or other means of concealing your passport and valuables while traveling
- Sturdy water bottle (i.e. Nalgene)
- Insect repellent and malaria medication (particularly during the rainy season)

The lighter your luggage, the easier it will be to get around in more remote areas where cobblestone roads are not particularly friendly terrain for roller bags and the like.

Getting There

ENTRY REQUIREMENTS

A passport and visa are required when traveling to Cape Verde. Visa approval can take several days and Cape Verde issues two types of tourist visas: a single-entry visa valid for up to 90 days or a multiple-entry visa valid for one year. Overseas, inquiries should be made to the nearest Cape Verdean embassy or consulate. Visit the Cape Verde virtual portal online at www.virtualcapeverde.net for the most current visa information.

Visas at the Airport

Embassies located in Praia encourage travelers to apply for a visa before traveling to Cape Verde. In the rare instance that a foreigner is allowed to travel without a visa, it is required that they apply for and purchase an entry visa upon arrival at the airport. These "airport" visas cost more and are restricted to a 7-day period of stay; to extend a visit beyond those seven days, a visitor with an "airport" visa must purchase a regular single or multiple-entry visa at the office of immigration police.

BY AIR

Traveling to Cape Verde is easy but requires planning as flights to and from Cape Verde arrive daily but from different cities and on different days of the week.

Airports in Cape Verde have become a necessity for the economy as well as for the development of the country. In response to the need for income that tourism and international investment provides, almost every island (with the exception of Brava and Santo Antão) now has a domestic airport, and additional international ones are currently under construction in an effort to promote local tourism potential and expand business and investment opportunities for growth.

Praia Airport, which opened for international flights in 2005, is typically the main point of destination for the large Cape Verdean diaspora, whereas the international airports of Sal and Boa Vista cater mostly to tourists. In 2009, the São Pedro Airport on the island of São Vicente became the new São Pedro International Airport, though international flights are on hold until the completion of construction that will bring it to international standards.

As flights in-country can often be unreliable, it is a good idea to fly into an airport that is closest to your island of destination (i.e. travelers to Fogo should fly into Santiago's airport, while those journeying to Santo Antão should go

Consulates & Embassies

United Kingdom Cape Verde Honorary Consul; Mr. Joao Roberto; 18-20 Stanley Street, Liverpool L1 6AF; Tel: 0151 236 0206; E-mail: Joao.Roberto@capeverdeconsul.com

Netherlands Cape Verde Consulate; Mathenesserlaan 32b, Rotterdam, 3021 HX; Tel: 1 04 77 89 77

Germany Botschaft der Republik Kap Verde, Stavanger Str. 16, 10439 Berlin ; Tel: (030) 20 45 09 55 (from 09:00 to 17:00); E-mail: info@embassy-capeverde.de

Germany Honorarkonsul im Saarland; Herr Rolf-Dieter Müller; Saargemünder Straße 136; 66119 Saarbrücken; Tel: 0681-39 80 98; E-mail: info@honorarkonsul-kapverde.de

USA Embassy of the Republic of Cape Verde; 3415 Massachusetts Avenue, NW, Washington D.C. 20007; Tel: (202) 965-6820

USA Consulate General of Cape Verde, Boston, MA; Tel: (617) 353-0014

through São Vicente). There are regularly-scheduled flights on Portugal's airline TAP, as well as the national Cape Verdean carrier TACV, and Air Senegal.

Reservations can be made at any time but confirmation is subject to availability. Please note that the country is undergoing rapid changes and that all travel information within this section is therefore also subject to change and should be verified by contacting a preferred airline agency or nearest travel agent.

Transportes Aéreos de Cabo Verde (TACV), the official airline of Cape Verde, has daily flights to and from the islands from many points of origin throughout the world. Cape Verde is also serviced by *Transportes Aéreos de Portugal* (TAP), Air Senegal, South African Airways (SAA), and chartered Air Luxor and Condor flights. Both airlines increase the number of flights during the peak travel season, which is June through September.

Though TACV is known for its safety record, the same cannot be said about its punctuality; the airline is notorious for delays as well as early departures, so this must be taken into consideration when planning an international journey. Travelers interested in using TACV should check for up-to-date information.

FaleCom TACV–Customer Service TACV *Cabo Verde Airlines; Praia Airport; P.O. Box Nr. 1, Praia, Cabo Verde; Tel: + 238 260 88 03; falecomtacv@tacv.aero*

From the United States

TACV has a weekly flight from Boston's Logan Airport to Sal and twice-weekly service from Boston to the international airport in Praia. Visitors from the United States can also travel to Cape Verde through Europe on the airlines below or through Dakar, Senegal via Air Senegal or TACV.

To receive further flight information, visit the TACV web site at www.flytacv.com (click on the American flag in the upper right-hand corner for English).

TACV Boston *1245 Hancock Street, Suite #3, Quincy, MA 02169; Tel: 1-617-472-2227*

International Airports

ISLAND	CITY/TOWN	AIRPORT CODE	AIRPORT NAME
Boa Vista	Rabil	BVC	Rabil Int'l
Sal	Espargos	SID	Amílcar Cabral Int'l
Santiago	Praia	RAI	Praia Int'l

basics

From Europe

TACV has direct flights from throughout Europe. Please consult your local airport for direct flights and up-to-date travel information.

TAP Portugal connects most major European cities through Lisbon, which has daily flights to Sal and Santiago. Flight schedules vary, so visitors from Europe or those wishing to connect in Europe should begin making flight reservations early. Condor and Volary Air offer chartered flights from Frankfurt and Rome during peak season.

Thomson has chartered flights through Sal and Boa Vista for travelers from the UK with booked packages. Contact through www.thomson.co.uk.

From West Africa

TACV and Air Senegal offer flights from Dakar, Banjul, Nouakchott, Guinea Bissau, Ouagadougou and Abidjan. Flight schedules vary according to season and demand.

INTER-ISLAND TRAVEL BY AIR

During peak travel season, travelers who connect to other islands via the the inter-island plane service may experience delays in receiving their luggage at their final destination due to a limited carrying capacity of inter-island planes. Travelers should be sure to carry a change of clothing and all valuable or essential belongings in their carry-on bags in order to avoid frustration upon arrival in the country. Inter-island travel is generally through 45-seat propeller planes or ferries. Not all flights between islands are direct. During the windy season (late December to late March), inter-island plane service may be cancelled due to poor visibility and related safety concerns. The island of Brava is not accessible via plane.

Transportation Within the Islands

BY VEHICLE

Intra-island service usually consists of minivans (typically Toyota *Hiaces* that seat up to 12 people...or more) or converted pickup trucks that have benches along the edges of the pickup bed. Cars generally leave from a central location (outlined throughout each section) with no regular schedule. Most cities have taxis (again, consult specifics that are detailed in each section) but only Praia and Mindelo have a limited bus system.

In Cape Verde, traffic moves on the right side of the road, as in the United States. Under Cape Verdean law, seat belts must be worn at all times by the driver as well as the person in the front passenger seat. Children under 12 must sit in the back seat. Motorcyclists must wear helmets and use headlights at all times.

Intra-island service can be dangerous because some drivers overload their vehicles, exceed the speed limit, and drive after drinking alcohol. Before entering any transport, riders should pay close attention to the behavior of the driver, particularly while traveling at night.

The availability and cost for transportation once within the archipelago varies from island to island and is outlined in each individual chapter. It is common for *Hiaces* and taxis to circle the town squares of urban areas. *Hiaces* often maintain no particular schedule, as they typically circle the town until the car is filled up. If you are traveling by *Hiace*, it is beneficial to search for a car that is relatively full before getting in, to avoid sitting in one for hours in search of other passengers. Cars often are available more frequently in the mornings and evenings, to service commuters coming in to the city from outlying villages. Midday is the hardest time to find a vehicle.

Bus services are available mainly on the islands of São Vicente and Santiago, and are predominantly restricted to their main cities of Mindelo and Praia. As such, depending on time and convenience, it may be preferable to rent a car through local car hire companies found on each island.

BY BOAT

There is regular daily inter-island ferry service between Santo Antão and São Vicente. There is also ferry service between Santiago, Brava, and Fogo, however, these ferry links do not offer daily runs and the schedule frequently changes.

Ferry schedules and island-by-island specifics are referenced throughout the book, but a fairly reasonable guide to the ferries that are and are not running can be consulted online at: www.bela-vista.net/Ferry.aspx

Specific information on transportation varies from island to island and is outlined in the Getting Around section of each chapter.

CAR HIRE AND TAXI SITUATION

Sal

Due to Sal's relatively small size (the island is only about 30 miles or 48 km long), it is possible to cover a considerable amount of distance and to become acquainted with a large portion of what the island has to offer in as little as a day. Since it has an international airport and is considered one of the more cosmopolitan islands, transport is made easy with the help of taxis and rented cars that are available in Espargos.

Please refer to each island section in this book for specific car hire and taxi information.

Until recently taxis were not known to overcharge tourists, but current reports claim that this may be changing for non-Portuguese speakers. Therefore, it is important to check the price with multiple sources before settling with one car. Also, for a price, 4X4 quad rentals are available for those who wish to visit deserted beaches and cross sand dunes where normal cars cannot.

São Nicolau

Cars are available with more frequency in the main towns of Vila and Tarrafal (the trip should costs approximately 150$), though there are steep winding roads that can be navigated on foot as well.

Santiago

A recent government mandate states that all taxis should be labeled as such and painted crème. Taxis within Praia (your point of origin when arriving from anywhere by plane to Santiago) range in price from approximately 150-100. After dark, however, prices increase from 50-100. It is also possible to take the bus to most destinations across the large and varied island. A taxi ride across the island (from Cidade Velha to Praia, for example, should cost around 2000$ round-trip.

São Vicente

São Vicente has relatively good roads and cars can easily be hired in Mindelo.

Santo Antão

In Santo Antão the cobblestone roads and numerous mountains are often dangerous for driving and in disrepair. Local drivers know where the worst potholes are, but at night, taxis are considered the safest option of transport.

Boa Vista

On Boa Vista, drivers expect foreign tourists to rent cars and may sometime overcharge or expect high prices for short journeys. A half day trip visiting one of the remote beaches can be costly. It is essential to bargain the price ahead of time. Visitors who opt to rent cars should be sure to get a good 4X4, as vehicles often get stuck in desert sand dunes and drifts that block the roads.

Fogo

It is recommended for visitors to get a taxi from the port or airport into the city of Sao Filipe. If you find a good taxi driver that you like, it is best to keep their contact information for future use. There are taxis, Hiaces and covered cars in the main squares.

A taxi to the volcano can be expensive, but may be worth it to those who prefer comfort and promptness. The ride takes half the time in a crowded, covered and inexpensive car, which can take up to three hours to reach its destination due to multiple stops along the journey.

Cars on Brava meet the boat from Fogo with a relatively planned schedule.

Maio

Taxis are very rare here and you may end up paying for a private one. If you can find where they stop in Vila do Maio by the local grocery shop and after a long enough wait you can share to be driven up the Coast past the airport. There are very few hire cars.

basics

Traffic Safety and Road Conditions

Cape Verde has a fairly extensive road system on most islands. Asphalt roads used to be relatively uncommon, but now on Santiago, Sal, and São Vicente, Santo Antão and São Nicolau many roads in the cities and along main routes are paved. On the other islands (Fogo, Brava, Maio, and Boa Vista), the roads are more narrow, winding, and mostly consist of uneven cobblestone.

There are many current projects in the process of converting cobblestone roads to asphalt. The new roads allow for speedier transport, but can be more dangerous since these roads are smoother and lack speed bumps, which results in a tendency for drivers to speed. During the rainy season, cobblestone roads can be slippery, and mudslides and large falling rocks are common on roads that go through mountains.

A majority of houses are located along main roads, so drivers must be aware of children and livestock. Roads and streets are often unlit, so driving at night is hazardous and not recommended. Most accidents result from aggressive driving, excessive speed, and passing around blind curves.

Driving while under the influence of alcohol is a problem. The peak time for drunk drivers is on Sundays, but one can encounter them at any time. Also, extreme caution should be exercised after celebrations, festivals and open-air concerts as well as during holiday periods, such as Christmas, New Year's, and Carnaval.

Service stations are available and quite modern. Taxis and buses generally offer clean, dependable service on all islands. Bus service in Praia is reliable and inexpensive, and most buses are fairly new.

In the event of an accident or emergency, call 131 for fire or 132 for police.

Communication & Staying in Touch

INTERNET AND PHONE ACCESS

The internet in Cape Verde is gradually becoming more available, reliable, and affordable, though it is still difficult to find in rural areas. The connection is generally decent, and it is important to remember that a higher price for access does not necessarily ensure a better connection. A reasonable price at Internet cafés is 200-400/hour. Viruses are still a major problem, so visitors should exercise caution and inquire about virus protection on computers before inserting pen drives into portals. International calls are becoming more available with VOIP (voice over internet protocol), which can be as low as 8-10$/minute. Some WIFI is available in public spaces and are recognized throughout this book.

In urban areas, there are a number of established internet cafés that offer international calling. International services in Cape Verde are dependent on transatlantic fiber-optic cables, but internet-based calls are making international phone calls considerably more affordable. In the case that this option is not available, CV Telecom sells international calling cards at their offices and through the *correios* (post offices). Visitors who need reliable communication to other countries may consider bringing satellite-based voice and/or data equipment. Phone booths are not common, but many shops, hotels and restaurants have phones for local, public use (generally advertised with a sign *"telefone public")*.

The international country code for Cape Verde is 238.

CV Telecom is currently the only provider for fixed-line voice, data service, and Internet service (dial-up, ISDN, and ADSL). Mobile phone service is on the GSM standard, and is available from CV Telecom and T-Mais (T+). The recent insurgence of T+ has made mobile communication much more affordable and available to the general public. For an extended stay, it may be in your favor to obtain a contract. Fixed and mobile line numbers all have seven digits. Land lines begin with the number two, and mobile numbers begin with the number nine. Phone service in Cape Verde is improving. However, due to variable factors such as the electrical power quality and weather conditions, travelers may encounter some difficulty when making international calls.

CELL PHONES

If you intend to stay for more than a week and will be travelling from island to island or hotel to hotel, it may be in your best interest to invest in a local mobile phone. This way if there is a change in flight times of hotel reservations, you can easily be contacted. Contracts are available through CV Telecom/CV Movel and T-Mais for a minimal fee. SIM cards are readily available and mobile phones may be purchased for less than 5000$.

MAIL

Cape Verde does not enjoy a high standard of mail service equivalent to that or the United States and Europe. A letter sent from another country takes, on average, three weeks to arrive. Though it is rare, it is not unheard of for some mail to not arrive at all. It is advised that all letters sent to and from the country to include "Air Mail" and "Par Avion" on their envelopes, as well as "Via Portugal" at the bottom of the address.

It is discouraged for visitors to send money, large packages, or airline tickets through the mail. There are no customs duties if sent by airmail; however, postage costs may be high. Packages sent in bubble manila envelopes have a better chance of arriving, though larger packages may often mysteriously disappear in transit. It is recommended that post cards are sent within envelopes to ensure that they arrive at their intended destinations.

basics

Accommodations

In terms of accommodations, visitors can expect a large range of varying options and choices in Cape Verde. There is everything from home stays, in which one may stay in an extra bed or room in a family house (a much more culturally significant experience to see how Cape Verdeans live), to *pensões*, which are basically small bed & breakfasts that resemble hostels.

Residencials provide a B&B/apartment option for a high level of privacy, and places like ApartHotel provide a range of accommodations, sometimes with a kitchen, but always with the option of staying for longer periods of time.

Hotels are often of a higher caliber with quality rooms, ranging from small to massive (some are par with international standards, some are not) and high-end resorts are often all-inclusive, and up to international standards.

Specific accommodation options based on location are listed throughout the island sections of this book.

Money

Cape Verde is mainly a cash-based society. Most large hotels and resorts will accept Euros and/or American dollars, but unless otherwise noted, be prepared to pay with cash. It is possible to exchange money at the airport and in any of the banks—*BCA, Banco Interatlântico, Caixa Economica or BCN*—for a standard rate that is updated daily. In larger towns and cities there are generally Western Union posts where you can transfer and exchange for a steeper fee.

The unit of currency is the Cape Verdean Escudo (CVE), broken down into 100 centavos. The CVE is tied to the Euro at CVE 110.27 =1 Euro and CVE 100 = $1.35 (USD). There is a *bureau de change* at the airport and local banks will change travelers' checks and foreign currency, although there is a high commission on travelers' checks. ATMs can be found at the airport and in Sal, Praia and Sâo Vincent. Major credit cards, particularly MasterCard and Visa are currently accepted in a few main resort hotels and restaurants. Banks will give cash on credit cards but commissions are high. To avoid additional charges, carry travelers' checks in US Dollars or Pounds Sterling.

Black Market Money Exchange

In Praia, it is possible to avoid the lines in the bank and change money on the street for a slightly lower exchange rate. As you walk along the main street of Plateau in the area of the market you will find groups of men standing around with fanny packs stuffed with money. Anyone perceived not to be Cape Verdean will likely be approached and offered to exchange currency in a variety of languages. Due to the sheer number of men competing for your money, the rate is fairly normalized, but it is not a bad idea to verify exchange rates beforehand. Despite relatively normalized rates, the reliability of the exchange can be doubted as an increasing number of counterfeit bills make their way into circulation.

Safety and Security

Visitors traveling to Cape Verde who are engaged in water sports or other water-related activities such as swimming, boating, wind surfing and fishing should do so with caution. The ocean currents along the beaches of Cape Verde are extremely strong, particularly in the southern islands of the archipelago. There have been numerous incidents of drowning and several small fishing boats were lost at sea in recent years.

In terms of safety precautions, the volcano on the island of Fogo is still active. It erupted numerous times over the past century, the last in 1995. Though it is a rare occurrence, travelers who wish to climb the volcano (a particularly popular activity among those who travel to the island) should be aware of the possibility of future eruptions.

Political campaign rallies and public demonstrations are usually peaceful, however, travelers should do their best to avoid large crowds such as political gatherings.

For the latest security information, those traveling abroad should regularly monitor the U.S. Department of State, Bureau of Consular Affairs' web site, where the current Travel Warnings and Travel Alerts, as well as the Worldwide Caution, can be found. Up-to-date information on safety and security can also be obtained by calling 1-888-407-4747 toll-free in the U.S. and Canada, or for callers outside the U.S. and Canada, a regular toll-line at 1-202-501-4444. These numbers are available from 8:00-20:00 Eastern Time, Monday through Friday (except U.S. federal holidays).

Travelers are urged to take responsibility for their own personal security while traveling overseas. For general information about appropriate measures travelers can take to protect themselves in an overseas environment, see the U.S. Department of State's *A Safe Trip Abroad.*

CRIME

basics

The most common type of crime that occurs within Cape Verde is theft and burglary, which is most prevalent in crowded urban areas such as markets, musical festivals, and parties. Those most often targeted are affluent-looking foreigners, regardless of nationality. Current statistics in Cape Verde demonstrate a small increase in crime in the cities of Praia and Mindelo. Of those found guilty of crimes, the most common perpetrators are large groups of street children, so it is recommended that visitors avoid large amounts of children who appear as though they have no adult supervision.

It is important for visitors to remember that muggings and thievery occur most often at night in more isolated areas. Since there is often inadequate lighting in public areas, as well as common power outages, it is encouraged to carry a small flashlight, not walk alone, avoid dark and isolated places, and be particularly aware of surroundings once the sun goes down.

Although foreign citizens are not targeted specifically, being flashy and demonstrating a high level of wealth and excess is a key way to attract the attention of criminals. It is not unknown for joggers to have iPods stolen from them, or for shoppers in Praia's popular Sukapira market to encounter instances in empty stairwells. To avoid such instances, remain in groups, do not carry a bag or purse in urban areas, keep belongings close, and be aware of surroundings at all times. It should be mentioned, as well, that alcohol is often involved in instances of violence or rape. Women should exercise particular caution, and it is not recommended that they travel alone unless they are familiar with the area they are visiting.

Information for Victims of Crime

If a passport is lost, it should be reported immediately to the local police and the nearest embassy or consulate. If you are the victim of a crime while overseas, in addition to reporting to local police, please contact the nearest embassy or consulate for assistance. The embassy/consulate staff can help you receive proper medical care, as well as contact family members or friends. Although the prosecution of crime is the responsibility of local police authorities, consular officers can help you to understand the local criminal justice process and to find an attorney if needed.

The emergency line in Cape Verde is 132 (police) and 131 (fire).

Registration

Individuals living or traveling in Cape Verde are encouraged to register with their country's nearest embassy or consulate through respective country of origin's travel registration web site so that they can obtain updated information on travel and security within Cape Verde.

Health

Medical facilities in Cape Verde are limited, and some medicines are in short supply or unavailable. There are hospitals in Praia and Mindelo, as well as most large towns across the islands, with smaller medical facilities throughout the rural parts of the country (known as *posto sanitarios*). The islands of Brava and Santo Antão no longer have functioning airports so air evacuation in the event of a medical emergency is nearly impossible from these two islands. Brava also has limited inter-island ferry service.

Malaria does exist in Cape Verde, although it is not nearly as common as in mainland Africa. The island of Santiago is the only island at risk, particularly from the months of July to December. It is recommended that travelers take preventative measures while visiting Cape Verde in these areas, and at these times by purchasing and taking malaria pills, using insect repellant, and utilizing mosquito nets.

There are no HIV/AIDS entry restrictions for visitors to or foreign residents of Cape Verde, but that does not mean there are no instances of infection. The national percentage of infected citizens is low, but it is difficult to know how accurate such figures are.

Information on vaccinations and other health precautions, such as safe food and water precautions and insect bite protection, may be obtained from the Centers for Disease Control and Prevention's hotline for international travelers at 1-877-FYI-TRIP (1-877-394-8747) or via the CDC's web site. For information about outbreaks of infectious diseases abroad, consult the World Health Organization's (WHO) web site. Further health information for travelers is available from the WHO.

VACCINATIONS

Be sure to make an appointment with your physician at least 4-6 weeks before your trip in order to allow time for vaccinations to take effect. Even if it is less than 4 weeks before departure for your trip, it is still important to consult with a doctor in order to receive shots, proper medication, and information about illness and injury prevention while traveling.

Recommended Vaccinations

The following vaccines may be recommended for your travel to Cape Verde. Make it a point to discuss specific travel plans and personal health concerns with a healthcare provider to determine which vaccines you will need.

- **Hepatitis A** or immune globulin (IG). Transmission of hepatitis A virus can occur through direct person-to-person contact; through exposure to contaminated water, ice, or shellfish harvested in contaminated water; or from fruits, vegetables, or other foods that are eaten uncooked and that were contaminated during harvesting or subsequent handling.
- **Hepatitis B**, especially if you might be exposed to blood or body fluids (for example, healthcare workers), have sexual contact with the local population, or be exposed through medical treatment. Hepatitis B vaccine is now recommended for all infants and for children ages 11–12 years who did not receive the series as infants.
- **Meningococcal (meningitis)**, if you plan to visit countries in this region that experience epidemics of meningococcal disease during December through June.
- **Rabies**, if you might have extensive unprotected outdoor exposure in rural areas, such as might occur during camping, hiking, or bicycling, or engaging in certain occupational activities.
- **Typhoid** vaccine. Typhoid fever can be contracted through contaminated drinking water or food, or by eating food or drinking beverages that have been handled by a person who is infected. Large outbreaks are most often related to fecal contamination of water supplies or foods sold by street vendors
- As needed, booster doses for tetanus-diphtheria, measles, and a one-time dose of polio vaccine for adults.

Required Vaccinations

- A certificate of yellow fever vaccination is required from all travelers over one year of age and traveling from an infected country.

Medical Insurance

Travelers should contact their medical insurance companies before traveling in order to inquire whether their specific policies cover overseas medical costs and whether they cover emergency expenses such as a medical evacuation. You may also consider purchasing comprehensive travel insurance. If nothing else, purchase it solely for emergency medical reasons that may arise, covering the cost of medical evacuations from the country. Many packages also offer extended services to baggage, flight departure, and other travel related issues that may arise.

Etiquette Tips for Travelers in Cape Verde

- When entering a building – whether it be a restaurant, bank, or someone's home – it is customary to greet others as you enter with a general *bon dia* (good morning), *bo tardi* (good afternoon), or *bo noti* (good night). Those who do not are considered rude.

- While visiting smaller communities, do not eat in public unless you have brought enough to share with those around you.

- At your discretion, it is encouraged to accept an invitation to visit, engage in conversation, and get to know the people of Cape Verde, particularly in rural areas where communities are close-knit and relatively safe.

- If you are unable to attend an event you have been invited to, it is proper to use non-literal phrases such as "*N tinha dor di cabeça*" ("I had a headache") to explain absences, rather than give excuses.

- Do not risk drinking water from someone's house – this includes juice that has been mixed with powder and water, which is commonly served. If you feel uncomfortable eating or drinking something, tell your host that your stomach is not well – "*Nha barriga sta mal*" and all will be forgiven.

- If you are a vegetarian, it is easiest to refuse meat by claiming you have a health problem and the doctor told you not to ("*N ka podi kume por causo di saude*").

- Cape Verdeans take pride in their attire and personal appearance. It is seen as a sign of respect and an indicator of class. Though much of the rural Cape Verdean population is poor, they are sure to neatly press their attire before going out and covet name brand clothing sent from abroad. It is typical to see youngsters stepping out of shacks, dressed to the nines, looking like they've stepped out of a hip-hop music video.

- Cape Verde is a small place. You shed your anonymity when you step onto Cape Verdean soil. Bear in mind that whatever you do will be observed and will represent your own culture. It is important to conduct yourself in the way you wish for you, and your country, to be perceived.

- Women should be aware that in some communities women who drink, dance in public, and wear revealing clothing is an invitation for men; in other areas it is the norm. For safety reasons, it is vital for women traveling in Cape Verde (especially those traveling alone) to observe what other women are doing to gauge what is culturally appropriate, and safe.

Santo Antão

The towering mountains of Santo Antão are visible from neighboring São Vicente and, as you approach on the ferry, their majestic presence becomes more and more clear. From the coast, a long slow ascent rapidly turns steep, creating a fortress around the interior of the island. Protected within the walls of this fortress are breathtaking views, year round supply of water, a rare peace found only in the most obscure places in the world and a thriving population famed for resilience, abundant agriculture and the production of *grogue.*

Santo Antão is most commonly visited by adventurous hikers as the size and varying terrain provide seemingly endless places to explore. In recent years, this draw for tourists has sprouted an increase in available guided tours and activities; including diving, fishing, cycling and climbing.

GEOGRAPHY

At 300 sq miles (779 sq km), Santo Antão is the second largest island in the archipelago of Cape Verde. It is also home to the second highest peak with Tope d' Coroa reaching a staggering 6,942 feet (1,979m). Despite falling short of reaching first in either of these categories, it is regarded by many as first for natural beauty.

Like all of the islands, Santo Antão is of volcanic origin. A continuous mountain range runs through the island from the northeast to the southwest making it one of the most difficult islands to traverse. The mountains of the northeast capture cloud coverage and moisture creating two separate climates on the north and south ends. Though the two ends are equally jagged and steep, residents of the northern half have adapted to the terrain, introducing terraces and cultivating land along the steep walls of the valleys.

> The island is split into three *conselhos:* Porto Novo, Paúl and Ribeira Grande.

HISTORY

The island was discovered on 17 January 1462 and used for almost a century as only a property divide between the land-hungry Portuguese and

Spanish colonizers. In 1494, the Treaty of Tordesillas created an imaginary line off the coast of Santo Antão splitting the Atlantic Ocean and her islands into West (Spanish) and East (Portuguese).

The importance of Santo Antão went largely unrecognized through much of the period of colonization and development. "Ownership" of this island changed hands many times under the Portuguese crown as leased land, but it wasn't until the Marquess of Gouveia destroyed generations of management under successive Counts of Santa Cruz by mortgaging the land to England after fleeing with the kidnapped Mariana de Penha de França. This foolish act caused a ripple of excitement on the sleepy island as the Portuguese joined together to drive off English prospectors.

In 1852, Santo Antão briefly became the capital of the north. This position of importance was designated for its status as most populated and wealthiest due to the abundance of water and prosperity of agriculture. These positive characteristics were quickly outweighed by negatives as the treacherous landscape and lack of infrastructure prevented products from making their way in and out of Tarrafal, the best port and most difficult spot to access. In 1934, Santo Antão was again demoted as São Vicente took the seat as capital of the north.

Despite these challenges, Santo Antão has continued to flourish. Current projects are underway to improve the roads and increase access of remote communities. A new road was recently inaugurated along the northwest coast connecting Porto Novo directly with Paúl and Ribeira Grande. There are also efforts underway to make more effective use of the island's precious resource, water.

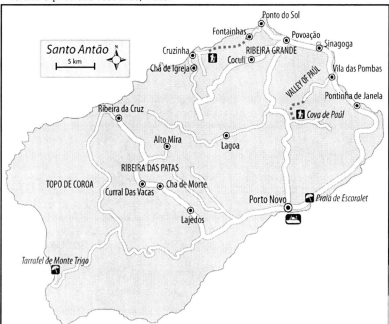

GETTING AROUND SANTO ANTÃO

Though it would be a long and arduous journey, you would only be able to circle the island by foot. It is best to imagine that Santo Antão is like a hand. The port, sticking out into the Atlantic, is the thumb and Porto Novo, the broad palm. From Porto Novo, the roads spread out in different directions, like fingers, covering separate areas of the island. Though some roads now connect, it is best to approach each individually as each is different from the other.

From Porto Novo, public cars head in and out of the city following the boat schedule. Within each district Ribeira Grande, Vila das Pombas and the west of Porto Novo—you will be find cars making circuits around the area, but it can be difficult to get in and out of Porto Novo between boats. Head to the port when the ferry arrives to find a public car to your destination of choice. There are a few tour style buses, but most transportation is by Hiace (15 passenger van) or in the back of a truck. It is also possible to hire a driver to take you to any destination—price ranges from 3000$ to 10000$ depending on location. Taxis are available within the city of Porto Novo and are also happy to take passengers along the coastal road as far as Ponta-do-Sol, but can get expensive. If you are hiking along a main road, you can flag down a car to save your feet and may get a free ride.

Car Rental

Porto Novo Car *Tel. 222.1490*

Motacar *Tel. 222.1021*

Holiday Houses Rent-a-Car *Tel. 222.2800*

Popular Hikes

Northeast

Ponta do Sol to Cruzinha/Chã de Igreja *Scenic coastal hike, a must do.*

Coculi to Chã de Pedras *In the heart of Santo Antão, a glimpse of life in the lush valleys sheltered by towering cliffs.*

Vale de Paúl (Cova to Vila das Pombas) *From (nearly) the top of the island to the coast, a most do if only for the view looking down Vale de Paúl.*

Chã de Igreja to Boca das Ambas Ribeiras *From the nearly coastal town up ando ver the mountains to the heart of Santo Antão*

Northwest

Curral das Vacas along Bordeira de Norte *A walk along the top of the island.*

Chã de Morte to Alto Mira *A trip that takes you over the mountan ridge to the islated valley of Alro Mira on the Northwest side of the island.*

Topo de Coroa *Ascent to the highest point on Santo Antão.*

EXCURSIONS

Santo Antão is revered by Cape Verdeans and visitors alike as one of god's most stunning creations, the sacred crumb that slipped between his fingers. The dramatic landscape and invariable peace that transcends the majestic peaks also makes it one of the most compelling.

> Many hotels and *pensões* offer guided tours or have information about tour guides. Be sure to speak with the proprietor in advance to see if this option is for you.

Local Guides

A great way to experience the beauty of Santo Antão is with a local guide. The names below represent a growing association of trained and experienced guides native to Santo Antão. In addition to guided hikes, they offer an insider perspective and stories only a Cape Verdean can provide. They are located throughout the island, but will happily meet you where you are staying. All guided hikes are 4500$/day, but they also offer one to two week trips covering the island.

CaboVerde Safari Though based in São Vicente, Cabo Verde Safari also offers incredible, personalized tours of Santo Antão. There are three different programs available: the north, the west and the entire island. Prices range from 6500$ to 24000$ depending on the duration of the visit and number of travelers. It's guaranteed to be an informative and eye opening experience that you will not soon forget. *Tel: 231.0299 / 991.1544 caboverdesafari@cvtelecom.cv; www.caboverdesafari.com*

 Alfred "Alemão" (Alfred the German) is actually Alfred the Austrian, but has become a local over his 20+ years in Cape Verde. In addition to some of the best food and *grogue* available on the island, Alfred offers an intimate introduction to life on Santo Antão through personalized tours of Paúl, *grogue* production and agricultural practices—both traditional and innovative. Alfred's initiative won him the honor of the International Environmental Award in 1995 given by the German Travel Association recognizing his commitment to protecting the environment while supporting tourism. Alfred continues his work at O Curral in Chã de João Paz and is expanding his reach to the community of Lagoa up in the mountains on the way to Ribeira Grande (see box "Strada Bedju" on pg 71). *Alsatour: Tel: 225.1213; alfred@alsatur.de; www.alstour.de*

Santtur Located up the hill from the port beyond the Shell station in Porto Novo, Santtur arranges excursions, guides and transportation. *santtur@cvtelecom.cv; santtur@hotmail.com; Tel: 222.1276*

CVB Naturã Growing interest in Adventure Tours has aided the development of Cabo Verde Bikes at the bottom of Avenida Principal in Ponto do Sol. In addition to renting bicycles (1500-4000/day), CVB Naturã offers guided hikes, discovery tours, boat tours and a variety of climbing expeditions. Run by André and Eduardo, expertise is guaranteed. *Tel: 225.1526 / 982.5059 cvbnatura@yahoo.com; www.caboverdenolimits.com; SKYPE: andreCVB*

Hetty Guddens *Tel: 988.3137; cabo_latina_lady@hotmail.com; Languages: English, French, German, Dutch, Potuguese, Kriolu*

Paulo Monteiro Dias *Tel: 951.2410; paulodias279@hotmail.com; Languages: English, French, Portuguese, Kriolu*

Ailton Jorge Silva *Tel: 970.7500; ailtonsilva01@hotmail.com; Languages: English, French, Portuguese, Kriolu*

Rony Da Cruz Ramos *rony_ramos_2@hotmail.com; Languages: English, French, Italian, Spanish, Portuguese, Kriolu*

Porto Novo

Pronounced *Port Nov* and known to locals as "Port," Porto Novo is the largest *conselho* in size, but not in population. Despite the small population, it is the center for hustle and bustle as the ship comes from Mindelo twice a day bringing with it family, visitors and supplies from the more populous island. The growing city didn't ask to be the business hub and can't help it either. If you never leave Port, you may question the beauty that brings this island its fame, though you will have a clear view of the ominous mountains not far out of the city. If you are planning to explore the entire island, Porto Novo is a good home base as you will be able to access transportation to all areas, but don't limit yourself to this area as there is much more hidden from view.

The city sprawls upward, but the commercial area and most movement is concentrated on the road that runs along the coast. The city is essentially split into two halves; the eastern half dominated by the port and the western, Abofador, is famous for a string of bars and markets that line the street. For all intents and purposes, the "center" of town is where these two sides meet by the old soccer stadium.

Despite being the urban center of this largely rural island, life very much runs on traditional hours here. Everything, including markets, close between the hours of 13:00 and 15:00 and you will be hard pressed to find anything open. The best thing to do if you should find yourself in this situation is follow the local example; find a nice restaurant or a good place to sit, grab a bite to eat and a few cold drinks and watch as life passes by. During the week, flocks of uniformed students fill the streets as the school day changes from morning to afternoon classes.

IMPORTANT INFORMATION

Bank There are a few different of banks in Porto Novo. The BCA is currently under renovation, but the doors are still open. BCN has opened at the eastern half of town on the way to the port. All banks are open Monday-Friday from approximately 8:00-15:00.

Hospital: Tel: 222.1130; Off the main road at the top of town,

Pharmacy *Farmácia São João Baptista,* Tel: 222.1393, north of town on the main road; *Farmácia Porto Novo*, right next to the municipal market.

Post Office *Correios* Open Monday-Friday either from 8:00-12:00, 14:00-17:00 or 7:30-15:00; Up the street from the Shell station on the left.

Police *Polícia* Tel: 222.1132; Up by the *correios*.

STAYING IN TOUCH

The two most prominent internet spots are Cyber Caffe (up a back street) and Nats Café (along towards Abofador). Nats doubles as a *papelaria* (office supply/paper store) and general technology hub, but if you can get a seat, internet is half the price of Cyber Caffe. There is a third along the main road, but it seems to keep strange hours. If you catch it open, it's worth a look.

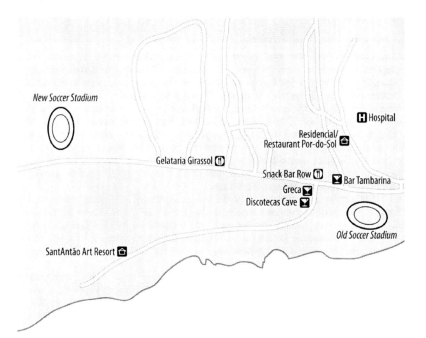

New Soccer Stadium

H Hospital

Residencial/
Restaurant Por-do-Sol

Gelataria Girassol

Snack Bar Row

Bar Tambarina

Greca

Discotecas Cave

Old Soccer Stadium

SantAntão Art Resort

WHAT TO DO

There is a new soccer stadium that has been built on the road going west out of the city. If you hear of a match, it is a guaranteed excitement. Bars and clubs fill up on the weekend, or you can spend some time in the street down by the old stadium and take in the crowd. There is a pleasant enough beach, Praia de Escoralet, along the new road to Ribeira Grande and less attractive sand strewn along the coast of the city. Within the *conselho* outside of the city there are a number of small towns with abundant hiking and exploring.

Don't Miss!

Up Avenida 5 de Julho before you reach the pharmacy you will pass Merceria Rural. It doesn't look like much from the outside, but inside there is *grogue* factory run by Jair Rocha, a local school teacher. Open from 8:00-13:00 and 15:00-18:00, here you can sample and purchase various liquors from his family farm in Ribeira Grande. This is a new location for the store and they are hoping to soon expand to include *doce* (jams), goat cheese and meats also from the family farm.

WHERE TO EAT

Many of the *residencials* in Porto Novo double as restaurants and are often the best places in town. Smaller restaurants may keep strange hours and can be unexpectedly closed. It is always possible to get a quick snack (*toasta mista* or pasteis), but sit down meals are generally only served during lunch

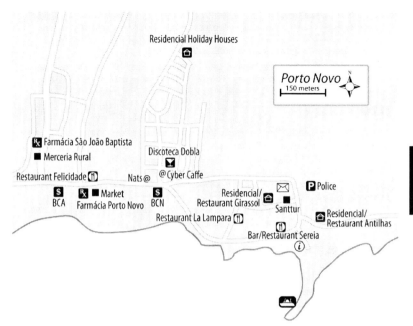

Porto Novo

150 meters

and dinner hours (12:30-15:00 and 18/19:00–22:00 respectively). Late night bites are readily available at a variety of kiosks, grills and food vans in "snack bar row" down by Disco Cave and the old soccer field in the center of town.

Restaurant Antilhas Even if you don't stay at Antilhas, be sure to stop by this patio restaurant downstairs. Lunch and dinner prices are steeper than most other options, but food is made with a bit of creativity and flair that is sometimes lacking in simpler traditional dishes. If heading off for a long hike, grab the breakfast *cachupa*; it's like filling your tank with premium high performance fuel. Arguably the best *cachupa* in Cape Verde, it is the *picante* (hot sauce) that makes the difference. $$ *Tel: 222.1193*

Por-do-Sol Located on the top floor of the *residencial* of the same name, this restaurant offers similar plates as Antilhas but at lower prices. The food and view are well worth the climb to the top. $$ *Tel: 222.2179*

Restaurant Felicidade Impossible to miss along the main road in the center of town, Felicidade is considered one of the more upscale restaurants in Porto Novo. The menu is extensive, but subject to availability. Prices are reasonable and portions are very generous, but in this case, quantity often takes the place of quality. $$ *Tel: 222.1167*

Restaurant La Lampara If you are looking for something a little different, this restaurant offers Cape Verdean dishes with an Italian twist and straight up Italian items on the menu. It is tucked away off the coastal road on the way to the port. Open mainly for dinner, it is definitely the best place to get lasagna in Porto Novo. $$$

Bar/Restaurant Sereia Looking out over the port, food is served during meal times, but it is most commonly used as a watering hole. A great place to sit with a drink and watch as the city comes to life and returns to a state of rest while the boat comes in from Mindelo. $-$$

Gelataria Girassol Open sporadically in Abofador, you may or may not be able to pop in here for ice cream. The city gets hot, so when it's open, it's definitely worth the trip. If not, you can likely score a *fresquinha* at a nearby shop. $

NIGHTLIFE

During the weekend, there is generally a crowd hanging around in the area of **Discotecas Cave** and **Greca** and the cluster of snack bars. The clubs may never really fill up (due to entry fees), but you are guaranteed a crowd in the street. Grab a drink at **Bar Tambarina** nicely set under a massive tamarind tree; you will be able to see the excitement without getting stuck in the middle of it.

On the other end of the city, check out **Discoteca Dobla**. A little classier than the other options, there is generally a good crowd on Friday nights. Don't make the mistake of showing up too early or you will be disappointed. People don't really start pouring in until midnight.

WHERE TO STAY

Residencial/Restaurant Por-do-Sol Error! Bookmark not defined. Por-do-Sol is a well established place to stay. The rooms are reasonably nice and reasonably priced, comparatively a good deal. For nightlife, it is well located just up to street from the center of town. $$ *Tel: 222.2179; pordosolpn@cvtelecom.cv*

Residencial/Restaurant Antilhas Antilhas is likely the first building you will see as you drive up from the port. This location has added to its popularity, but its good reputation is not unfounded. There are a variety of rooms to fit a variety of needs and prices vary according whether or not the rooms have a balcony or apartment. The staff is more than happy to help arrange tours and tour guides for guests. $$-$$$ *Tel: 222.1193; residencialantilhas@hotmail.com*

Residencial Holiday Houses Holiday Houses is in the process of expansion to include more rooms, but there are currently a variety of single and double rooms. If you're traveling on a budget, you can book a room with a shared bathroom. For a little extra, you can book a room with an ocean view. There

Festival of São João Baptista

Porto Novo shares the patron saint of Saint John the Baptist with Brava and throws a party that matches the smaller islands enthusiasm and veneration. Beginning on the 23rd of June, *koladeras* (singers/dancers of praise) start in Ribeira das Patas and lead the 12.5 mile (20 km) procession into Porto Novo. Cape Verdean *kola/cola* is a musical tradition of praise for patron saints grown out of the 17th century that generally consist of a group of men keeping a constant beat on well worn drums of old while a group of women sing out their troubles, aspirations, praise and prayers. The procession symbolizes sacrifice in the name of São João and the following celebration includes food, drink, music and dance in Porto Novo through the 25th when the festivities return to Ribeira das Patas for *SãoJoãozinho*.

are also beautiful apartments with kitchens available for rent (price reduction for stays of more than one week). The staff is happy to arrange excursions and provide car hire. single $, double/apartment $$ *Tel: 222.2800; holidayhouses@hotmail.com; www.capeverdehotelholidayhouses.com*

Residencial/Restaurant Girassol Up on a back street overlooking the port, some rooms have a nice view, while others have a view of the neighboring buildings. From Girassol, you have easy access to the port and transportation around the island that largely follows the boat schedule. Rooms are simple, but clean. $$ *Tel: 222.1383*

SantAntão Art Resort This is the first of what is likely to become multiple resorts and it has done its best to set a good standard. Unfortunately, it is far out of the main areas of the city and is situated in what is becoming a bad neighborhood. However, if you are looking to spend your days exploring the reaches of this beautiful island and your nights resting in the lap of luxury, this is the place for you.

It's located along the coast at the far western end of the town down by the new stadium and appears a bit out of place. It has been open for two years, but the bright paint is already fading. Facilities are all inclusive with everything you could want from a resort at comparatively good prices for Cape Verde. There are larger rooms and suites available at an additional price and children are given half price. $$$ *Tel: 222.2675/76/77; santantaoartresort@gmail.com www.santantao-art-resort.com*

To The West

As you leave port heading west, you will likely not understand why Santo Antão has been called lush, verdant and an agricultural center. In fact, you may feel that you have been dropped on the moon or any other uninhabited surface covered with eerie, sand blown decaying lava flows.

Right on the outskirts of the city, you will pass a new cold storage facility funded by the Millennium Challenge Corporation to help prevent the waste of excess produce and meat There are a few signs and roads that seemingly lead off into nowhere and there is evidence of pilfering of sand for use in construction and a few corrals for livestock. Further along, the road splits: the first right takes you up to the small villages of Ribeira Fria and Poio. The second right takes you into Ribeira das Patas and up over the mountains to the northeast coast.

Festivals and Hoildays on Santo Antão

Januray 17 – Ribeira Grande, Municipal Festival

May 3 – Coculi, Santa Cruz

June 13 – Paúl, Santo António das Pombas

June 23/24 – Porto Novo, São João

June 29 – Chã de Igreja, São Pedro

August 15 – Janela, Nossa Senhora de Piedade

September 24 – Ponta do Sol, Nossa Senhora de Livramento

October 7 – Riberia Grande, Nossa Senhora de Rosário

November 29 – Ribeira da Cruz, Santo André

Santo Antão

Ribeira das Patas

The beauty of Ribeira das Patas is often overshadowed by its more verdant western neighbors, but the landscape and communities here are not without merit. Once you turn off the main road, you begin the slow ascent that eventually leads up and over the mountains and down into the sparsely populated northwest side of the island.

LAJEDOS

Just after turning north (away from the coast), you will pass through the small, but active community of Lajedos. International funding put toward the *Projecto Desenvolvimento Comunitário de Lajedos* (Project for the Development of the Community of Lajedos) has built a beautiful restaurant, Babilónia, created a local homestay program for hikers, visitors and tourists, and started the development of a women's association.

Stop by the Esplanada São João (on the side of the road, impossible to miss) and check out the store that is entirely run and stocked by the hard work of these women. Inside you will find *doce* (jams), liquors, coffee, fabrics and other items produced in and around the community. The time and effort put into production is evident in the beautiful presentation of the products. If you are lucky enough (or plan well) and arrive on the first Saturday of the month, you will find yourself in the midst of the monthly open market/fair displaying products from throughout the region such as goat cheese, seasonal vegetables, juices, liquors, jams and meats. It is guaranteed to be an experience.

Where to Stay

The women of the Lajedos homestays have received training on sanitation, cooking and minimal language skills through the association. They also have facilities within their homes that meet a certain standard to house tourists for one or multiple nights. The houses are not marked, but easily found by asking around. All houses charge 1000$ for one guest and 2000$ (as of late 2009) for two. Breakfast is an additional 200-250 and other meals may be available on request.

Lajedos Homestays
Sónia: 227.1049
Lola: 227.1008
Miriã: (also works at the restaurant) 227.1005
Lauinha: 227.1009
Andreza: 227.1021
Francesce: 982.0154

Where to Eat

 Babylónia Though visible from the road, this beautiful restaurant is set up along a path. Enter across from the small blue building before the school and you will feel like you have disappeared into an old agricultural fairytale. The short path winds through fields of sugarcane and wildflowers. Definitely call in advance as the only customers are tourists and passers-by, but there is a full menu with delicious plates at a reasonable price *Tel: 227.1054* $/$$

Lajedos Project

There's a project going on in Lagedos that is working on increasing tourism and marketing local goods. It's been there for about 7 years but there's still a lot of work to be done. Right now a group of local women use the fruits grown in the village (apples, guava, papaya, mango) to make *doce*, juice, and flavored *ponche*. The problem is that when tourists come to Santo Antao, they arrive in Porto Novo, but usually jump right on a Hiace and go to the other side of the island. Right now there is a UN volunteer living in Lagedos, working on a project to train thirteen local Cape Verdeans from six villages in our area. They will take classes in local culture, geography, history, environment, and English. The hope is that when groups go through the local villages here, there will be trained guides to take them around. This, in addition to the Feira on the first Saturday of the month, will give the locals income generating opportunities by selling their homemade goods, like goat cheese, baskets, grog, etc.

Tomorrow is the Feira that Lagedos does the first Saturday of every month. This includes lunch, and vendors who sell food and handmade goods. The students are "hosting" the Feira tomorrow, giving presentations on their towns based on the work they've done so far.

This past Wednesday, the whole group of students, the UN volunteer, and myself, all got into a car at 8:00 and went around to all of their villages where they each had the opportunity practice guiding. In the first village we went to, Chã de Coxete, we took a walk to the house of a poet from the 1930s. The students gave a talk about the history and about the poet's life, and we talked about what kinds of information tourists may want to know. Then we went to Alto Mira, a village split into 3 zones. We walked for about an hour, talked about the agriculture (sweet potatoes, garlic, mangos, papayas, and much more), and went to see the church. After, we drove to Ribeira da Cruz, another rural town, and down to the bottom of the *ribeira* where we then walked for about 20 minutes leading to the most beautiful black sand beach. We ate goat cheese and made a fire, grilled fish, and drank homemade apple juice. Then walked back to the car, drove up to the next town, Cha di Norte. This was the first time I had ever been to Cha di Norte, and I definitely got an eye opener. The people there live in much harder conditions; they have a difficult time getting water, it's extremely dry, there's no electricity, and only one person has a car for the entire town, about an hour's drive from Ribeira da Cruz on a very dusty, rocky road. It's so far removed that high school students live in Porto Novo during the school year because there's no daily transportation. Some of the houses had walls made out of plastic tarps. The dust from the Sahara that blows over here to Cape Verde was so thick over the mountains in Cha di Norte that you couldn't even see the sky, and by the end of the day my skin was covered in a layer of sand.

students are amazing-- smart, interesting, and friendly. It feels good to be part of something that will hopefully turn out to improve the lives of the locals and increase tourism on this side of the island. I know that everyone loves Ribeira Grande because it's so green and "tropical," but this side of the island is really spectacular too.

- Lauren Knauss

Santo Antão

LAGOA

As you continue north along the main road through Chiã do Morte, a quick turn marked by a painted mural takes you to the small agricultural area of Lagoa. This circular route can be started by car, but finished only on foot. As you head away from the main road, you will pass a massive, steep rock formation that resembles a finger. The foot path takes you up and over a hill through a cluster of houses called Cartão. There is something mysterious and charming about this little area as you haul yourself up the steep steps and realize that the residents do this every day. As you pass beyond the village, the path becomes rough until you come upon the well groomed agricultural area of Lagoa. Fields of sugarcane, papaya trees and assorted other fruits and vegetables are sustained through irrigation. It is possible to walk back around to Chã do Morte, or (if it is open) you can stay the night in the quiet *pensão*.

Where to Stay & Eat

There is a small *pensão* being built in Lagoa by a German man. Contact him at Tel: 980.4985 for more information.

CURRAL DAS VACAS

Overlooking the new school in Chã do Morte, Curral das Vacas is a small peaceful community on the way to the ridge that separates the west from the northwest. There may not be an immediate draw to stay here unless you look to climb Topo d' Coroa and explore the northwest. From this area, there are a few trails that lead up over the ridge and on to the daunting peak.

Where to Stay & Eat

Pensão At the time of research, this house was in the final stages of being converted into a *pensão* and had not yet been named. The rooms, however, are brand new, well furnished and refreshing. Price includes half board and they are happy to supply a picnic lunch for 250$ each. $ *Tel: 227.2000 (Tchiquinha)*

The Northwest

The road leading over the ridge forks before the pass and taking you to either of two isolated communities in the northwest. Ribeira da Cruz, the "end of the line" of the western fork is a small, but proud, village that relies on careful irrigation of small areas to produce crops. The soccer field just outside of town is the pride and joy of the youth, drawing crowds religiously for practice and games. From here, it is possible to hike down to the coast and around to Tarrafal. The eastern fork in the road takes you through the valley of Alto Mira. A few small villages are sprinkled along the road and from here, you can ask for directions to the long and tiring trek that leads to Chã di Igreja (guide recommended).

Tarrafal de Monte Trigo

Those from the island who have been to Tarrafal claim it is the most beautiful beach they have seen. Though it may not match up to the seemingly endless miles of beach along the shores of Boa Vista or the brilliant white sand beaches of Sal, Tarrafal is a departure from most of this island's rocky coastline. The sand is a sort of off-black color and the grains are thicker and rougher than the fine sand found elsewhere. It is a not an abrasive sand, but rather a welcome beach partner as it is easily cleaned from the body and any other items brought to the shore.

Up the hill and outside the village, there is an oasis sprung from a natural water source that is not common on this half of the island. Residents take full advantage of this rare resource by planting corn, beans and select fruits.

Getting There

It is said that the sweetest fruit is always the one out of reach, and that may be partially true of this isolated "paradise." It is hard not to wonder if the joy and glory around the beauty of Tarrafal is not partially due to the joy and beauty of surviving the trip. If you intend to spend your entire vacation exploring the reaches of Santo Antão, then Tarrafal is a must as you traverse a large expanse of the unexplored west and reach heights second only to the climb to the crater of Chã das Caldeiras of Fogo, but the road is long and rough, often washed out during the rainy season. Unless a reluctant driver with the right vehicle is hired for 10,000$, it is impossible to make the trek in one day. Because it usually ends in an overnight stay, it is best to book accommodations in advance as there are a limited number of rooms.

There is public transportation that makes the trip once daily heading in to meet the morning ferry and returning after the afternoon ferry. Hang out at the dock and ask around for cars to Tarrafal to arrange a ride that will likely be packed with supplies and a few passengers.

WHERE TO STAY & EAT

Residencial Mar Tranquilidade A small cluster of cottages run by a German couple, it is reputed as one of the nicest places to stay on Santo Antão. This cluster of cottages offers a beautiful place to relax. $$-$$$ *Tel: 227.6012; info@martranquilidade.com; www.martranquilidade.com*

Dona Marie Alice and Jamie da Cruz This local couple caught wind of the success of Mar Tranquilidade and opened a small *pensão* overlooking the beach. Simple rooms are without hot water or private bathrooms. $$ *Tel: 227.6002*

Excerpt from "Great Heights" by Nadia Fazel

When you get off the ferry, you arrive in a town that looks like it was leftover from the development of Mindelo. It is similar because it is immediately accessible from Mindelo and therefore a little more 'modern' with amenities slightly easier to obtain. As you drive away from the Port town and into the mountains, you climb higher and higher until you can see Mindelo from across the channel. This side of the island is browner, and even looks a little like the Rocky Mountains in Arizona. But the drive itself is amazing. You continue to climb until you reach the clouds and there is so much moisture in the air that it is practically raining. You find yourself driving through the clouds and the air is thicker than any other fog you have ever been through. But then you reach a point where the clouds are below you and in fact only on one side of the island, running like a waterfall over the mountains to the other side.

To the North

Thanks to the Millennium Challenge Corporation, there are a number of new roads throughout Cape Verde. In Santo Antão, there are now two ways to get to the northern half of the island. The old road (*strada bedju*) leaves through the center of Porto Novo and heads up through the mountains, descending into Povoação of Ribeira Grande on the other side. The new road leaves Porto Novo to the east of the port and winds up and along the coast, coming around through Paúl before connecting to Ribeira Grande.

Ribeira Grande

If you enter this great area via the old road, the name "large valley" will immediately make sense. Though Ribeira Grande comprises less than 1/3 of the island, it is home to almost 2/3 of the population and boasts some of the most stunning areas. A more apt name would probably be Ribeiras Grandes as the *conselho* stretches across multiple ridges and valleys once connected by daunting foot paths. Despite efforts to connect and improve roads and bridges, heavy rains in 2009 washed out sections of the new road in Coculi and along the way to Chã de Igreja.

Ribeira Grande is known for its agriculture and traditional way of life. In this area, many live untouched by modernity that is spreading throughout the islands. Intricate terracing and antique irrigation methods have allowed the population to bring life from the soil, and the increasing presence of modern techniques and technology have created a conflicting presence that questions tradition that has allowed for survival in harsh and demanding conditions.

It is possible to spend days exploring all the hidden valleys of Ribeira Grande, but the most prominent areas and starting/stopping points are the Povoação, Ponta do Sol, Coculi and, increasingly, Chã de Igreja. Keep in mind that from each of these points, it is possible to hike to another off the road on a myriad of stunning explorations. Some paths may require a guide, but others, such as Ponto do Sol to Cruzinha/Chã de Igreja, are easily followed with just a companion.

POVOAÇÃO

Povoação is an absurdly busy little village despite its feeling of isolation. Nestled between looming mountain ridges are roads that wind freely, with houses and shops lined along the cobbled roads. When walking the streets, one may hear echoes of a small mountain village in Europe. Many little *praças* (town squares) are scattered about the village. At any given time, you are likely to run across a group of old men, school children playing in the street, or a growing group youth just "hanging out." Despite being a small city, it is possible to pass hours walking up and down the narrow streets and through the neighborhoods separated by ridges and valleys.

Important Information

Bank: There are two banks in Povoação, BCA and Caixa Económica. Banks are open Monday-Friday from approx 8:00-15:00.

Hospital: Tel: 221.1130 The new hospital funded by the Luxemburg Corporation has opened along Rua Luxemburg.

Pharmacy: *Farmácia São Lucas* on the corner by the hospital.

Post Office *Correios*: Open Monday-Friday either from 8:00-12:00, 14:00-17:00 or 7:30-15:00.

Police *Polícia*: Tel: 221.1132

Rent-A-Car: Spencer Construções & Imobiliára: Tel: 221.2323, m 991.2412; sci@cvtelecom.cv, www.sci.cv.

Points of Interest

Born in Povoação in 1837, Roberto Durate da Silva became famous for his work with Chemistry in France. Recipient of the *Prix Jecker* (Jecker Prize) from the Paris Academy of Sciences in 1885 for work with Organic Chemistry, da Silva worked with other famous chemists such as the American James Mason Crafts and his French colleagues, Adolphe Wurtz, Henri Sainte-Claire Deville, Marcelin Berthelot e de Jerôme Balard. His house still stands (*Casa de Roberto Duarte da Silva*, House of Roberto Duarte Silva) in the center of town across from *Residencial* 5 de Julho and *praça* Marcal, although there is nothing more than a plaque denoting this significance.

Another interesting site is the recently restored *Igreja de Nossa Senhora do Rosário* (Church of Our Lady of the Rosary), which was originally built in the 18th century and consecrated in 1755 by Bishop Valente who fled from the troubles of Santiago.

Shops & Whatnot

Like any village of any importance with a significant population, the streets of Povoação are ripe with a variety of Chinese run *lojas* that, more often than not,

Strada Bedju, **Experiencing Ribeira Grande by Car**

If you are not interested in spending the day hiking, but would still like to experience the stunning landscape, hire a driver to take you along *strada bedju* "the old road" that climbs straight up from Porto Novo. When you reach Cova, take a slight detour to the right and head out toward Pico da Cruz, one of the highest points on the island. At 5953 feet (1814m), on a clear, you will look out over São Vicente to Santa Luzia, São Nicolau and beyond.

From Cova, it is possible to hike down through the valley of Paúl, possibly one of the most stunning views in Cape Verde. The path is long and winding, but there are many hidden gems within the valley.

If you return to the road, continue on to Lagoa, hopeful site of the newest project of Alfred Alemão (O Curral, Chã de João Paz, Paúl Tel: 223.1213) where he plans to educate the community in organic farming and wire the entire community for broadcast over the internet. Lagoa is in the process of development with the incorporation of agricultural and water resource management by building cisterns and setting up irrigation infrastructure. The goal of this project is to connect the isolated village in Cape Verde to the outside world and offer visitors the opportunity to learn more about life in Cape Verde before, during and after their stay. (see www.alsatour.de for more information)

If you stay the course to Povoação, you will pass by small agricultural communities with beautifully terraced fields on frighteningly sheer slopes. Though at times the curves in the road seem impossibly sharp and the valleys impossibly steep, trust in your driver as until 2009, this was the primary road. They are entirely used to this treacherous trek.

carry mostly the same items. If you are running low on supplies, these can be a savior as you will often find clothes and other products at low prices.

For a quick bite or a snack for the road, there is also a good supply of bakeries and small markets around. Along Rua da Horta, check out **Padaria da Luz** for fresh bread and **SISA,** the market run by the association that not only sells food, but serves quick snacks.

Where to Eat

Café 5 de Julho Outdoor patio attached to the *residencial* of the same name in front of *praça* Marcal, this is a popular place for locals and tourists alike. Prices are a little steep, but the food is very good and portions are generous. Probably the best *cachupa* around. $$ *Tel: 221.1345*

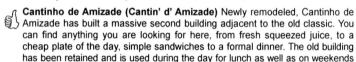

Cantinho de Amizade (Cantin' d' Amizade) Newly remodeled, Cantinho de Amizade has built a massive second building adjacent to the old classic. You can find anything you are looking for here, from fresh squeezed juice, to a cheap plate of the day, simple sandwiches to a formal dinner. The old building has been retained and is used during the day for lunch as well as on weekends for grilling and occasional *tocatinho* (musical performance). $-$$ *Tel: 221.1392*

Lanchonette Flôr & Eventos More of a snack bar than a restaurant, this little place across from the primary school along Rua da Horta offers something virtually unheard of in Cape Verde—a child's play space. This is no McDonalds' supermaze, but it is an interesting initiative. $ *Tel: 221.2939*

Restaurant Trópical Certainly the most expensive, this is also likely the nicest place to have a meal. The fare is typical to other restaurants in Cape Verde and may or may not be worth the extra cash. Specialties include lobster and other seafood. $$-$$$ *Tel: 2211129*

Pizzaria Rosa/Lanchonette Rosa This small pizzeria off a side street by the Nazarene Church has expanded to a second location along Rua Luxemburg. It is still possible to grab a delicious pizza at the original restaurant, but you can now enjoy a more extensive menu in a larger space that is also available for parties and catering. The music can sometimes be a bit loud. $$ *Tel: 221.2572, m.986.7877*

Municipal Market Also down the side street by the Nazarene Church, the second floor of the municipal market is one of the best places to grab a quick lunch at a reasonable price, a heaping plate-of-the-day. $

Green&Purple Right across the street from the new Cantinho de Amizade is a tall building with green and purple vertical stripes. On the ground floor is a garage that has been converted into a bar/restaurant. It may not look like much, but it is a great place to grab a few drinks and some fresh, delicious fried *moreia* (moray eel). Various other plates are also served depending on availability/request. A local favorite. $

Nightlife

Povoação is not known for its nightlife which can be hit-or-miss at best. An evening well spent in this sleepy village may be at any of the assortment of bars watching a soccer game, popping in on Capoeira lessons at the primary school or, the local favorite, walking up and down the main street.

Try the **Shell** for a cold beer or a coffee. It may sound strange, but the Shell station is the best stocked store and is often the place to be.

In the past, Povoação has hosted Sete Sóis Sete Luas, an annual celebration/presentation of music and arts from Mediterranean and Portuguese speaking countries. Generally held in November, there is a permanent stage at the edge of town. For more information, log on to www.7sois7luas.com.

Where to Stay

 Residencial Top d' Croa Set back from the heart of the village, climbing to the top of this *residencial* may feel like the ascent of Top d' Coroa, but arriving at the rooms make it worth the trip. Slightly less expensive than Trópical, Top d' Coroa is a peaceful and welcoming place to stay. $$ *Tel: 221.2794, m. 991.7414; viagitur@hotmail.com*

Residencial/Restaurant/Bar Trópical Supposedly a nice place to stay, the owner can be a bit abrasive. The restaurant is known as the most expensive, but also nicest place to eat. Price varies by room size and location/view. $$ *Tel: 221.1129*

Residencial 5 de Julho Even if you don't stay here, the maze of a building is worth exploring; it will likely take you the duration of your stay to figure out how to get in and out of the building. It is clearly an old building, but the rooms are very well maintained and varying. There are 14 rooms, 4 with private bathrooms. A double with breakfast runs 2000$, and a single is 1700$ with breakfast and 1200$ without. *Tel: 221.1345*

 Residencial Biby From the outside, the building does not look like much, but inside are ten simple rooms that are well kept and offer private bathrooms with hot water. Just up the street from Hotel Trópical, this is a much more affordable option with a familial feel (breakfast included in price). single $, double $$ *Tel: 221.1149; residencialbibi@cvtelecom.cv*

Residencial Aliança May or may not be functioning. Nice location toward the center of town, but building appears to be under renovation. $ *Tel: 221.1246*

Ponto de Levada

At the end of Rua da Horta is Ponto de Levada (meaning the carrying off point). Spencer Construções & Imobiliára dominates the end of the unassuming street that starts the path into the mouth of the *ribeira*. Not much is visible from this humble street corner beyond the massive holiday house construction project (Spencer), but beyond this, the road meanders through the valley ultimately climbing halfway up the furthest reaches at Horta da Garça. Before you catch one of the cars heading into *ribiera*, grab some delicious sugar cookies at the little bakery/snack bar on the corner.

Within this large valley for which Ribeira Grande undoubtedly gets its name, there are a multitude of villages and houses scattered up along the mountainous walls. Similar to Paúl, you could spend a week's vacation just within the valley, hiking to the many different villages.

COCULI

The unassuming "center" of the *ribeira*, at first glance, there doesn't seem to be much here worthy of note. A new school was opened in 2006 for the many students that come from as far as Cruzinha. Many shops, a post office and internet café are lined along the street, saving the weary traveler from the trip into Povoação. Beyond Coculi, the road splits with a left taking you into Chã de Pedras, a village living in the past, where you can stay the night in the guesthouse **Antero Chantre de Olivieira** (Tel: 224.1133) and check out the *trapiche* that is still pulled by oxen in the traditional manner to produce *grogue*.

Take a right at the fork to continue your trek deeper into the heart of the island. About 6 miles (10 km) up into the *ribeira*, you will enter Boca de Caruja, a sunny, quiet village kept modest in its dramatic backdrop.

Where to Stay & Eat

Pedracin Village (Boca de Caruja) Designed and built by native of Boca de Caruja, the cottages are built of stone with thatched roofs in a traditional manner using local methods. Despite the antique look and feel, there is no shortage of modern comforts. The water in the pool is regularly replaced with the supply of rain water. There is a full restaurant, and guides and excursions can be arranged. Horseback excursions are also available. Breakfast is included, lunch and dinner available for order. Single $$, double $$$, suite $$$$ *Tel: 224.2020; pedracin@cvtelecom.cv*

Beyond Boca de Caruja, the road splits again at Boca das Ambas Ribeiras (the mouth of both valleys). From here, a path is barely visible on the right that leads up and over the mountains into Chã de Igreja. It is possible to continue straight along the road into Horta da Garça that eventually leads to Chã de Igreja/Cruzinha, or bear left to Caibros where you can stay perched in the middle of the mountains at **Casa Zeca** (Tel: 221.1720) or the house of **Benvindo Nascimento Lima** (Tel: 224.1174) or return to Povoação and head to Ponta do Sol.

PONTA DO SOL

The tried and true tourist destination on Santo Antão, Ponta do Sol has a little bit of everything and is a great starting point for many hikes in the northeast of the island. The town itself is built on a slope that grows abruptly steeper at the foot of the mountains. A road snakes across the top of the village, stunting upward growth beyond the landmark cemetery. The bottom of the village is limited by the sea, and marked by the disused airport, fenced off with an impossibly short runway cutting through the tiny peninsula.

Interest in Ponta do Sol has waned in past years, but its long history as a destination has allowed for the development of a fairly solid infrastructure. Here you will find established hotels and pensões, as well as innovative new places. There is charm in the peaceful isolation of this, the municipal seat of Ribeira Grande. There is also access to the sea as well as the mountains and is the starting point for one of the most famous "must do" hikes on the island: Ponta-do-Sol/Fontainhas to Cruzinha/Chã de Igreja.

Lingua-de-Vaca

Lingua-de-Vaca, *Echium stenosiphon*, means literally "the cow's tounge" is named for the rough texture of the toungued leaves. It can be found pushing out from impossibly rocky ground from 500m upwards on Santo Antão, São Vicente and São Nicolau and will be recognized by the impossibly bright pink and purple flowers. On the island of Fogo, look out for the variation unique to the Chã das Caldeiras (*Echium vulcanorum*). The leaves are similar to the variation found elsewhere, spade shaped and rough, but the flowers are larger, bell shaped and blueish-white in color.

Airport of Ponta do Sol

Looking at this stunted airstrip, it may be hard to believe that planes ever landed there. The use of this airstrip was halted after the fatal crash on August 7, 1999. Bad weather conditions did not allow the plane to land and in an attempt to return to the take off point in Mindelo, the landing plane was blown off course and crashed into the nearby mountains.

Transportation

If you would like to arrange transport anywhere, Cecílio (Tel: 992.3634) has developed a transportation empire in Ponta do Sol.

Staying in Touch

For reliability, Cybernet Café in the pink building next to the *Câmara* is your best bet. Price is charged by the minute.

What to Do: Hiking

The hike between Ponta-do-Sol/Fontainhas to Cruzinha/Chã de Igreja is probably the most famous trek in Santo Antão, and for good reason. It is at least a four hour trek filled with some grueling moments of ascent and descent, but the views are well worth the sweat. It is possible to hike in either direction, but it is said that the hike is best done from Ponta-do-Sol as the ups and downs by Fontainhas can be brutal after a few hours on the trail. Despite stretches of near abandonment, the trail itself is well maintained and easily navigated. A few populated villages appear as if out of a fairytale and the abandoned buildings just add to the mythical appeal.

Shopping

EKI-EKO This shop above CVB Naturã was opened by a French woman who visits all the islands seeking products that are art specific to Cape Verde. There is some information and maps available, but all of the art and souvenirs are "authentic" to Cape Verde. *Tel: 225.1526; eki_eko.capvert@yahoo.fr*

Where to Eat

BeiraMar (Chez Fatima) The tables are crowded on top of one another and the décor is a bit tacky, but it is famous around town for the seafood specialties. Other food is fairly typical Cape Verdean fare. Dinner is available after 19:00 and reservations are recommended. $$-$$$ *Tel: 225.1008*

 Por-do-Sol Arte Exceptional meals that are inspired by both French and Cape Verdean cuisine. Open only for dinner and very limited seating, reservations are required in advance. $$-$$$ *Tel: 225.1480*

O Valeiro This boat inspired restaurant is certainly the most uniquely shaped restaurant here as the seats and bar literally hang out over the sea. The food is fairly typical, but the prices are very reasonable. A great spot for lunch or an afternoon refreshment. $-$$ *Tel: 225.1480*

 Por d' Sol/Restaurant Panoramica Up along the coast, the Senegalese run restaurant is open for lunch and dinner and, though the prices are a bit steep, the food is excellent, well cooked and have a variety of flavorful influences. Open for lunch and dinner. $$-$$$

Cantinho do Gato Preto A relatively new addition to the restaurants of Ponto do Sol, the owners, an Italian woman and a French woman, have done an excellent job integrating and grabbing onto an untapped niché in the market. The food is a delicious mix of French, Italian and Cape Verdean. The beautiful indoor patio is a great place to enjoy lunch or dinner. $$-$$$ *Tel: 225.1539*

 Bar/Restaurant Sol Portense Definitely the most affordable and authentic (Cape Verdean) place to grab a bite to eat. Stop by or call an hour before and your meal will be on the table waiting for you. $ *Tel: 225.1004*

Escondidinha A little café with a big name. Located in the newly built "mall," you can grab a coffee or a quick snack here and sit outside and watch life go by. $

Nightlife

There is one established night club on the edge of town facing the airport, but movement is sporadic and unpredictable. Historically, nightlife is a bit more active than Povoação, be sure to ask around on Fridays or Saturdays to see if there is anything happening. In addition to the club, there are some restaurants that stay open a bit later and there are a number of small bars scattered around the town.

Oceano A typical Cape Verdean club, Oceano is hit-or-miss. Generally open on Saturdays, look for fliers and ask around for upcoming events, otherwise you may be one of a handful of people in the club. *Tel: 225.1347*

Paulu Mar This little bar is a popular spot at night. A short walk up the hill towards the road to Fontainhas, take a right at the Jardim (*Alice in Wonderland* mural) and it will be on your left.

Lúcia's Ask around for Lúcia's. A popular spot with locals, Lúcia is also happy to take in groups of tourists for small meals and drinks.

Where to Stay

Residencial Chez Pasquinha Located a few streets back from the sea, the upper rooms have a nice view of the coast. Established eight years ago, the building and rooms have been well maintained. Each room has two twin beds and breakfast included. single $, double $$ *Tel: 225.1091*

Residencial Leila Leite Across from Hotel Blue Bell, this small place looks like nothing in comparison. The rooms, however, are charming, clean and quaint for a decent price. There are eight rooms, four with doubles, three twin and one single with a shared bathroom, breakfast included. $ *Tel: 225.1056*

 Casa Familial Dedei The little sign hanging above the door does no justice to this gem. Dona Maria da Rosario (Dedei) and her husband Advilo run a neat little *residencial* with a beautiful room in their house and five additional rooms in a large, restored house down the street. The rooms are open and clean, all with desks, but not all with private bathrooms. Hot water is supplied by use of solar panels on the roof. Breakfast included. $ *Tel: 225.1037*

Chez Fatima/BeiraMar Dona Fatima, daughter of Dedei and Advilo, has opened a large *pensão* on the corner by the sea. The eight rooms are mostly twins with one double bed. There is a lovely veranda with an excellent view and a rusty, rundown bar. The rooms are also a little tired looking, despite the upkeep. Breakfast included. $$ *Tel: 225.1008*

Hotel BlueBell The largest hotel in Ponta do Sol, BlueBell has held this title for a while (and it shows). The hallways and rooms are immaculate, but the furniture and décor is mismatched, tired and falling apart in some areas. This is, however, the only place where you will find extras like a restaurant, bar, gym, laundry and a safe for valuables. The staff will also be happy to arrange tours and excursions for both guests and nonguests. There are 27 rooms, eight twin, twelve double and two suites. Price varies by room and number of guests. $$-$$$ *Tel: 225.1215; bluebell@cvtelecom.cv*

Residencial Ponta do Sol A newer addition to the *residencial* family in Ponta do Sol, the 14 rooms are clean and welcoming with all amenities including private bathroom, hot water and fans. On the road coming into the village, you will have easy access to cars leaving for Povoação and Porto Novo as well as an even quieter visit. There are eight doubles and six twins, some with a veranda. Breakfast is included. single $, double and triple $$ *Tel: 225.1238 residencialpsol@cvtelecom.cv*

 Por-do-Sol Arte This small, unique guesthouse is an absolute gem on the edge of the city looking out at the sea. The four rooms are all different and the beautiful, handcrafted furniture is built specific for each one. Contact for price and availability depending on duration of stay. The staff is very helpful with information or assistance arranging an excursion. It is also home to one of the best restaurants in the area. $$-$$$ *Tel: 225.1121; porsolarte@yahoo.fr*

Fontainhas

If you are not up for the intense four hour hike along to coast from Ponta-do-Sol to Cruzinha/Chã de Igreja, a trip to Fontainhas is a must. Less than an hour out of Ponta do Sol along the northwest coast, you will round a corner to find a narrow strip of houses perched in the depths of the *ribeira*. Looking at the houses, it is impossible to imagine who thought to build them so precariously, but from a glance into the valley far below where the ocean meets land, you may be able to spot the pulley system that has been set up to aid in what seems an impossible cultivation.

CRUZINHA

This little village would remain undiscovered if it weren't for the spectacular hike from Ponta-do-Sol or the small, swimmable spot right outside town, *Praia da Ribeira Seca* (Beach of the Dry Valley) that has been dubbed "turtle beach" for the turtle sightings in the months of August and September. During the day, you will find small groups of boys and men sitting along the wall looking out over the water either waiting for the catch to come in or for something interesting to happen.

> A handful of small houses cluster around the bay, with one hotel/restaurant.

Where to Stay & Eat

There is only one place to stay and eat in Cruzinha, so it's a pretty easy decision.

Pensão/Restaurant SonaFish This little *pensão* doesn't have a shortage of rooms or seats in the restaurant, but the ten rooms look, feel and smell every bit of their ten years of use. That said, the rooms are clean and well-kept and the owners are pleasant, happily taking advantage of the monopoly. Four rooms have a private bathroom and the other six share three additional bathrooms. Half-board included in price. single $, double $$. *Tel: 226.1027*

CHÃ DE IGREJA

A twenty minute walk from Cruzinha, this tiny village sits perched on a cliff side, virtually in the middle of nowhere. Home to just a few hundred residents, its popularity is growing faster than the meager population. The town is built around a small church with a small kiosk in the center, a few stores and a private club (The Dancing Trapiche) that opens once a year for the town festival (Dia de São Pedro, June 29). Perhaps it is the small town feel and peace that is increasingly drawing a tourist crowd. One thing is for sure, you will get a good night's sleep under the thick blanket of clouds and country silence.

Getting There and Away

Most visitors hike into Chã de Igreja along the coast or over the mountains, but there are a few cars that make the trip from Chã de Igreja to Porto Novo in the morning (700$) and return in the afternoon. You can ask around in Porto Novo, Paúl or Povoação (350$).

Where to Stay & Eat

Senhor Rodrigo A returned immigrant, Senhor Rodrigo has rebuilt his family home into a much larger place, renting extra rooms to tourists and guests. Breakfast is included and half board is available. $ *Tel: 231.6360*

Senhor Arimndo Similar story as Senhor Rodrigo, Armindo has created a little haven for his family and guests fully equipped with a lush garden and relaxing seats in which to enjoy it. Depending on the season, there may be a minimum stay. Kitchen is open to guests (meaning, "Make your own breakfast"). $ *Tel: 996.8942*

Senhor Delgado First tall building on the road to Horta da Garça, breakfast and hot water included, dinner optional. $ *Tel: 262.1162*

The Northeast

If you choose to bypass the treacherous journey over the mountains into Riberia Grande, it is now possible to head to the northeast along the new coastal road. Inaugurated in 2009, the asphalt road runs along the northeast coast of the island, connects the three *conselhos* and will take you through stunning landscapes and past the few points of interest along the way.

PRAIA DE ESCORALET

This small beach is along the road within walking distance from Porto Novo. During the summer, it is possible to enter the water here, but beware in the windier seasons (November-May) as the sea becomes quite rough and the beach is often swallowed by the tide.

PONTINHA DE JANELA

Within the conselho of Paúl, but situated between Porto Novo and Paúl, Pontinha de Janela is a tiny place, but may be of some interest. Here you will find the *Farol Fontes Pereira de Melo* (lighthouse of Fontes Pereira de Melo) known commonly as Boi lighthouse inaugurated in 1886. You can also make your way up to Fajã de Janela to see the mysterious *Rocha*

Scribida (inscribed rock). There is much debate whether the writing on this rock is from the many Portuguese that passed through in the 15th century or, a newer theory, that it was a mark left by the Chinese in their expedition of 1421 to "discover the world." There is no conclusive evidence either way, but the second theory would mean that the Portuguese did not, after all, "discover" Cape Verde.

CONSELHO DE PAÚL

The *conselho* of Paúl is slowly developing into a hotspot for tourism on Santo Antão. Vila das Pombas is deceptively uninteresting, for it is truly the depths of the *ribeira* that give Paúl its growing popularity. The valley itself is famous within the island for its almost permanent source of water and much of the islands agriculture comes from the its well irrigated mountain sides. Though it is possible to catch a car along the new road, the best way to reach this valley is by foot, hiking down from Cova de Paúl along the old road to Ribeira Grande (see below). If this is not an option, there are many shorter hikes that are easily reached by car/foot along the road that climbs all the way up to the community of Manuel dos Santos.

What to Do: Hiking

Cova de Paúl is the well preserved eastern crater now used for agricultural purposes. Take a car to Corda along the old road from Porto Novo. When the car completes the ascent up into the mountains, the road will fork. To the far right, you can head to Pico da Cruz, where, on a clear day, you can look out over the eastern islands. The road continues straight around Cova, but you can follow the middle road down into the crater and climb up the other side. When you reach the pinnacle of the trail, the wind is fierce and clouds rush over the surrounding peaks. Despite the physical assault of wind and cold, it is the view down into the valley that will take your breath away. On a clear day, you can see all the way down through the valley and out to the ocean. The lone path that takes you down switchbacks below you, disappearing at some points and reappearing impossibly far away. The hike itself takes three to four hours and is arduous, downhill the entire way, but entirely unforgettable.

VALLEY OF PAÚL

If you hike down from Cova, the path eventually merges with the road in Cavoquinho. You can continue on your way down to Vila das Pombas—most cars will offer a ride—or spend some time in the peaceful, verdant valley. Here you will find much of the islands sugar cane and *grogue* production as well as abundant fruits and vegetables. Notorious in Cape Verde for its year-round supply of fresh water, it is an agricultural paradise in comparison with many of the other islands.

Within the valley, there are endless paths to explore and hikes for the tireless adventurer. Many of the establishments here—Cavoquinho, Casa das Ilhas—offer guided tours and a list of available hikes. As one of the agricultural centers of SantoAntão, there is not much hustle and bustle on a day-to-day basis, unless it is time to plant or reap the labors of the season. For the traveler looking to get away from the hectic pace of life and step into a peaceful, beautiful environment, fully removed from the pressures of city life, this is the place to come. Spend an afternoon sitting on the wall, kick a soccer ball with the local kids or go on a mango hunt to get a taste of the slower pace of life.

Where to Stay

With the growing popularity of Paúl, there has also been an increase in places to stay, many of which are located up in the valley for easy access to hikes.

Residencial Cavoquinho Waiting to greet you at the top of the road where the path from Cova and the road to Vila das Pombas meet, Cavoquinho is a good bet for anyone who starts the hike down from Cova late or is looking to explore the higher reaches of the valley. $$-$$$ *Tel: 223.2065, m: 998.9919; www.cavoquinho.com*

Casa de Sandro Lacerenza This establishment has been here for five years and seems to be growing. The artisan shop is tempting, despite the long walk to Vila, but the rooms may be more tempting after a long hike. Many young people of Manuel dos Santos are employed here and will do their best to have you sample local *grogue* or have a bite to eat on the patio overlooking the southern side of the valley. $$ *Tel: 223.1941 m: 980.0139 sandro_lacerenza@yahoo.fr*

Casa Sabine Jahnel This well established homestay is located in Eito, closer to Vila, and is a good option for those who want the best of both worlds. The four rooms are cozy and peaceful and offer a glimpse into the daily lives of a family in Paúl. $ *Tel: 223.1544*

Casa das Ilhas This charming refuge is tucked away from the road a few kilometers up into the valley. The nine cottages represent the nine islands and come in as many shapes and sizes (with almost as many languages spoken!). The price varies by the size of the room, but all rooms include half board with personally designed dinners. All the furnishings and rooms were developed and built locally and the owners continue to give back to the community by offering a kindergarten for otherwise forgotten local youth. $$$ *Tel: 223.1832, m: 996.7774; casadasilhas@yahoo.fr*

O Curral Impossible to miss on the hike down from Cova and a shame to miss if you are passing through, O Curral has become a staple in Paúl and on Santo Antão in general. It is hard to say if it is Alfred, his *grogue* or his food that is more famous, but this coupled with ground-breaking sustainable practices have certainly made their impact. $$-$$$ *Tel: 223.1213 / 223.1520; www.grogue.de; www.alsatour.de*

VILA DAS POMBAS

Vila das Pombas never asked for popularity and probably doesn't deserve it. A thin row of houses line the coastal road and spread inland up into the *ribeira.* Along the coast, the sun breaks through the clouds and the heat bears down much more than in the valley. It is a quiet place where you will find men playing *oril* and cards in the evenings and children wandering the streets. You will likely be approached by a few grubby children looking for spare change or a piece of chewing gum. The growing popularity has given rise to begging, but also an increasing number of quality restaurants and places to stay.

Important Information

Bank There are two banks in Paúl, BCA and Caixa Económica. All banks are open Monday-Friday from approximately 8:00-15:00.

Health Center Tel: 223.1130

Pharmacy Tel: 223.1972; To the right of the police station.

Post Office Correios Open Monday-Friday either from 8:00-12:00, 14:00-17:00 or 7:30-15:00.

Police Polícia Tel: 223.1292

Staying in Touch

P@úl Mystik Located up behind the *correios* and next to the Palácio de Justíca, you can find fairly reliable internet access and international phone calls.

Cyber Jantar Not yet open at the time of research, Cyber Jantar is under construction on one of the side streets below the church. A garage has been converted to include an internet room with privacy screens, international and local call booths and a variety of products on display for sale.

What to Do

At the mouth of the road heading up into the *ribeira*, take the path on the left to climb up to the towering statue of Santo António, the patron saint of Paúl. Here you will be afforded a good view of the coastal town and up into the *ribeira*.

Where the road into the valley meets the coastal road, head left (facing the water) and you will soon pass Trapiche Ildo Benos (Tel: 223.1364, m. 996.7131). Stop to watch as sugar cane is processed into the infamous *grogue* in the traditional manner, using oxen to pull the *trapiche* (press) that milks the sugar cane for its precious juice. If you pass by at the wrong time, you may still get a quick tour of the facilities and process, including a quick sample.

Continuing along the road from Traphiche Ildo Benos, stop in Docel (Tel: 223.1428 / 22.31205), the small shop run by the Associação das Mulheres (Women's Association) for some souvenirs. You will find a selection typical to most general stores, but along the wall by the register are a variety of *doces* (jams) and liquors made by the women of the association with local products.

Where to Eat

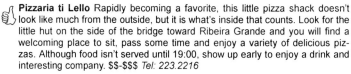

Pizzaria ti Lello Rapidly becoming a favorite, this little pizza shack doesn't look like much from the outside, but it is what's inside that counts. Look for the little hut on the side of the bridge toward Ribeira Grande and you will find a welcoming place to sit, pass some time and enjoy a variety of delicious pizzas. Although food isn't served until 19:00, show up early to enjoy a drink and interesting company. $$-$$$ *Tel: 223.2216*

Morabeza Morabeza is open 7 days a week from 8:00-22:00 and has been for years. The menu offers a variety of Cape Verdean style dishes and other, unique options. Tourists are drawn here for the delicious meals and the art produced locally by Odair, but it is also a popular local hangout. $$-$$$ *Tel: 223.1790 m. 991.5926; atgoncalves49@hotmail.com*

Santo Antão

O Valeiro Only open for six months, it is hard to say if O Valeiro has yet reached its full potential. Open from 9:00-23:00, you will mostly find typical Cape Verdean restaurant fare. One thing is certain and that is that the location is unbeatable. Stop for a coffee or beer and look out into the wide Atlantic. $-$$ *Tel: 952.0364*

Restaurant Vale do Paúl On the top floor of the *residencial* of the same name, dinner is served here by request only. Be sure to make a request/reservation well in advance and you will likely be able to specify what you hope to eat. Fish is generally a good bet. $$-$$$ *Tel: 223.1319*

Nightlife

As is typical in Cape Verde, nightlife is hit or miss. You can check out **Discoteca Beira Mar**. The building is impossible to miss from the massive posters that line the sides, but you may or may not find anyone inside. You are more likely to find some action in any little hole-in-the-wall bar.

Where to Stay

Residencial Vale do Paúl Good in a pinch and on a budget, Dona Cláudia Costa offers five simple rooms-two double and three twin, all share two bathrooms. The highlight is probably the restaurant serving traditional Cape Verdean fare overlooking the ocean (reservations required). Breakfast is an additional 250$. $ *Tel: 223.1319*

Aldeia Jerome Though set in the center of town, it is easy to forget where you are as you walk through the front gate and pass through a small banana plantation that muffles all but the low roar of the ocean in the distance. Follow the path back to the three brightly painted buildings where you will find five double rooms, two suites and one apartment with accommodations for six. There is also a small kitchen area. Single/double $$, suite/apartment $$$ *Tel: 223.2173; aldeiajerome@yahoo;.it www.aldeiajerome.it.gg*

Mar E Sol Tia Melo has rented these six simple, but clean, rooms for the past five years at a great price. Though she is still doing so, she is also looking for a potential buyer. There is space below for six more rooms and the location is unbeatable—looking out across a promenade straight to the ocean. Breakfast is an additional 250$. $ *Tel: 223.1294*

Residencial Familiar Tak Rida A new addition to the collection of *residencial*s in Paúl, Tak Rida offers bright, fresh, clean rooms and a beautiful terrace with a great view to enjoy breakfast. Some rooms have a private bathroom and some shared (price varies by accommodations). $-$$ *Tel: 223.1129, m: 995.6228*

SINAGOGA

An isolated point between Paúl and Ribeira Grande, Sinagoga is now a popular spot for swimming in the summer months with a small black sand beach, but was once home to exiled Portuguese Jews in the early 19th century and later became a leper colony. There had been Jewish presence in Cape Verde throughout its development with men from all walks of life dipping into the prosperity of the slave trade, but it was the Spanish/Portuguese Inquisition that sent many Jews to hide in the mountains of Santo Antão. Not much remains from this intriguing past beyond a few Jewish graves, but there is an effort to unearth some of the history that may be buried alongside these bodies. For more information, see www.capeverdejewishheritage.org.

São Vicente

Known as "the northern capital," São Vicente is, without a doubt, the hub of the *Barlavento*. The majority of the population of this island resides in the municipal seat/capital of Mindelo. Here you will find a rich cultural mix and history that spreads beyond the city streets and across the varying volcanic landscape.

Whether arriving by plane or by boat, the first thing you will encounter are the outstretched arms of the bay. Remnants of a volcanic crater, the sides seem to be reaching out to embrace neighboring Santo Antão. Though the distant island will never enter these welcoming arms, they greet and protect thousands of incoming ships since the years of British colonization. Residents today reflect this hospitality with symbolic warmth.

GEOGRAPHY

São Vicente covers 88 sq. miles (227 sq km) of largely deforested and arid land. São Vicente suffers desert conditions similar to Sal, Maio and Boa Vista, but is different in that there is more varying terrain. Monte Verde is the highest point on the island at 2460 feet (750m), but there are many lava scarred mountains and valleys in the furthest reaches of the island.

The *conselho* (municipal area) of São Vicente encompasses the entire island as well as Santa Luzia and the islets of Branco and Raso. The land is governed as one *conselho* (municipal area), but the majority of the island's 80,000 residents live within the city of Mindelo and its immediate suburbs. There are, however, small communities that subsist off minimal agriculture and a fairly substantial fishing industry in the further reaches of the island.

HISTORY

Despite the promising bay, the harsh environment rendered it useless to the Portuguese colonizers. Though discovered on January 22, 1462, the island remained largely uninhabited until the late 18th century. Like so many other islands, the hillsides were populated by goats before humans.

After a failed settlement attempt by the Portuguese in 1795, the British realized the potential held in the great bay of Mindelo and established a small colony. Coal was brought and charcoal produced for trade with passing ships and the city became a major stopping point to stock up on coal, water, goat meat and fruits. At the height of its reign, Mindelo ranked among the top coaling stations.

Despite the success of business within the bay, non-British residents received little of the profits. It is said that incoming ships would often be swarmed by small boats with people begging for a bit of work or to attempt some kind of swindle. Within the city, many relied on the sale of liquor, prostitution and begging to get by.

This unruly existence accelerated the downfall of São Vicente as trade lessened due to the expansion of ships' cargo space and the eventual switch to oil. With no options, many residents immigrated to Europe or São Tomé in search of opportunity, but many stayed in São Vicente, suffering the harsh conditions abetted by drought and famine.

One saving grace for the island was the transfer of the Seminary of São Nicolau to Mindelo in 1911. This helped establish Mindelo as one of the intellectual centers of the archipelago and created an environment for the eventual overthrow of Portuguese colonial rule.

GETTING THERE

By Air

The airport in Mindelo was recently upgraded to support international flights, but international service is a step behind (expected to begin in 2010). Currently, you can fly into Mindelo on daily flights from Sal or Santiago through TACV. The airport is about 10 km outside of the city just outside of São Pedro. Taxis cost about 800$ into Mindelo.

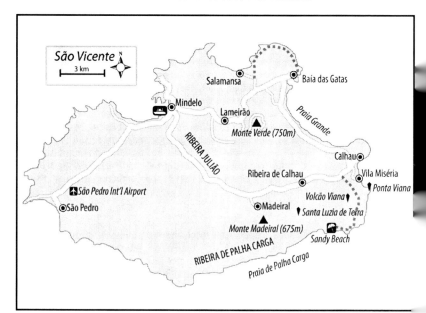

By Sea

The *Sal Rei* ferry runs a Praia-São Vicente-São Nicolau circuit once a week. Check the schedule with STM shipping. Also try online at www.bela-vista.net/ferry.aspx

Agentur S.T.M. (Praia) *Tel: 261.2564*

Agentur S.T.M. (Mindelo) *Tel: 232.1179; Avenida 5 de Julho*

GETTING AROUND

There are only a few roads leading out of Mindelo. On the western side of the city, you can circle the bay and head to the airport and beyond to São Pedro. On the other side of the city, there are two additional roads leading out through the interior to Baìa das Gatas and Calhau, recently connected along a coastal road. Though there are public cars, transportation in and out of the city is not easy to come by. Most cars head into the city in the early morning and back out by mid-day. If you head out by foot, you may have a hard time getting back.

During the summer, there is a bus that heads to and from Baía das Gatas and there is more general traffic throughout the island as many emigrants visit from abroad, but the best way to travel around the island is either on a guided tour or with a rental car.

Within the city, there are marked taxis that circle around looking for passengers. Additionally, there are buses that will take you through the city and on to the adjacent suburbs. The main stop is by the shore at the *praça* in front of Casa Café Mindelo. Bus # 1 will take you to Laginha Beach and #5 will take you into the suburb, Monte Sossego. The commercial center of town is easily covered on foot.

Rental Cars

There are a number of car rental agencies for independent island/city exploring.

Ocident Rent-A-Car *Tel: 231.7920 m. 991.4088 / 993.5584; ocidentrenta-car@hotmail.com; Located in Pracinha de Igreja*

Atlantic Car *Tel: 231.7032, m. 991.6229; Located on Rua Baltazar Lopes da Silva*

Avis *Operated in conjunction with the Hotel Porto Grande.*

Alucar *Tel: 232.1295 / 232.5194; alucarsv@cvtelecom.cv; Located in Monte Sossego.*

EXCURSIONS

CaboVerde Safari Based in Mindelo, Cabo Verde Safari offers incredible, personalized off road tours of São Vicente, Santo Antão and, weather permitting, Santa Luzia. João Coelho speaks many languages (English, French, Portuguese, Spanish and a bit of Romanian) and will take small groups around in the company jeep for a day to explore this largely overlooked island. The day starts heading off into hidden valleys, long lonely beaches and a beautiful, stark landscape that culminates at sunset atop of Monte Verde. City tours also available. *Tel: 231.0299, m 991.1544 / 991.2721; caboverdesafari@cvtelecom.cv; www.caboverdesafari.com*

Cape Verde Travel A British tour company. The office in Mindelo offers island and inter-island tours and information. A good resource for yachts and boats as well. *m. 998.2878; capeverdetravel@cvtelecom.cv*

Big Game Fishing/Boating Excursions Run out of the Residencial Alto Fortim, this Cape Verdean woman and her French husband offer a variety of boating excursions for fishing or venturing to other islands. Call or check out their website for more info on available packages. *Tel: 992.3656; biggamecaboverde@gmail.com; www.biggamecaboverde.com; SKYPE: gabrielamendes*

AVENTURA Based out of the Gallerias, AVENTURA advertises tours and excursions. Call for a representative to meet with you at your hotel and make arrangements. *m. 996.9110*

Blue Discovery Diving and watersports training hosted out of Foya Branca Resort in São Pedro. Contact Foya Branca (see pg 100) for more information.

Mindelo

Mindelo is the heart of "culture" in Cape Verde. Home to the world renowned Cesária Évora (see box on pg 90), it is no surprise that music, theater, *Capoeira* and the arts pulse through the city, bringing life to what is otherwise a somewhat mountainous strip of desert in the Atlantic. Known for live music and a vigorous nightlife, many would argue that Mindelo is heart of Cape Verde, not the southern capital of Praia. Though comparatively Mindelo is much smaller, you will find many of the same amenities—five star hotels, universities and large markets—as are available in Praia, but with less crime and pollution.

As the sun comes up in the morning, the city slowly comes back to life. A flock of women in green smocks fill the streets. Equipped with brooms and pans, they set out to sweep away the previous night and prepare for a new day. Children and adults fill the sidewalks on their way to school and work while businesses prepare to open their doors. Despite this early surge, things don't really start moving until around 10:00. As the day goes on and the temperature and sun begin to rise, the movement in town increases accordingly. To get anything accomplished—banking, travel arrangements—get an early start and you will likely beat the crowd. The culture here is very much one of a relaxed pace, coffee breaks and minimal stress. As the sun goes down in the afternoon, crowds switch from coffee breaks to beer and the hard workers of the day unwind in a variety of ways.

> By the fish market, watch as the fishermen come in and play *oril* or the popular card game *biska*.

Crime

Like Praia, the multitude of people crammed into a small area has had a negative impact on the once peaceful climate. Unlike Praia, violent crime is not as common, but begging, pick-pocketing and muggings are becoming increasingly prominent in the city. Walking long distances alone or in small groups at night is not recommended. Crime is especially common, even during the day, down toward *Praça Estrela* and the fish market. Be especially vigilant during times of festivals.

Boats

What will forever etch this country in my mind is the sense of isolation, of being in another world that pervades. A place that achieves a kind of beauty in the way that human beings have managed to eke out a way of living on terrain so obviously not intended for their habitation. So rugged and detached, it gives the sense of a place forgotten by all those who leave for more promising locales. Half-finished buildings, cobblestone roads built on the sweat of slaves. I think too of the way that altruism can turn so many places into a dumping ground. Murals lecturing about AIDS permanently looming over soccer games and community events in the polivalent (soccer field), a long dormant dumpster with a faded UNICEF proudly emblazoned on the side, men proudly strutting around town in jerseys commemorating Superbowl wins that never took place. It is a strange beauty.

I will never forget the first trip I took from the airport in the northern island of São Vicente into the city. It was my first time on Cape Verdean soil outside of the main island of Santiago and I was determined to take it all in. As my car sped along the coast, we whizzed by a line of old boats. They were seemingly shipwrecked right there yards from the road; hulking, rusty relics of an earlier time. I did not know how long they had been there, but I highly doubted that they were part of any kitschy attempt to Disney-ify the surroundings, an attempt to add a pirate theme to the tourists' experience. These shipwrecks were authentic.

Flash forward a few months later. I am pleasantly surprised to find a new, modern-looking airport servicing the island. Several times the size of the cramped building that served as the previous airport, it comes with a pleasant café where one can pass away the inevitable delay. This is an improvement from forlornly sitting in the parking lot at the old airport. Sepia-toned photographs of olden times in Mindelo abound on the walls. It made me feel good about the investments being made in infrastructure here, investments that could bring a better beginning of tourism and foreign investment.

But returning from all that comfort at the airport, the boats are no longer along the coast. I suppose they probably did seem a bit unseemly to folks coming straight from a plush terminal, especially if it begins taking direct flights from Europe as is the rumor. I am sure they likely were a hazard to the untold number of bored Cape Verdean kids who played among the ship wreckage in search of a way to pass a dusty afternoon. But what was once striking to me as a gateway to some other world now looks like any other beach I have seen. It is kind of a shame, if you ask me. Maybe the question of the boats is too obvious a metaphor for the challenges of development in a place like Cape Verde - trying to be respectful of culture and tradition while improving lives and leading toward progress. But you see what I'm getting at.

- Daron Christopher

São Vicente

IMPORTANT INFORMATION

Bank There are multiple branches of the major banks through the city. Caixa Económica is along Avenida 5 de Julho. BCA and Banco InterAtlântico have branches along *Praça Nova (Praça Amilcar Cabral)*as well as in the center of town. All banks are open Monday-Friday from approximately 8:00-15:00.

Currency Exchange For small amounts, the best place to exchange currency is on the side street across from the post office.

Hospital Baptisto: Tel: 232.7355 / 231.1879

Pharmacy There are a number of pharmacies scattered throughout the center of town, the most prominent just up the street from the municipal market.

Post Office *Correios* Open Monday-Friday either from 8:00-12:00, 14:00-17:00 or 7:30-15:00; On the side street between the tourist kiosk and Aparthotel Avenida.

Police *Polícia* Tel: 231.4631; Between the fish market and *Praça Estrela.*

TACV Tel: 232.1524; Open 8:00-12:00, 14:30-17:30; headquarters is on Avenida 5 de Julho.

HalcyonAir Tel: 232.2960; On Rua Sena Barcelos by the *correios*

Agência Nacional de Viagens (National Travel Agency) Tel: 231.1115; Located on Avenida da Republica

WIFI WiFi is available in *Praça Nova (Praça Amilcar Cabral)* by the Porto Grande Hotel. There are also a number of internet cafés scattered throughout the city.

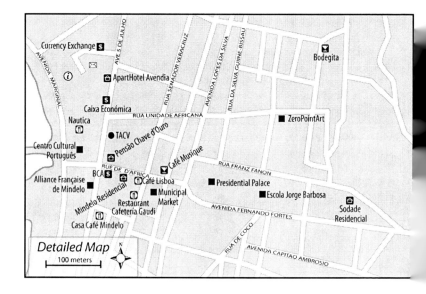

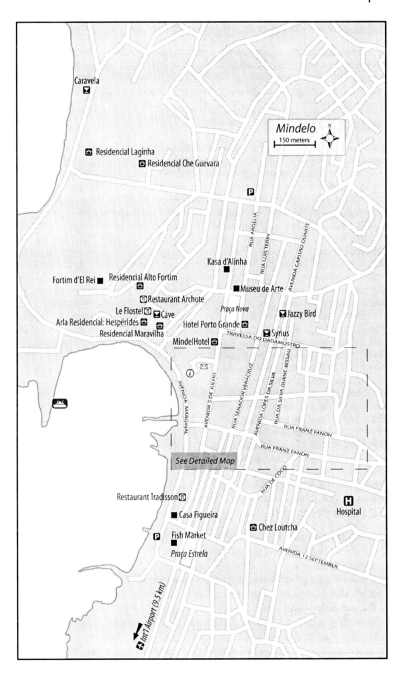

Caravela

Residencial Laginha

Residencial Che Guevara

Mindelo
150 meters

RUA ARGÉLIA

RUA LUÍS TERRY

AVENIDA CAPITÃO DUARTE

Kasa d'Alinha

Fortim d'El Rei ■   Residencial Alto Fortim

■ Museu de Arte

Restaurant Archote

Praça Nova

Le Flostel Cave
Arla Residencial: Hespérides   Hotel Porto Grande

Jazzy Bird

Residencial Maravilha

Syrius

MindelHotel

TRAVESSA DO DADAMOSTRO

AVENIDA MARGINAL

AVENIDA 5 DE JULHO

RUA SENADOR VERA-CRUZ

AVENIDA LOPES DA SILVA

RUA DA SILVA GUINE-BISSAU

RUA FRANZ FANON

RUA FRANZ FANON

See Detailed Map

RUA DE COCO

Restaurant Tradisson

■ Casa Figueira

Chez Loutcha

H
Hospital

Fish Market
■

Praça Estrela

AVENIDA 12 SEPTEMBER

Int'l Airport (9.5 km)

São Vicente

TOURIST INFORMATION

A small tourist information kiosk is located along Avenida Marginal at the corner of the side street leading to the post office. They may not be able to answer all your questions, but they can help if you are lost and sell a number of books and maps for navigating Mindelo, São Vicente and the other islands.

WHAT TO DO

With much of the population of São Vicente crowding around the bay, there is no shortage of sights and sounds in the city. One of the best ways to get a feel for it is to spend a morning or afternoon walking along the neat, tree-lined streets. Smaller than Praia, efforts to keep the city clean have been much more successful and though there is a slight dinginess associated with urban areas, the city is orderly and well-kept.

Fortim d'El Rei keeps watch over the city and offers a stunning view of the bay below. There have been plans in place to renovate the ruins of the fort and build a restaurant/hotel/casino. At the time of research all that existed of these plans was a line of construction tape flapping in the breeze. This is a well-known tourist destination for the view, and is a common spot for robberies. If you choose to walk, be warned that you may be watched. A small group should be able to ward off any threat, but no guarantees.

There are many parks and plazas (*praças*) scattered throughout the city and it is worth it to go around and explore. The **municipal market**, built in 1874, is a remnant of colonial times. It is clean and well kept, though most fruits and vegetables are shipped from Santo Antão or abroad. The city itself is a marvel—the central downtown architecturally giving homage to the British colonial past.

The pink **Presidential Palace** sits proudly in the middle of town, although it is not open to the public. Originally built in 1873, the second floor was added in the 1930s. Beyond it lies the **Escola Jorge Barbosa**, the only high school in Mindelo. It was first built in 1859 when the seminary in São Nicolau was closed, education was moved to this school. Though it was responsible for educating what would become Cape Verde's leaders of independence, the building has seen a variety of uses including an army barraks and hospital over the years.

Cesária Évora: The Voice of Cape Verde

Haunting melodies and the bittersweet sounds of *morna* delivered in her thick, rich voice have put the name Cesária Évora and Cape Verde on the map for many countries. One of few Cape Verdean artists recognized throughout the globe, when you hear her sing it is not difficult to understand why. Now 68, Évora did not even begin her music career until her late forties. In 2004, *Voz d'Amor* received a Grammy nomination for Best World Music. Évora still owns a house in the center of Mindelo and—though she does not perform much in the city—apart from the music festival Baía das Gatas, she has not let her age slow her down. There are currently a number of shows lined up for 2010 and a new album, *Nha Sentimento*, was released in 2009.

ARTS & CULTURE

Mindelo's theater group, **MindelAct**, throws a month-long celebration of theater in September. If you visit during this time (and throughout the year) keep an eye out for upcoming performances.

A largely Catholic country with strong Brazilian influences, **Carnaval**—the festival marking the beginning of Lent—is one of the busiest times of the year, the city of Mindelo swells to almost twice its size in an attempt to contain the festival. The streets fill with music, dancing and celebration as the town dresses up Mardi Gras style and different groups compete for best float, music and choreography.

The old style gazebo in *Praça Nova (Praça Amilcar Cabral)* hosts a weekly concert for the public on Sunday evenings starting around 19:00. Sunday's are generally a leisurely day, so the excuse to wander out in the evening is embraced by families throughout the city.

Capoeira, the Afro-Brazilian martial arts form, has taken root in Cape Verde over the years, originating in the history of trans-Atlantic trade. Combining music, dance and martial arts, capoeira is a dynamic circle controlled by the changing rhythm and beat with a perpetual cycle of participants. It is enchanting to the eyes, ears and soul. Stop in the *Associação Capoeira Liberdade Expressão* next to the Portuguese Cultural Center on Avenida Marginal to watch training and performances and to find out about public events. Contact Djé (m. 984.3130; djecapoeira@hotmail.com) to arrange an evening event for groups.

São Vicente

Museums

Museu de Arte (Museum of Traditional Art)
There are a number of cultural artifacts as well as contemporary works of art. Admission is 100$. At the top of the *Praça Nova (Praça Amilcar Cabral). Open Monday-Friday from 9:00-12:00, 15:00-18:00.*

Kasa d'Alinha (Casa de Avozinha, Grandma's House)
Not open at the time of research, this appears to be a cultural preservation effort. It is up the street to the left of the Museu de Arte Traditional and worth a look.

Centro Cultural Português (Portuguese Cultural Center)
This large building has a library, souvenir/book store and vast rooms frequently used for exhibits or events. Stop by for postings of upcoming events. Along the coast in the old customs house where Avenida Amilcar Cabral turns to Avenida Marginal. *Open Mon-Fri from 8:00-12:00, 15:00-19:00*

Alliance Française de Mindelo (French Cultural Center)
Around the corner from the Portuguese Cultural Center, the French Cultural Center is open Mon-Fri from 7:00-19:00 and Sat from 8:00-12:30 is also known to host events. There is a library and café (La Pergola) where live music is regularly hosted.

Casa Figueira
Home of the artist Manuel Figueira, you can sometimes enter to view and purchase his paintings. The house is hard to miss along Avenida Amilcar Cabral as the name is painted in large white letters on the bright blue wall.

ZeroPointArt 👍

Brand new to Mindelo, this gallery/wine bar opened the doors with an intimate piano concert and exhibit of Alex's, the proprietor, art. According to Alex, it is his attempt to revive the culture of art and performance in Cape Verde by offering gallery and studio space to aspiring artists in the colonial house where he was raised. He also looks to bring artists from abroad. If you are interested, please contact Alex at m. 995.5681. www.xakuka.com; www.zeropointart.org; alex@zeropointart.org

WHERE TO EAT

Mindelo has a culture of going to cafés and restaurants that is not as prominent on other islands, so the city center is literally teeming with cafés, bars and restaurants. Below is a selection of recommended places worthy of note or somehow unique. This list is nowhere near exhaustive.

👍 **Café Lisboa** This hole in the wall is almost always teeming with customers. In the morning hours, a few regulars stake claim on the outdoor chairs as people from all walks of life flow through the door for morning coffee. As the sun goes down, the volume of the music goes up and drinks change from coffee to liquor. A great place to soak up the environment and watch the world go by, you are guaranteed an interesting crowd ranging from harmless beggars to the president of the *Câmara*. $

Restaurant Cafétería Gaudi This French restaurant is a key player during carnival, hosting meals and events. The menu is a bit pricey, but encompasses a range of dishes and is tailored by the French owner. $$$

👍 **Casa Café Mindelo** The bottom floor of the *residencial* of the same name, this café is a hot spot in Mindelo and draws and international crowd from all walks of life. A great place to sit and watch the flow of people through the city, enjoy some of the fresh baked goods or the delicious plate-of-the-day. $$-$$$

Fund d' Mar Meaning "Under the Sea," this bar/restaurant is actually underground. The décor is fitted to the name, food and drinks are a bit pricey, but the pizza is good. Music can be a bit loud, definitely a younger crowd. $$-$$$

Nautica Right on the main street between the Portuguese Cultural Center and the Capoeira Association, Nautica is known for regular live music and generally draws a good, but mixed crowd of predominantly tourists. Check the posting outdoors during the day to confirm nighttime performances. $$-$$$

👍 **Restaurant Archote** Up in Alto São Nicolau, Archote is one of the top restaurants in Mindelo, according to locals and tourists alike. The cuisine is a mix of traditional dishes with more inventive twists, specializing in seafood and fish. Live music Monday-Saturday (reservations recommended, especially for the weekend). $$$ *Tel: 232.3916, m. 994275; archote@cvtelecom.cv*

Restaurant/Pizzaria Mindel Hotel The restaurant of MindelHotel is located around the corner from the hotel entrance and is open to the public for meals and live music Thursday-Saturday. $$$

May O'Leary's The popular Irish style pub from Sal has made its way to Mindelo as well. Located on the side street by the *correios* that connects Avenida Marginal and Avenida 5 de Julho. Popular for happy hour and non-Cape Verdean cuisine. $$

Esplanada Maravilha A pleasant, outdoor restaurant/bar at the Residencial Maravilha offering fairly typical Cape Verdean cuisine in a comfortable, relaxing environment. $$-$$$ *Tel: 232.2203*

Le Flostel Open at night, Le Flostel feeds the clubgoers of A Cave some of the best pizza and chawarma in Mindelo. With 24 different pizzas (more variety than you will encounter anywhere else), you can't go wrong. $$-$$$

Restaurant Tradisson This bar/restaurant along the coast toward the fish market is well marked and known for live music Wednesday through Saturday (closed Monday). Open for dinner, music starts around 21:00. $$$

Chez Loutcha The restaurant under the hotel of the same name offers consistently good food and a popular Cape Verdean night on Wednesdays and Fridays (reservations recommended). Fare includes a buffet of Cape Verdean cuisine and live music. Also check out the Sunday lunch buffet in Calhau (reservations required). $$-$$$ *Tel: 232.1636 / 232.1689*

Restaurant Lua Azul A part of the *residencial* Casa Azul, the French cuisine here is superb and served in the beautiful covered terrace. Open from noon until things wind down, Wednesday-Sunday, reservations are required. Pricey, but not without cause. $$$-$$$$ *m. 983.2346*

Sodade Restaurant On the top floor of the *residencial* of the same name, the restaurant offers a panoramic view of the city and typical cuisine. $$-$$$ *Tel: 230.3200; residencialsodade@hotmail.com*

Tapas
There is a new Tapas style restaurant located somewhere up by Alto Fortim. At the time of research our team was unable to visit, but we have heard that it is good, typical Tapas fare albeit fairly pricey. $$$$

NIGHTLIFE

Mindelo is known for live music, and is well aware that this draws tourists. The best time to visit (outside of Carnival) for vibrant nightlife is during the summer months (June-September).

Syrius Located just up the street from *Praça Nova (Praça Amilcar Cabral)*, Syrius boasts regular movement, but tends to draw a younger crowd (late teens to mid-twenties). A typical nightclub in Cape Verde, doors don't open until 21:30/midnight.

A Cave Up in Alto São Nicolau below the Residencial Maravilha, Cave also draws a good crowd on the weekends. Partygoers at Cave tend to be an older, more affluent crowd than that of Syrius.

 Caravela Right along Laginha Beach, this gazebo style bar/restaurant is fairly consistent for live music on Friday and Saturday nights. Regularly draws a good crowd for sit-down drinks.

Jazzy Bird Tucked away on Rua Baltazar Lopes da Silva, Jazzy Bird has a longstanding reputation as a place to be, but without regularity. Running into a crowd is hit-or-miss, but even if you have the place to yourself, it's a nice place to sit down for a drink.

Bodegita This Spanish style watering hole is way up from Syrius by Rua Camões. Comfortable seating, great decoration and killer Mojitos. Food available as well.

Café Musique Across from the municipal market, Café Musique has a reputation for live music on Friday and Saturday nights, but can be hit-or-miss during the off season.

São Vicente

WHERE TO STAY

As it is a large city, there are a number of places to stay. The list below is not exhaustive, but includes some of the best places for every price range.

 Casa Café Mindelo Located above the café of the same name, the rooms are as well renovated and decorated as the popular café. The renovated colonial house from the 1830s now offers four large rooms and a welcoming sitting room. Shower space is outside of the room due to design. $$-$$$ *Tel: 231.8731; info@casacafémindelo.com; www.casacafémindelo.com*

Pensão Chave d'Ouro Right in the center of downtown along Avenida 5 de Julho, Pensão Chave d'Ouro claims to be the oldest hotel in Mindelo with 80+ years of service. When you enter some of the rooms, it is easy to believe. The rooms vary greatly from one to another, but despite upkeep, age and countless visitors have left their mark. Regardless, it is a great place to stay on a budget. Shared bathrooms and breakfast included. $-$$ *Tel: 232.7050*

 Mindelo Residencial Just around the corner up Rua de Lisboa, this is a great find right downtown. The balcony and rooms that overlook the street are the pride of the *residencial* during carnival as they offer a fantastic view of the festivities. The nine rooms and two suites (with kitchen) are pleasant and well-kept. The staff is pleasant and does their best to accommodate guests. $$-$$$ *Tel: 230.0863 djiblam@cvtelcom.cv; www.mindeloresidencial.com*

 Residencial Maravilha Located in Alto São Nicolau by the nightclub A Cave, Residencial Maravilha offers an excellent view of the city and the bay below. There are a variety of rooms ranging from simple singles to a large, comfortable suite for two and one triple on the top floor. All of the rooms are tastefully decorated and well kept with all amenities (en suite bathroom with hot water, minifridge, A/C, TV). Rooms with a view run more than those without. $$ *Tel: 232.2203/232.2216; maravilha.caboverde@gmail.com*

Arla Residencial: Hespérides Also in Alto São Nicolau, Hespérides is adjacent to the nightclub A Cave. The noise nuisance and water damage from a particularly rainy 2009 have lowered the price of some of the basement rooms, slightly resembling a cave. The rooms upstairs are bright and open with private bathrooms and hot water. $$ *Tel: 232.8688, m.995.1812; www.arlaresidencial.com*

Residencial Jenny This French-run *residencial* in Alto São Nicolau offers some of the best views of the bay from half of the twenty rooms. A repeat award winner of the petitfute award, it is easy to see why. The rooms are impeccably clean with great light coming in from the open veranda. Price varies by location, rooms with sea view and balconies are more expensive. Staff offers assistance with guides/transportation. A 10% discount is offered for more than two nights stay. Rooms with a view $$$, rooms without $$. *Tel: 232.8969; hstaubyn@cvtelecom.cv; www.petitfute.com*

New Year's Eve

In addition to Carnival and the music festival of Baía Das Gatas, Mindelo also hosts a nationally famous New Years Eve celebration. There are separate parties throughout the city (some more expensive than others), but if you arrive early, you will be surprised to find that the guests will be underdressed. It is tradition that at midnight, people from all over the city flock to the coast to welcome the New Year in the ocean.

Hotel Porto Grande Part of the Oasis Atlantico family, this long standing hotel looks out over *Praça Nova (Praça Amilcar Cabral)* and the buildings blocking the view of the bay. The fifty rooms meet international standards and prices for a four star hotel: The pool is welcome respite from the sun. Breakfast buffet included. $$$$$-$$$$$$ *Tel: 232.3190; pgrande@cvtelecom.cv; www.oasisatlantico.com*

MindelHotel This four star hotel is longstanding in Mindelo. The rooms are a bit small and sterile, but up to international four-star standard with all ameni-ties plus satellite TV and hairdryers, an anomaly in much of Cape Verde. Transportation provided to and from the airport and major credit cards are accepted. The building and sometimes functional roof-top pool look out over the bay and *Praça Nova (Praça Amilcar Cabral)*. $$$$-$$$$$ *Tel: 232.8881 / 232.8886; mihotel@cvtelecom.cv*

ApartHotel Avendia Easily mistaken for a commercial complex next to Min-delHotel, ApartHotel Avenida offers a variety of rooms ranging from simple singles to full apartments. Despite the simple accommodations, rooms fill up regularly, so book ahead. Breakfast is included, but there is no restaurant. Rental cars are also available for 5000$/day. Rooms $$ (+1000$/additional person), suites/apartments $$$ *Tel: 232.3435; aparthtlavenida@cvtelecom.cv*

Residencial Solar Windelo Up in Alto Santo António, Solar Windelo is a fairly new addition to the collection of places to stay in Mindelo. Cozy and tastefully decorated, the rooms vary according to different needs. Price varies remarkably based on room, number of nights and guests. There is a detailed link on the page outlining costs. $$$$ *Tel: 231.0070; windelocapvert@gmail.com; www.windelo.com*

Residencial Che Guevara Along Avenida Che Guevara across from the *Es-cola Técnica*, the *residencial* of the same name offers a variety of rooms in a maze of a building. The building is a bit old, but is currently under renovation, sprucing up the eleven single/double rooms, triple and suite. $$ *Tel: 232.2449; cheguevara@cvtelecom.cv; www.res_cheguevara,tripod.com*

Residencial Laginha Right up the hill from Laginha beach, this bright blue building has rooms that range in price depending on number of occupants. The bar was fairly well stocked and nicely decorated, which may or may not reflect the rooms (unavailable for review at time of research). $$ *Tel: 232.5468, m. 997.2417*

Residencial Alto Fortim Up in Alto Fortim, affords a generous view of the bay. The ten rooms are stylishly decorated and reasonably priced. Rooms are equipped with AC, fridge and a couch. Breakfast is included, but half and full board are available. Big game fishing excursions can be organized from here. $$-$$$ *Tel: 232.6983; altofortim@hotmail.com; www.altofortim.com*

Sodade Residencial/Restaurant Located behind the primary school on the way up Rua Franz Fanon, the rooms increase in price and appeal as you head up. The rooftop restaurant affords a fabulous view of the city, as do the upper rooms. Breakfast included, but amenities vary by room. Rooms $$-$$$, suite $$$$ *Tel: 230.3200; residencialsodade@hotmail.com*

Chez Loutcha On Rua da Côco by Praça Estrela, Chez Loutcha offers 24 rooms of a vast variety, but equally good standards. There are single rooms, doubles with twin or double bed and two, two person suites. Breakfast in-cluded. $$-$$$ *Tel: 232.1639 / 232.1689*

Casa Azul Outside of the city proper (about 2.8 miles/4.5 km in the direction of Baia das Gatas) take a left at Lameirão and follow the road up the hill, Ca-sa Azul offers beautiful views over the city. It's close enough for convenience and far enough for tranquility. Price varies depending on accommodations and season. $$$$$ *Tel: 231.0124; www.casa-azul-mindelo.com*

Getting Around São Vicente

In the past, three main roads headed out of Mindelo in different directions. To the west, São Pedro. To the southeast, Ribeira Julião/Calhau. To the northeast, Baía das Gatas. Calhau and Baía das Gatas were recently connected with a paved road along what used to be a footpath through the dunes of Praia Grande, making it possible to circuit the northeast half of the island.

Southeast

As you head out of Mindelo toward Calhau, you will pass through the outskirts of the city. Like most cities, it cycles through a section of poverty and into the wealthy "suburbs." Houses are popping up along the road as quickly as grass spurts up during the rainy season. Beyond these hopeful homes, the scenery settles into a somewhat predictable desert landscape.

Unlike its barren counterparts—Sal, Maio and Boa Vista—São Vicente is a younger island and still marked by jagged peaks and dramatic valleys. The road takes you along behind Monte Verde which can be seen most days with a thin cluster of clouds caught on the one peak high enough to disturb their meander across the sky. On the southern side of Monte Verde, there are clusters of houses that were once sustained by water run-off from the mountain. Today, most everything inland has dried up.

As the road to Calhau continues through Ribeira Julião, there is a short road off the right that leads to the mostly abandoned cluster of houses, Madeiral. Like many of the off-shoot villages on São Vicente, it was never prosperous, but it was once able to subsist during more verdant times. Beyond the village and southwest of Monte Madeiral is Ribeira de Palha Carga. After a bumpy, off-road trek, you reach a high point looking out between two opposing mountain ranges and down across the wide valley leading to the sea. Though it is not the rugged and winding type of valley that brings Santo Antão its fame, the vastness of virtually untouched soil framed by mountains and graced by the expanse of the sky will take your breath away. Far in the distance, Praia de Palha Carga lies parallel to the horizon.

The name *palha carga* means to pick up/gather a load. It is said that the wind whipping through the valley would blow the grasses out to sea. The life-giving ocean would then return to grass to the coast, washed up in neat bundles. The people that once lived in Mardeiral may have made this trek to gather the valuable resource to use as feed and building material. To the west of the expanse of mixed black and white sand, a cluster of palm and tall acacia trees, an ineffectual rock wall and crumbling building are dwarfed by the extreme of the western ridge.

RIBEIRA DE CALHAU

Beyond the turn for Madieral, the *ribeira* widens, making room for the small village and its desperate agricultural attempts. Before reaching the coast, there are groups of houses along the road with patches of irrigated farm land. Windmills pull water from the thirsty soil. The village in the *ribeira* is small and isolated, hardly more than an afterthought of development. The area was originally settled by the British that came for the business in coal. It was once the site of a small forest, but all that remains are low clusters of acacia trees, planted in hopes of reforestation.

VILA MISÉRIA/CALHAU

As you head toward the sea, there is a left turn that will follow the coast to to the beaches of Praia Grande and Baía das Gatas. If you stay straight, the road splits, and you can continue heading to the coast to the last bit of Calhau or, off to the right, Vila Miséria. Separated only by the bay, these two small areas consist mostly of weekend and holidays homes, but they also shelter a few of the hidden gems of São Vicente: In Vila de Miséria there is one of the most beautiful hotels on the island, Residencial Goa, and in the last bit of Calhau are two exceptional restaurants (see following descriptions). Though the horizon is vast and Calhau has an unshakable feel of isolation, Santa Luzia is visible in the distance, and on a clear day, Branco, Raso, São Nicolau and Santo Antão appear to remind that you are not alone.

What to Do

In addition to the restaurants and hotel, there are some natural wonders within walking distance from this area. Just a short walk from Vila de Miséria is Ponta Viana, named for the crater of Volcão Viana which lies just inland. It is possible to hike up the peak and look into the nearly perfect crater, or you can spend hours looking out on Ponta Viana where two opposing currents rush together, churning the water and crashing upwards in spurts.

There is a beaten path leading away from the village that takes you further along the coast to Praia Branca, a small white sand beach used by sea turtles to lay their eggs in August and September. A few kilometers beyond Praia Branca is Sandy Beach, a strip of white sand that is pristine during the week, but fills with surfers and families out to enjoy the uninhabited coastline during the weekend. There is a road to get here from Calhau, but it is washed out and rough.

On the other side of the coast is another small cluster of houses—the last of Calhau—and a couple of restaurants overshadowed by Volcão de Calhau. The houses here are almost entirely weekend/holiday homes, but fishermen from Calhau make use of the small bay to launch boats and dive for lobster. Unless you come during the weekend, you are likely to encounter only a small group of people milling around, waiting to help take in and clean the catch of the day. If you spend the weekend, the small town swells to take in families from Mindelo. From here, hike up Volcão de Calhau or back to the main road and along to Praia Grande.

Where to Stay & Eat

Residencial Goa This hidden gem is in a modern building with sparse, but tasteful decoration. The grand patio invites guests to relax after a long day of wandering and exploration. The building and French owners strive to provide comfort and peace while being gracefully incorporated into the environment. $$$-$$$$ *Tel: 232.9355, m 996.2696; www.goa-mindelo.com*

Bar/Restaurant Hamburg From the outside it doesn't appear to be much. Inside, a covered patio decorated with paintings by an artist from Calhau that met an untimely death from overuse of local *grogue*. Though the paintings are bright

São Vicente

and intriguing, it is the food that brings Hamburg fame. On the wall, a small menu lists the options for the day based on what has been caught. Probably the best place for seafood in São Vicente, try the *buzio* (conch) or *polvo* (octopus). All dishes are made to order, so you can call in advance, stop by, or sit and enjoy the environment while your food is prepared. $$-$$$ *Tel: 283.0196*

Chez Loutcha Run by the owners of the *pensão* of the same name in Mindelo, this restaurant opens its doors only on Sundays for an all afternoon celebration of Cape Verdean food and music. Entrance fee includes the opportunity to sample and enjoy the spread of over 15 different dishes while relaxing to live music and rubbing elbows with the Mindelo elite. $$$$

Moving On

In 2009, the road connecting Calhau with Baía das Gatas was completed. Just out of Calhau, the road crests and looks out over Praia Grande, an expanse of beautiful sand dunes kissed by the wild Atlantic. Baía das Gatas is visible just under 3 miles (4 km) away. The road itself is part of the series of paving projects to improve transportation and mobility around the islands. This particular road was planned for an inland route, and changed for visual appeal. Small patios are set off to the side of the road with picnic tables looking out over the expanse of ocean, but at points, the sustainability of the road can be called into question. The dunes of Praia Grande extend inland, at times crossing paths with the winding road. It makes for a beautiful trip, but one that may have harsh environmental consequences.

BAÍA DAS GATAS

The spot of the action during the weekend of the first full moon in August, the rest of the year, Baía das Gatas is a sleepy, cluster of houses. The town itself juts out into the water on a small peninsula that breaks the tide and keeps the water fairly calm. Inland, the houses, mostly weekend and holiday homes for emigrants and folks from Mindelo, sit together tightly. During the weekend, cars run from Mindelo (100$ each way), bringing flocks of people to take advantage of the excellent swimming and fishing conditions.

The permanent stage for the festival of Baía das Gatas stands out on the coast looking over the bay. In the early days of the festival, it was just a chance for people to pass time and enjoy some music. In the past, a small stage was assembled and dissembled for that one weekend each August, but as Cape Verdean music has gained footing abroad and the festival has developed an international reputation, it has grown exponentially. It is said to be the best music festival in Cape Verde as it draws performers from all over the archipelago as well as Brazilian, Portuguese, French and American artists. The entire island uproots and temporarily moves to the peninsula for the weekend of the festival. Under the full moon, food vendors line the streets and everywhere you look people are drinking, dancing, singing—enjoying the peace of the tiny town on the beach.

Where to Stay & Eat

Restaurant/Residencial Atlanta The restaurant and *residencial* are located in different buildings, but during the off season, it is affordable and available. A peaceful place to get away. $$$ *Tel: 232.7500*

Baía Verde A large restaurant that was open at the time of research, but also hanging a "for sale" sign. $$-$$$ *m. 996.8470*

Foya Grill An extension of Foya Branca Resort in São Pedro, the grill is open for lunch most days, but may depend on use by resort guests. Contact Foya Branca Resort for more information. $$$ *Tel: 230.7400*

SALAMANSA

Just along the road from Baía das Gatas, there is a right turn that will take you to the village of Salamansa. Despite the small crowds of people you encounter—children playing in the street, groups of young boys kicking around a sickly soccer ball, men sitting in the street playing cards, women chatting, chasing children or braiding hair—there is an echo of silence in the air. Only a few hundred people live here and their livelihood is almost entirely dependent on the success of the men who launch their boats out of Baía das Gatas, spending up to an entire week on Santa Luzia catching fish and eel and supplying most of São Vicente with the fresh fish that is in such high demand on menus.

One may wonder why they stay here in this small town almost 3 miles (5 km) away from where the boats are launched. But even with the echo of silence, there is vibrancy here that, most of the year, is entirely lacking in Baía das Gatas.

Here you can experience life for so many Cape Verdeans: sit, watch and wait to see what happens. There are a few small shops where you can grab a drink and try to chat with any of the locals who are also sitting, watching and waiting to see what happens.

MONTE VERDE

At 2460 feet (750m), Monte Verde is the highest point on São Vicente. Frequently covered in a coat of clouds, this is one of the few places where you will still find terraced crops and a few resilient Cape Verdeans toiling during the rainy season that is so underrepresented on this increasingly barren island. The road forks to the left on the way back into São Vicente, winding past aging houses up to the peak. Rock walls line the road and the landscape is marked by jagged peaks and rolling valleys. At sunset, you can look out over the bay of Mindelo and its crowded houses in the distance as the sky changes to brilliant reds, pinks and oranges, illuminating the clouds and welcoming the coming purples of the night sky. To reach the peak, walk or drive up the cobbled road.

Lameirão

Beyond the road for Monte Verde, you will pass the road to Lameirão, location of the popular hotel Casa Azul (see description on pg 95) and a few quiet houses. In the valley below, abandoned and not-quite-yet abandoned houses hold firm on land that was once prosperous. Small pineapple, banana and mixed crop farms survive on meager water supplies. In the distance, Seixal is home to a significant aloe vera farm.

West of Mindelo

As you head out of the city toward the airport, the small suburb of Lazareto populates the western side of the bay. Signs point to large buildings, remnants of a more industrial era and its hopeful revival. Three lonely

São Vicente

wind turbines stand in the distance, another hopeful beginning. The Cape Verdean energy company Electra built this small wind park in 1989 in hopes of harnessing the element that is so much a part of life in the archipelago. This small park offers promise, but inconsistency in wind speed and direction interrupt the regularity of the source.

About a half mile beyond the airport (6.2 miles/10 km outside of Mindelo) lies São Pedro, a beautiful little beach with a small fishing village and growing tourist development. The small community doesn't offer much beyond its humble existence on the beach and a few small shops and bars, but Foya Branca Resort has introduced elements that previously did not exist here.

Where to Stay & Eat

Foya Branca Resort This massive resort complex attempts to integrate into the surrounding area. All together there are 12 suites, 4 triple rooms, 52 double rooms and 6 villas varying in size. The resort itself offers swimming pools, horseback riding, tennis, a full gym and transportation to and from Mindelo. The staff will also happily help you arrange a fishing tour. Bicycles, surf boards and wind surfing equipment are available for rental. Prices start at 7500$ for a single and gradually increase depending on number of people and style of room. (complete guide to pricing available on website). Full and half board available. $$$-$$$$$ *Tel: 230.7400; foyabranca@cvtelecom.cv; www.foyabranca.com*

Festivals on São Vicente

January 22 – Mindelo, Municipal Day

February (the week of Ash Wednesday) – Mindelo, Carnival

May 3 – Santa Cruz

June 24 – Ribeira Julião, São João

June 29 – São Pedro, São Pedro

August 8 – Nossa Senhora da Luz

August (the weekend of the full moon) – Baía das Gatas, Music Festival

August 13 – Ribeira Julião, Santo António

September – Mindelo, MindelAct Theater Festival

December 31 – Mindelo, New Years Eve

São Nicolau

Flying in to São Nicolau, the plane curves along the southern-most point, a narrow ridge of land, and descends narrowly between this ridge and a volcanic crater. For a moment, it is impossible to determine where the plane will land. Good faith, however, in the pilot is required and without any sign of an airport or civilization, the plane touches down. As you disembark, Vila is visible from the airport, but is about a 15 minute ride along a winding road.

The airport is nothing more than a couple of small buildings where baggage is passed through a window and crowds of people jam in the corner with empty carts causing an impressive traffic jam—the worst traffic you will encounter during your stay. When you are able to wrestle your bags from the mess, a crowd of drivers await at the door. Be sure to get in a public car as the cost is about 1/3 of a "chartered" car. The jagged peaks and valleys along the road make for a dramatic entrance and the few rustic houses scattered along the path give a feel of the tranquility that reigns over the entire island; a feeling that will stay with you beyond your visit.

GEOGRAPHY

At 343 sq km (132 sq miles), it is neither the largest nor the smallest of the islands, but it is certainly the most uniquely shaped. The western half eerily echoes the African coastline while a long and largely uninhabited finger reaches off to the east as if pointing to the continent that played a large part in the country's development.

The island itself is comprised of two mountain ranges, one running north to south and the other stretching out to the northwest, culminating at Monte Gordo. The name "fat mountain" refers to the rounded width of the peak, but it is also the highest peak on São Nicolau. At 1,312m (4,304 feet), it is said that on a clear day, you can see almost all of the islands.

Today, much of the island is dry and red-grey rock can be all you see for miles, but Monte Gordo provides a consistent supply of water to the valley of Fajã. Hidden in the mountains, the expanse of green here can be jarring after the long, dry ride from Vila.

HISTORY

The depth of São Nicolau's history may not be immediately evident today, but this island was once the Portuguese stronghold in the archipelago. Though discovered in 1461, it was initially populated with goats. When people decided to settle in the early 1500s, they came in small groups and the population did not begin to grow for almost 200 years.

Tarrafal was the initial site of the Portuguese concentration camp for political prisoners, but was soon abandoned for the city of the same name on Santiago for the more accessible port and more tranquil waters. The difficult terrain of São Nicolau kept the island from the complexities of trade and commerce. Because of this, it became a place of religion and intellectualism—a history that is still held up with importance if not with great continuation.

In 1866, Dr. Julio José Dias, a native of São Nicolau, offered his house to establish a seminary in Ribeira Brava. Within the seminary, a secondary school was formed that offered subjects of the same caliber as schools in Portugal. This gave some of the brightest students of São Nicolau the opportunity to pursue careers within the church and Portuguese civil service. It strengthened the ties between Cape Verde and Portugal with a mutually beneficial relationship.

As the educated population increased, radical ideas followed. Focus shifted from strong ties between Portugal and Cape Verde toward the improvement of conditions for Cape Verde and her people. Though revolution was not manifested until the following generation, the father of Amilcar Cabral, Juvenal Cabral and the father of Aristides Pereira were educated within the seminary. These revolutionary seeds were well planted in their sons, who led Cape Verde to independence.

When church and state were separated in Portugal in 1911, the secondary school was moved to Mindelo where it was felt that more students would receive better opportunities. The seminary closed soon after in 1917, reopened and then closed again permanently in 1933. Now, the impressive buildings sit up on the hill awaiting a future.

Today, São Nicolau has the most rapidly decreasing population as the educated youth and more fortunate head to other islands or abroad to pursue other opportunities. Those who stay are engaged in agriculture, government, education or maritime pursuits. Transportation to the island can be difficult, so the tourist industry is in the long, slow process of development. Despite evident lack of infrastructure, there is no lack of things for visitors to see and do or places to stay. São Nicolau is a place to take the time to get to know. A quick glimpse or brief passing would not do justice to the many hidden beauties and mysteries of this unjustly forgotten island.

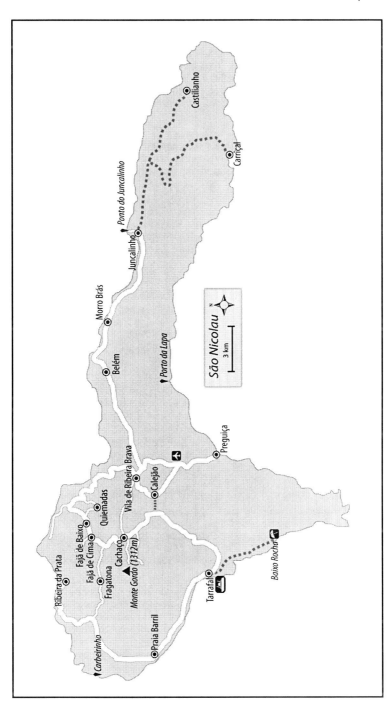

São Nicolau

GETTING THERE

São Nicolau is often dubbed *the* "forgotten island" of these forgotten islands. It is overlooked in many respects because the attractions—hiking, fishing and exploring—are sometimes more readily available on other islands. Transportation to São Nicolau is more irregular than the more common touristic destinations, but those who make the trip will be pleasantly surprised.

By Air

Flights are available a few times a week through TACV from Praia, Mindelo and Sal. The number of flights and availability increase during the summer months (July-September) and around the time of Carnival. Check at any of the agencies in Praia or through TACV directly.

By Sea

The *Sal Rei* makes a Praia-São Vicente-São Nicolau circuit about twice a week. The boat ride from Praia costs 7000-9000 and is about a 15 hour trip. Check www.bela-vista.net/ferry.aspx for fairly updated information on the ferry. Other options include:

Polar Shipping Tel: 261.5223 / 261.5225; Rua Cândido dos Reis on Plateau in Praia; polarp@cvtelecom.cv

Agentur S.T.M. S.T.M. is the main agency in Praia, but the office has been moved off of Plateau. Ask around for the new location or contact them directly at Tel: 261.2564.

Agentur S.T.M. The agency is next to Aparthotel Avenida on Rua 5 de Julho in Mindelo. Tel: 232.1179

GETTING AROUND

Cars leave regularly from Vila de Riberia Brava to Tarrafal. If trying to get out of Vila, your best bet is to get an early start. At all hours in the morning, you will find cars lingering around the praça by the church/library in the heart of town. Ask around for your destination of choice. There are no real "taxis," but many drivers can be chartered for the day.

To get to more remote parts of the island, like Carriçal, it is essential to have four-wheel drive, and an experienced driver. The road is often impassible, so confirm before making any plans. Recommended Driver:

Toi D'Armanda (speaks some English, excellent driver/guide) *Tel:* 236.1804, *m.* 994.5146; toilopes@hotmail.com

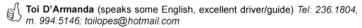

Vila de Ribeira Brava

The majority of the population of São Nicolau is nestled into this quaint mountainside village. Looking down into the valley, it is beautiful, and it lives up to the view on closer examination. The cobblestone roads twist and wind in a disorienting maze that echoes a small European village. Houses extend up both sides of the valley and meet in the commercial center along the floor of the *riberia*. The floor of the valley is littered with small planted parks with statues and tributes to legendary people from the island. A dirt part cuts through the middle where water flows in the rainy season and horses run in competition during Carnival.

Things generally run fairly smoothly in Vila as transportation consistently makes the trip to and from Tarrafal. There are a number of vehicles readily available and more shops than the small village seems to know what to do with. The school and other programs receive a lot of support, but in 2009 the rains came repeatedly and with a fury not seen in years, destroying much of the city's infrastructure. Landslides and erosion tore through some of the beautiful city parks and washed out large sections of the newly completed road from Vila to Tarrafal. Some houses were destroyed and three members of a family were killed. Restoration of the road and city infrastructure is currently underway, but the island still needs all the help it can get.

IMPORTANT INFORMATION

Bank On São Nicolau, you will find BCA, BCN and Caixa Económica. All banks open Monday-Friday, approx 8:00-15:30 (may vary a little by bank).

Hospital Posto Sanitário Though it is a large hospital, all services are not available on São Nicolau. Located up a hill on the airport side of the *ribeira*. Tel: 235.1130

Pharmacy: Down in the dirt of the *ribeira* on the way toward Cachaço/seminary.

Post Office *Correios*: Open Monday-Friday

Police *Polícia*: Down by the Shell station, it shouldn't be too difficult to find a patrolling police officer. Tel: 235.1152

TACV São Nicolau: By the library at the top of the praça. Open Monday-Friday; 8:00-12:30, 14:30-18:00. Tel: 235.1161

STAYING IN TOUCH

Internet is available in a few locations, but may be inconsistent. The least expensive option is the CEJ (*Centro de Juventude,* Youth Center) on the second floor of the building opposite the municipal market. For 100$/hour, you can use the reasonably reliable and moderately fast internet. Alternately, visit Cyber Hebr@ico next to Bela Criola and pay almost twice as much for similar quality service. Internet is also available at Pensão Jardim for 160$/hour.

WHAT TO DO

In the afternoon and evening, you will find many people milling around in the *praças*, particularly down by the *Câmara Municipal.* If there is a soccer game, it is sure to draw a crowd. There are a number of bars and shops where people tend to congregate.

The library is right in the center of town behind the tall monument commemorating Dr. Julio José Dias. Diagonally across the road is the **Igreja Matriz de Nossa Senhora de Rosário**, one of the oldest and most impressive churches in Cape Verde. It was rebuilt as a cathedral in the late 1800s. São Nicolau was the religious center of Cape Verde from 1866 until 1940. The seminary could be a major attraction, but is in the early stages of development. It has been renovated and you can try to enter, but there is no established museum or tribute to its historic revolutionary role.

São Nicolau

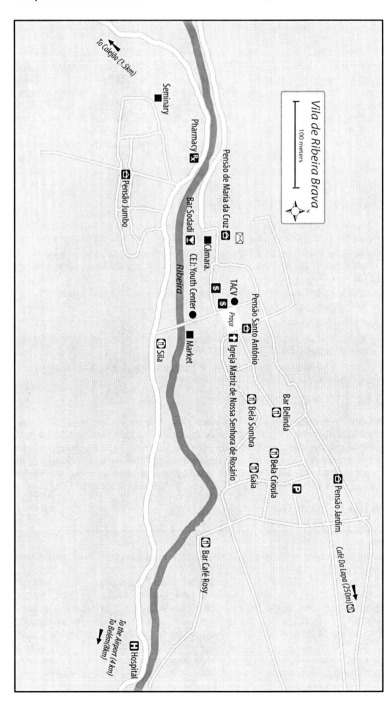

WHERE TO EAT

Snacks are easy to find in the many well stocked stores that line the winding streets of Vila. If you happen across a soccer game at the newly turfed *futebol* field, you will likely find a hoard of women out in the street selling a variety of fried or grilled seafood and chicken, *pastels* (tuna rolled in bread and fried) and homemade *donettes*.

As a general rule, restaurants do no have a consistent clientele and therefore may not have what you are looking for. There is sometimes a plate of the day available, but if you have a particular request, it is better to swing by and arrange a dish and mealtime.

Pensão Jardim Restaurant is located on the top floor of the pensão with a panoramic view of Vila. It is best to order food in advance. Lobster can be arranged if given enough notice. Invariably referred to as one of the best restaurants in town. $$ *Tel: 235.1117*

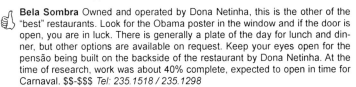

Bela Sombra Owned and operated by Dona Netinha, this is the other of the "best" restaurants. Look for the Obama poster in the window and if the door is open, you are in luck. There is generally a plate of the day for lunch and dinner, but other options are available on request. Keep your eyes open for the pensão being built on the backside of the restaurant by Dona Netinha. At the time of research, work was about 40% complete, expected to open in time for Carnaval. $$-$$$ *Tel: 235.1518 / 235.1298*

Bar Café Rosy All the way at the bottom of the city (take a right at the Shell), Rosy makes some of the best *cachupa* in town. Breakfast is until 11:00 and includes coffee, a heaping pile of *cachupa*, egg and half a fried fish for 200$. If you are feeling adventurous or stop by later in the day, ask to try some homemade *ponche*. $-$$

Pensão Santo António Located in the *pensão* of the same name, expect to pay a little more for a meal that is no better than anywhere else. Variety and reliability may be a draw. Open every day from 7:30-10:00, 12:30-14:30 and 7:30-20:00 (closed Sunday for dinner). $$-$$$ *Tel: 235.2200*

Bar Belinda Next to one of the many hair salons, it may be easy to pass by. This is a popular spot with locals for a quick, inexpensive plate-of-the-day. Serves breakfast, lunch and dinner. $

Sila On the other side of the bridge near the market, this spot was recently renovated by a couple of Italians who have converted the basement into a nightclub of varying popularity. They also introduced Italian style pizza and serve capirainhas. Expect to pay a little more than some other places. $$-$$$ *Tel: 235.1665*

Bela Crioula A nice open air space. The meals are not that impressive, but great for a coffee or snack. Recently changed ownership and name so there may be other changes to come. The real draw is the *tocatinhas* (live music) during weekends. $ *m. 983.8855*

Café Da Lapa All the way up in Lombona by the school, this small establishment is owned and run by Dona Da Lapa. All meals are available on request or made to order if you have a little time to kill. Stop in the front door and take a seat at the table and if you are lucky, you will be invited into the quintal away from the television. $-$$ *Tel: 235.1136*

Gaia Owned and run by a French man, the outside advertises *artisanto*, a restaurant and tours. Likely only open in the busy season, the view through the door is enough to make one want to take a better look. Food is rumored to be good, if a bit expensive. $$$

São Nicolau

NIGHTLIFE

Though there can be clubs open or parties thrown on Saturdays, Sunday nights are generally a popular night for people to gather in the street. A popular spot in the evenings is **Bar Sodadi** in the planted *praça* down by the *Câmara*. A quick *volta* loop around the downtown area will help determine the hot spot for the evening. Though São Nicolau is not known for its nightlife, there tends to be a little movement during the weekends. You are more likely to find fellow partygoers in Tarrafal than in Vila.

Sila The underground club is a little unnerving, but is popular throughout Cape Verde. As with all clubs in Vila, movement is hit-or-miss.

Bar Sodadi An open bar/café in the *praça* by the *Câmara,* this is old faithful for nightlife in Vila. Though you generally won't find a large party, you are almost certain to find a cluster of people out enjoying a few drinks and the evening air. Also a good place to get information about what else is happening.

Raconte A restaurant/bar/house on the way to Preguiça on the way out of Vila, there are generally parties hosted during "immigrant season" (July-September) to celebrate the homecoming of São Nicolau's many ex-pats. Ask around to see if there is anything happening, if there is, transportation will be readily available.

Bela Crioula If you are lucky, swing by on a night of *tocatinha* (live music).

Carnaval

In the weeks leading up to the beginning of lent, the entirety of Ribeira Brava is caught up in preparation for carnaval. Though São Nicolau does not receive the same acclaim of carnaval in Mindelo, this smaller celebration consumes the entire city and is far more personal and secure. The many groups spend the months leading up to the celebration preparing dances, costumes and floats to compete for the three day party.

WHERE TO STAY

 Pensão Jardim Owned and operated by Dona Valentina Jardim, this is probably the nicest place to stay in São Nicolau. Up the far hill toward the soccer field, the restaurant looks out over the valley. The 10 rooms are beautifully decorated and well maintained, all with a bathroom inside. There are also two rooms that connect for a suite. Prices are negotiable. $-$$ *Tel: 235.1117; pensaoresidencialjardim@hotmail.com*

Pensão Santo António Located right in the central *praça* across from the library, you pay for the convenience. The rooms are classy, if a little cold and the staff takes a little coaxing to smile. Reservations are available through travel agencies, but are less expensive if made directly. All amenities and breakfast included, less expensive if reserved directly through the hotel. $$ *Tel: 235.2200; manuelsantos@cvtelecom.cv*

Pensão Jumbo A short walk from the *Câmara*, this was once the family home of Georgina Soares. The restaurant of the same name was opened many years ago and after some success, the upstairs was converted into a pensão. The rooms are very simple and a bit old, but very well maintained.. Breakfast is not included, but is available upon request. $ (save 200$ on a room with a shared bathroom) *Tel: 235.1315*

Pensão de Maria da Cruz Used mostly by traveling soccer teams, rooms are available for rent in the beautiful old house. Because it is not regularly used, it may be a bit musty and Dona da Cruz can be a bit elusive, but for these same reasons, prices may be negotiable. $ *Tel: 235.1282*

Leaving Vila
It is possible to head into the interior or out along the finger. There is no round trip of the island, but all roads lead to Vila and, conversely, take you away to the furthest reaches of the island.

To the East

Heading east, you will pass through a smattering of small villages clearly marked by poverty and isolation. Pass through Belém and Morro Brás—small, windswept villages—to Juncalinho, another windswept village with a hidden natural wonder.

JUNCALINHO

At first glimpse, there is nothing special about this little town. A few houses of various degrees of completion line the road and extend back toward the ocean and opposing cliff faces. With around 300 residents, you pass through as quickly as you enter, but the jewel of this small community lies a few hundred meters away on the coast. The road to the coast is currently being repaired, but there may or may not be a sign indicating the turn off the main road. Pass through a few more houses until you reach the cliff overlooking uneven steps that have been carved into the rock face leading down to a natural pool nestled in the volcanic rock constantly replenished by the crashing tide.

> You can ask around in the morning for cars going to Juncalinho. If you are not successful, you can charter a car or talk with the proprietor of your *pensão*.

Where to Stay

Pensão Alves Jardim Built and owned by the same family as Pensão Jardim in Vila, this *pensão* is equally beautiful, though in the process of receiving finishing touches. A garden in the back keeps the rooms fresh and the communal washing area in front offers a glimpse of the never ending work of Cape Verdean women. Breakfast is available on request for a small fee ($) and transportation is available to and from Vila as well as for a variety of excursions. $ *Tel: 235.2800*

Where to Eat

Restaurant Alves Jardim Owned and operated by the Jardim family, the restaurant is located up the hill from the pensão. Be sure to order your meals in advance. $

Restaurant/Bar Lanchonette A small sign hangs outside a yellow house on the road to the lagoon. It doesn't look like much, but the family is more than happy to welcome you and serve you whatever they have available. Don't expect a full menu, but the generosity makes up for any perceived lack thereof. $

São Nicolau

CARRIÇAL

The small village of Carriçal hangs on to the finger of São Nicolau like a rough and jagged hang nail. The road there is long, steep, rocky and, once you pass Juncalinho, entirely deserted. Though work is being done, it is far from complete. Depending on conditions, it may be impossible to find a driver willing to take you out, but hiking is almost always a possible (not recommended during the rainy season as trails may wash out).

If hiking, plan to spend the entire day trekking to and from or call ahead and arrange to stay someplace for the night so that you can take your time to appreciate the tiny, isolated community. Follow the road, until you see a few abandoned buildings up ahead on the coastal side of the road. A distinct left turn will appear leading you along a trail down the coast to a little bay and then up the *ribeira*.

Along the road, a few abandoned settlements line rigid cliffs and a fenced agricultural area to let you know that you are getting closer. Shortly before the descent to Carriçal, the road splits and leads to Castilianho, possibly the most isolated location in the country. If you have time and are feeling adventurous, this road leads to a settlement of one family a few kilometers north of the lighthouse at the easternmost tip.

As you descend into Carriçal, you will look out over a few rows of government built, identical houses, the tip of the green oasis hiding down in the *ribeira* and the open ocean. A large tuna canning factory dominates the town, but unfortunately no longer functions. The factory was recently closed due to inability to compete with the factory in Tarrafal. Once the village's primary source of income, residents now rely entirely on remittances, government aid and the occasional sale of fresh seafood. Ask around to take a look inside.

It is impossible to imagine there was ever much bustle here, but the daily catch still brings a bit of activity to the port that was constructed by the *Câmara Municipal* in 2004/2005 and at any given hour you are likely to come across a group of children diving into the water (one of whom is featured on the cover of this book). From the port, you can gaze into the impossibly lush mouth of the *ribeira*, but don't walk up from the water as sea urchins cling to the rocks underfoot.

Fishermen will gladly take you out in their boats for a small fee to try your luck with the fishing line or to explore the uninhabited coastline. It may also sometimes be possible to travel from Carriçal to Preguiça (and vice versa) by boat. (May be a good option for tired hikers needing to get return to their base.)

Where to Stay & Eat

Though there is no established *pensão* in Carriçal, contact **Kulla** (Tel: 235.1693, $) to arrange a space in a house and a basic meal. Price will be negotiable, but this is one of few income generating opportunities in the community. Very little is available in the town's two run down stores, so be sure to bring any personal necessities (including water). Fish, on the other hand, is plentiful and inexpensive.

South of Vila

PREGUIÇA

On the road back from Carriçal/Junalinho, you can head back into Vila, or bear south toward the airport. This southern road also leads to the original port, Preguiça. One of the first settlements on São Nicolau, it was established as a safe port after the repeated infiltration of Porto da Lapa. The road leading down to the port is the oldest on the island, and it shows in the rustic houses that line the winding road that drops dramatically to the sea.

> It is possible to catch a car from Vila for around 200$ or you can walk.

Turn left in the descent before the pier and you will find scattered remnants of history. A low wall lined with a few scattered cannons are all that remain of the fortress built in defense against Sir Francis Drake and other looters. Looking out over the winding road and off into the ocean, the visitor is left wondering how the port was ever protected as the two monuments erected in honor of the passing of Pedro Alves Cabral in March of 1500 on his way to "discovering" Brazil tower over what remains of the once impenetrable walls.

At the bottom of the road, the port is endlessly bustling with activity. Relaxing on the pier and jumping off or diving for lobster are two of the main activities in the community. To the side of the pier, you will find the typical flock of bright fishing boats fully equipped with fishermen.

Where to Stay & Eat

Though there is no established *pensão* in Preguiça, it is possible to arrange for a meal or bed with **Dona Maria** (Tel: 235.1582, $). Her large, pink house stands out in the village (to the right when heading toward the ocean) and her food is just as notorious. A few years living in Italy have added a little pizzazz to her cooking that you won't easily find elsewhere.

CALEJÃO

On the way back from Preguiça or a short walk from Vila is Calejão, home of another abandoned relic. In addition to boasting the first institution of quality secondary education, Cape Verde's first orphanage in also here. The rain washed and wind-swept building looms large on the hill looking out over Caleijão and, below, the airstrip. Originally run by the Sisters of Amor

---

Porto da Lapa

Porto da Lapa, the first port, is nestled in the wide bay south of Vila, but has long since been abandoned. It is now a protected area for sea turtles nesting in the late summer, but it was once the easily invaded home of settlers from Portugal and Madeira. The infamous Sir Francis Drake who devastated Cidade Velha also visited São Nicolau inspiring inhabitants to flee into the protected valley and establish Vila de Ribeira Brava. This attack led to the building of the fortress in Preguiça.

The water here can be tempting, but it can also be dangerous. Be sure to ask around to see if the weather is right for swimming.

de Deus, the orphanage served young girls of São Nicolau and from throughout Cape Verde, offering them education and opportunities that would not have been accessible without a family. During the period of drought and famine in the 1940s, it was the only existing orphanage in the country and the rooms filled to almost double their capacity. Today, the building sits in a growing state of disrepair. There is talk of resurrection and establishment as a museum, like the seminary, but talk has yet to bring action.

The walk to Calejão involves a bit of climbing, but it is a short and interesting walk and it is worth it to examine the deteriorating building up close.

The Road North

This newly finished road has already been devastated in areas by the intense rains of the 2009 rainy season. Despite crumbling asphalt and potential landslides, drivers still pass in an effort to connect Vila with the western port in Tarrafal.

Even if you just make the trip between Vila and Tarrafal, it is worth travelling just to see the many different landscapes that exist, nestled within the mountains. The road snakes along the coast, weaving in and out until you reach the coastal town of Carvoeiros. As you approach the village, there is a well irrigated inlet which appears as a burst of green below the road. Banana, papaya, sugar cane and corn fill the gap between pavement and ocean giving a stunning contrast to what can be bone dry land. The curves along this part of the road are sharp and dangerous and have taken the lives of a few cyclists.

As you begin the ascent, Fajã and Quiemadas spread out like a carpet of green on the surrounding valley. After driving through the moonscape shoreline, this burst of green is welcome and almost seems out of place. These valleys are largely agricultural and the water provided by Monte Gordo is being utilized in a number of different ways to enhance productivity. Recent projects installing *gota-gota* (drip irrigation) have already made a significant mark on the effective use of the valuable resource of water.

It is here in Fajã that you will find some of the last naturally occurring Dragoeiro trees (*Dracaena draco*). Endemic to Cape Verde, there is a massive push on behalf of the natural parks and UNDP projects to protect existing trees and replant the tree that once flourished between elevations of 500 and 900 meters on Santo Antão, São Nicolau, Santiago, Fogo and Brava. The trees are said to live for a thousand years and the "blood" of the dragon tree has been used as a medicine to relieve pain and to flavor *grogue*.

The *Dragoeiro* Tree

Um simbolo d' resistêcia à seca	A symbol of resistence of draught
Florid na zona d' Fajã	Growing in the town of Fajã
Resisti tudo seca	Resisting all draught
Guenta tud mau tempo	Continuing through bad times
Tud táva pèlod	When all is bald and bare
Burro ma cabra nega pedra	Donkey and goat may ignore the rock
Es ka nega folha d'Dragoeiro...	But not the leaf of the Dragoeiro

CACHAÇO

Approximately half way between Vila and Tarrafal, Cachaço is the ideal base from which to explore the western half of the island. From here, it is possible to access the trails that criss-cross through the *Parque Natural*— the national park/protected area—and lead to many of the more isolated villages scattered throughout the mountain range. At the foot of Monte Gordo, Cachaço looks out over the verdant valley of Fajã and is graced with the fresh, cool air of gathering clouds on the peak.

Transportation

Take a car from Vila to Tarrafal and dismount at the *Casa do Ambiente* (150$). Alternatively, it is possible to walk to and from Vila and Cachaço on a steep, winding road that used to be the only way between the two villages.

What to Do

The park draws many for its stunning hikes and growing Information Center that offers information about the endemic species of São Nicolau, maps and guided hikes (detailed information available on website) as well as handmade souvenirs.

While relaxing in Cachaço, examine the famous Dragoeiro tree face-to-face, visit Igreja de Nossa Senhora do Monte at the foot of Monte Cintinha or the natural water source around the other side of the small peak. At night, join the local crowd at the *xafaris/chafariz* (public water supply) at the mouth of the trail leading to Vila for a game of cards, Arlinda's famous *ponche* a stunning view of the lights of Vila and to simply enjoy the cool night air.

Where to Stay

Pensão de Arlinda Spend a night or two in the best location on the island. Centrally located up in the fresh air at the foot of Monte Gordo, you will sleep peacefully-disturbed only by the occasional rooster-in the house of Arlinda's family. For a minimal price, you will get a taste of rural life in São Nicolau and a heaping pile of *cachupa* for breakfast. $ *Tel: 237.1176, m. 998.1533*

Where to Eat

Arrange something with Arlinda or talk to the staff at the *Casa do Ambiente* to arrange a meal at a local home. There are a few small stores around with a handful of snack ideas.

TARRAFAL

Throughout the islands, names of towns are repeated, but it is rare that the town's histories are also intertwined. It is believed that the three Tarrafals—one on São Nicolau, Santiago and Santo Antão—were named for the presence of the Tarrafe (*Tamarix senegalensis*), a tree that once flourished in the coastal mouths of *ribeiras*. Though it is not the most difficult to reach—Tarrafal in Santo Antão is many miles from Porto Novo down a long and arduous road—the Tarrafal of São Nicolau is subject to harsher conditions than that of Santiago.

Despite the harsh conditions, Tarrafal of São Nicolau has developed into one of the nicest port towns in Cape Verde. The port of Preguiça was abandoned in favor of Tarrafal which now harbors the irregular passenger and cargo boats. Fishing is still the main source of income for the town and the tuna canning factory adds additional income to this not-so-sleepy town. Though much of the catch goes to canning, it is possible to buy tuna, eel and whatever other catch of the day down at the dock for 150-200/kg when the boats come in. Look inside for fruits and vegetables.

There is a definite coastal town feel to this community with rows of shops and boutiques and colorful, unique buildings. People walk the wind-whipped streets at all hours of the day in bathing suits and the rushing tide provides a constant backdrop to the quiet city sounds. Nightlife in Tarrafal tends to be livelier than that of Vila and the stretch of dark, sandy beach comes to life every evening as youth and adults alike make their way to the coast to take in some fresh air and *toma banho*—bathe in the ocean.

Concentration Camp

In the 1930s during the reign of Salazar in Portugal, the construction of a concentration camp for political prisoners was ordered to be built in the colony of Cape Verde. Though it is Tarrafal of Santiago that is now famous for the uncanny prison, it was in São Nicolau that was initially slated for construction. Today, the camp in João Baptista of Tarrafal is nothing more than a few half started columns and walls, but the plans that still exist have inspired an initiative to finish some basic work to establish a historic site. Though it is unclear why the work here was abandoned, it is rumored that the conditions were too harsh even for political prisoners.

Where to Stay

 Residencial Natur Dona Maria Natur converted her family's house into a pensão eight years ago and has done well for herself ever since. Bright and clean with an open quintal and breakfast in the family kitchen, the only thing missing is toilet seats Breakfast is an additional fee ($) If available, request a room in the front for a cool ocean breeze and view of the garden across the street. $ *Tel: 236.1178*

Parque Natural de Monte Gordo

The village of Cachaço is probably most famous as the location of the natural park. Just up the street from Arlinda's house, the *Casa do Ambiente* (literal: Environment House, read: Visitor's Center) welcomes visitors and adventurers, offering information about endemic species, maps and guide service for hiking, sale of local *artesanto* (crafts) and any other services you can think of (including arranging a meal for when you return from your hike, hungry and tired).

The park is in the process of growth and development, but the services offered are top notch. In July of 2009, they were in the process of creating and posting signs on what could be confusing parts of hikes. The center does offer a small brochure with brief descriptions of plants and animals found in the park as well as a detailed map of hike with descriptions. For more information, visit: www.ecosaonicolau.cv.

Casa Aquário Down by the bay, this Dutch owned establishment offers six simple rooms and an exquisite cuisine. Former chef Henny Kusters will organize excursions, prepare your bed and serve up a masterpiece. Half-board only. $$-$$$ *Tel: 236.1099; info@casa-aquario.nl; www.casa-aquario.nl*

Pensão Alice This long established family run *pensão* has a welcoming feel and well decorated (if a little tacky) communal area giving it a feeling of home. All amenities are available, but not in all rooms. The price starts low for a simple single and goes up for a luxury double with A/C, television and mini-bar. Be sure to poke your head into the loja on the ground floor to visit Senhor Lídio, husband of Alice, and see the eclectic range of merchandise available. $-$$ *Tel: 236.1187*

Pensão Tocely This *pensão* is located right by the beach and A/C in all the rooms. Look out over some buildings to the ocean from the restaurant on the roof. The rooms are nicely decorated, but nothing special. $$ *Tel: 236.1220*

Where to Eat

Residencial Natur Dona Maria will be happy to prepare you a meal on request. Price is likely to vary depending on the nature of the request. $-$$ *Tel: 236.1178*

Pensão Alice If you opt not to stay here, stop in to enjoy a meal in the family living room. The decorations offer an eclectic view for diversion and entertainment while you wait for your meal to be prepared. $-$$ *Tel: 236.1220*

Restaurante Calibar Recently opened by a French couple, this small restaurant/bar is tastefully decorated with a thatched roof and furniture made in Cachaço. A variety of endemic plants and fruits keep the air fresh as the ocean breeze enters through the front door. Meals can be pricey, but enjoy a variety, including crepes, that is not available anywhere else on the island. Live music scheduled for Sunday nights. $$-$$$ *Tel: 975.2046*

Casa Aquário Open daily for lunch, please make reservations for lunch and give a day's notice for dinner, there is no way you will be let down. $$-$$$ *Tel: 236.1099*

Bar/Restaurant *Golfinho* (Blue Dolphin): Across from Pensão Tocely, the two floors of this eatery and watering hole are colorfully decorated and give a very beach feel. A popular spot to wait for the perpetually late boats. $$ *Tel: 236.1046*

Lanchonette Impossible to miss, this expansive restaurant is located right on the beach. The entire town seems drawn to the beach in the afternoon and evening hours making this place popular for a cold beer and some grilled chicken. The giant TV is also a drawing point for *futebol* games and the occasional Brazilian telenovella. $-$$

Restaurant Felicidade Up the hill from the beach, the menu appears to be varied, but it is really just different types of fish prepared in a variety of ways (fried, grilled, baked etc.). A favorite is *atun com natas* tuna in a cream sauce. All plates come with rice and french fries. Vegetables are available upon request. $$-$$$

Tarrafe

The Tarrafe *Tamarix senegalensis* is a fairly large tree, 2-5 meters tall, and is found in the shallow soil of the costal mouths of ribeiras. Though it was once common and wide spread, like all species of trees in Cape Verde, its number has been greatly reduced due to overharvesting for firewood as well as the destruction of its habitat by the extraction of sand for use in construction.

São Nicolau

Restaurant Evora Popular spot with locals for the shade and busy corner, the restaurant is located underneath Pensão Tocely, but is entirely separate. Don't look for a sign, just look for the chairs spilling out into the sidewalk and a group of men sitting around sipping on coffee and beer, playing *oril*, cards or just shooting the breeze. $

Buena Vida Restaurant Impossible to miss by the port, this restaurant was opened and is run by the Italian Bruno. Plates are undoubtedly more expensive than local restaurants and he is only open for dinner (18:00-close), but you would be a fool to skip the homemade gelato. Take a minute to admire the recycled paper menus made in Cachaço. $$-$$$

Beyond

South of Tarrafal there is a path to Baixo Rocha. The road is nearly impassable by car, so if you plan to visit, be sure to bring plenty of water for the hour and a half hike (one way). The road leads you along a lunar landscape of desolation and eventually drops into an oasis of white sand beach.

The road continues beyond Tarrafal heading back up around the other side of the mountains. As you leave Tarrafal, there is a massive holiday house complex that appears to never have been finished. One man from Tarrafal resides there as a guard watching over the forgotten investment.

As you head up the newly repaired road north of Tarrafal, there are a series of signs pointing to various beaches rumored to have medicinal sands. Of all the detours, Carbeirinho is most worth a visit.

Magical Medicinal Sands

Locals will swear that the dark sand of Praia Barril has healing powers for bodily aches and pains. To ease the pain of arthritis, rheumatism and general discomfort, one should be buried in the sand up to the neck for a cleansing period of sweating and relaxation. Though there may be nothing magic about them, consistently high temperatures, strength of the sun and darkness of the sand combine for nature's most powerful and probably dirtiest natural heating pad. Be sure to wear a hat and sunscreen and while you're there, check out the deteriorating lighthouse.

CARBEIRINHO

There are a number of signs along the road pointing out the beaches down along the coast, but if you only visit one, make it Carbeirinho. The dirt path leads up and over a rolling hill, suddenly dropping off toward the ocean. The walk down to the coast is steep and slippery and your destination is not visible until you have almost arrived. The last leg of the descent has been aided by steps carved into the rock. As you step down onto a ledge, the eroding stone behind you juts out like a wall of faces carved by an erratic hand. Below, the ocean swells into an open pool, sometimes rushing in with such fury that a burst of water rises up into view. If you climb down to either side, the ledge is surrounded by coves of an almost unworldly landscape. Fresh water drips down the damp, dark rocks giving birth to a green carpet along the walls.

At low tide, it is possible to swim in either of these coves, but as the tide comes in, the path back to the ledge is swallowed by the tide. Arguably the most stunning spot on São Nicolau, there is currently a push to make this a protected area. Inquire at the *Parque Natural* in Cachaço.

RIBEIRA DA PRATA

The road beyond Carbeirinho is in the process of revitalization, making it easier to access the few isolated communities that lay beyond. For some, it may be easier to hike down to Ribeira da Prata from Cachaço. The trail down from above leads through Fragata and Fragatona, two small communities that line mountain ridges like plates along the back of a stegosaurus.

Ribeira da Prata is itself known for the *Rocha Scribida* (rock with writing), similar to that of Santo Antão, though less intriguing, and the *Festival de Agua Doce* (literal: festival of sweet water) that is celebrated after the first significant rainfall in September. A small natural stage is set among the rock at the bottom of the *ribeira* and music is played, beer and *grogue* are drunk and food is eaten as the life giving water gushes past the stage on both sides.

São Nicolau

Festivals on São Nicolau

February – Carnival, the week leading up to ash Wednesday.

April - Pascoal, a festival celebrating Easter in Fajã

April 13 – Santo António in Preguiça

May – Nossa Senhora do Monte in Cachaço

June 24 – São João in Praia Branca

June 29 – São Pedro in Vila and Fajã

August – (first weekend) music festival in Tarrafal

August-September (after the first big rain) – Festival da Agua Doce in Ribeira da Prata

October – (first Sunday) Nossa Senhora do Rosário

December – (first Sunday) São Francisco in Tarrafal

December 6 – Municipal Day in Vila

The Bike Race that Shook the World

There are but a handful of events so momentous, so grand that they alter the course of humanity forever. The extinction of the dinosaurs, the ice age, the crucifixion of Christ, and "the Bike Race that Shook the World," or at least Cape Verde. That's right, for the first time in its more than 400 years of human history, since the Portuguese stepped foot on these islands, since the struggle for independence and the birth of democracy, finally, after all the waiting, the first cross island bike race has been held on São Nicolau.

The race began, shockingly, at the exact hour set; 10:00 on Sunday, July 12, 2009. The 26km race followed the National road on the island, from Vila de Ribeira Brava to the youthful fishing town of Tarrafal. From the central highlands to the ocean, the race covered all types of terrain; steep ascents, tear-jerking descents and flat, smooth coastal sections. With representatives from all parts of the island participating, the race crossed social and political classes, a diverse group taking steps toward world peace and bicycle safety.

Fifteen cyclists headed off after a "*Tres, Dois, Um, BAI!!!!*"(three, two, one, GO!) count down from the *Veriador de Desportivo* (sports director) in Vila. From the start, the riders completed an ascent that led into a roller coaster coastal section. With the Police in front, the road was cleared as the riders switch-backed up the steepest parts. The stronger cyclists shone as they pulled away from the crowd. Despite this early struggle, the most tortuous part of the race was upon them, nearly 10km of all uphill.

The leader was well ahead of the rest of the riders through the uphill struggles of Fajá, Lompelado, Canto and finally into Cachaço. From Cachaço, the uphill battle is over and a new set of skills are needed by the riders as they begin the 10km downhill bomb: braking curves and holding on for dear life as the bike reaches frightening speeds.

After an hour and thirty-five minutes, the leader from the start cruised past the finish line to a roar from the local crowd. Three minutes later, second place came in followed a minute later by third. Every minute another rider came speeding down the last hill to the finish line. By mid-day, the caravan had made it through, and whether a winner or slightly worse for the wear, were greeted by applause.

The race was an amazing success. All the riders used helmets, and one made a testament to its value. As the caravan made its way through Fajá, we learned that one of the bikers in the rear had taken a spill on a notoriously dangerous curve and had been taken to the hospital. While he didn't finish the race, he ended up with just a few scratches and his bike wasn't damaged. More helmets are going to be given out to those who weren't able to ride and everyone was already talking about the next race, the next time they can get together. The budding of a Bicycle Association was born on July 12th, 2009.

Although the bike race is completed, the work isn't done. Local organizations are distributing helmets, strengthening bike association, and creating an overall interest in the sport for future bike events being planned.

- Ross Guberman

Sal

Sal has long been a tourist destination in Cape Verde and is probably the most notorious of the three flat islands—Sal, Boa Vista and Maio. In many ways, Sal could be considered separate from much of Cape Verde as it is in the process of developing into a world of its own. The population of Sal has exploded with this development of tourism, almost doubling from roughly 8,000 to 15,000 since 1990 (nearly 50% of the nation's tourism is based in Sal). Cape Verdeans and West Africans flock to this barren island in hopes of finding employment, while Europeans relocate to Sal in hopes of finding some sun. There is an established ex-pat community that is active in developing and creating businesses in Santa Maria.

Politically, the *Câmara* is represented by an independent party setting it apart from the dominant political parties, PAICV and MPD. Despite this separation, much has been done on Sal to promote and welcome visitors. Within Espargos, the municipal seat, the streets are well signed and well kept with a well established tourism infrastructure.

GEORGRAPHY

Unless you catch a glimpse of Santa Maria when flying in, you may wonder what all the hype is about. Largely flat and desolate, the land is a muted red brown and the highest point, Monte Grande, just fails to reach 1,312 feet (400 meters). Sal is 18.6 miles (30 km) long and barely stretches to 7.5 miles 12 km wide with an area of 83.5 sq miles 216 sq km.There are minor variations in topography, but it is largely limited to small ridges, rounded volcanic remnants and rolling sand.

Sal is most well known for the southern bay of Santa Maria, which is a massive strip of sandy beach that has been developed into a tourist hotspot. On the west coast, Murdeira is also a developed bay known for the vibrant sea life. Along the southeast coast is Kite Beach, popular for kite-surfing. If you follow the east coast heading north, you will alternately pass dramatic cliffs and small, sheltered beaches.

Use care when swimming anywhere, even Santa Maria, as the tide can be remarkably strong.

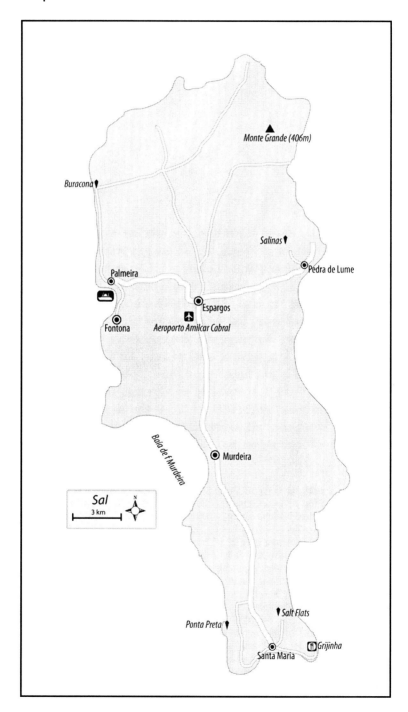

Monte Grande (406m)

Buracona

Salinas

Palmeira

Pedra de Lume

Espargos

Fontona

Aeroporto Amílcar Cabral

Baía de Murdeira

Murdeira

Sal
3 km

N

Salt Flats

Ponta Preta

Grijinha

Santa Maria

HISTORY

The island of Sal is the oldest island in the archipe-lago, estimated to have been formed roughly 50 million years ago. It was discovered on December 3rd of 1640, and named Llana, but was largely overlooked until the discovery of massive salt pans in Pedra de Lume.

> The name, Sal, is Portuguese for "salt."

The island was largely uninhabited for many years. A few brave souls survived here in the desert with goats, trading salt and salted goat meat to passing ships for supplies. In the 18th century, the Cape Verdean Manuel António Martins developed a salt extraction industry from the *salinas* of Pedra de Lume. Initially, donkeys were used to carry the salt over the lip of the crater, but a tunnel was later bore through the crater wall. In 1919, the business was purchased and a massive tramway system was built to increase the amount of salt transported.

When this industry was deserted in the early 20th century, the popula-tion of Sal once again dwindled. It wasn't until the development of the airport that interest returned to the barren strip of land. The use of Sal as a refueling station led to the rediscovery of Sal's other natural resource, white sand beaches and clear, turquoise water.

Aeroporto Amilcar Cabral, just outside of Espargos, was the first airport to accept international flights and has since been a stopping point for all kinds of visitors. Initially built in 1939, the project was funded by Italy as a refueling stop for flights to South America and South Africa. The airport was purchased by the Portuguese in 1947 and continued to be used as a refueling stop on-and-off for years, particularly for flights to South Africa during apartheid.

With the development of tourism and the increase of Cape Verdeans living abroad, additional flights have been introduced making Sal one of the more accessible islands.

GETTING THERE

Home to Cape Verde's oldest of a growing number of international airports, Sal is easier to get to than some of the other islands. Direct flights are available through TAP Portugal and the UK on Thomson and are rumored to be begin-ning through Delta from Atlanta, GA (USA).

If you intend to travel within the islands, it is recommended that you try to book the tickets before arrival in country. If traveling through a tour agency, see if they can book the tickets. Otherwise, try speaking to an agent at the airport upon arrival. During much of the year, especially summer months, internal flights can fill up quickly.

TACV and Halcyon offer flights to Santiago, São Vicente, Boa Vista and São Nicolau. Connecting flights to Fogo and Maio are available through Santiago.

Airport *Tel: 241.1468 / 241.1305*

TACV *Tel: 241.1656 / 241.1305*

TAP Portugal *Tel: 241.1195*

Halcyon Air *Tel: 241.2324 / 241.2374*

Cabo Verde Express *Tel: 241.2600*

TAAG (Angolan Airline) *Tel: 241.1355*

> All airline offices (except Thomson) are located at the airport.

GETTING AROUND

Taxis are generally available at the airport, as well as throughout Espargos and Santa Maria. A taxi from the airport is about 300$ to Espargos and 1000$ to Santa Maria. If you are on a budget and travelling light, it may be in your best interest to walk the few hundred meters to the road and wait for a passing car. Though you will have to pay, it is only 100$ to Santa Maria in a public car and a handful of change to Espargos.

There are a multitude of cars that run to and from Espargos and Santa Maria throughout the day and well into the evening. A one-way trip is 100$. For any of the other spots—Palmeira, Pedra de Lume/Salinas, Murdeira—you will need to ask around or go in a chartered car. Unlike many of the other islands, it is difficult to get a free ride on Sal. Cape Verdeans come here from all over trying to make a living and won't pass up any opportunity.

Car Rental

There are a number of places where you can rent a car to explore the island yourself. Price starts at 5000$ and you will need to add the cost of a deposit. Before taking the car, be sure to examine it to see if there are any visible problems. If you plan to visit Buracona or other reaches of the island that are not connected to the main road, be sure to request a 4x4. Be careful not to leave valuables in the car as they frequently fall victim to break-ins.

In Espargos

Luz Car *Tel 241.427*

Melicar *Tel 241.1666*

Porto Novo Car *Tel: 241.2880*

Rentaventra *Tel: 241.3519*

Mendes & Mendes *Tel: 241.2860, m. 991.8756; mendesemednes@cvtelecom.cv*

In Santa Maria

Mendes & Mendes *Tel: 242.1415; cpontao@cvtelecom.cv*

Alucar *Tel: 242.1187, m.991.5586; Near Morabeza, has a good reputation*

Avis *Tel: 242.1551; Operated out of the Hotel Novorizonte/Belizorante*

Hertz *Tel: 242.161; Operated out of the Hotel Crioula*

Cartur *Tel: 242.1700*

Quad Rentals

There are a number of companies that rent quad bikes and offer guided quad tours. Before renting, one should be aware that they are not meant to be taken on the beach or dunes (in fact, it is illegal). Quads are one of the causes for the decrease of turtle population. All places below are located in Santa Maria.

Cabo Quad *Tel: 242.1590*

Inco *Tel: 242.1994; On the beach across from Aparthotel Santa Maria, offers guided tours only.*

Fun Quad *By Enacol, offers buggy safaris.*

WHAT TO DO

The natural beauty and resources of Sal have been realized and are now used to the benefit of visitors. With miles of pristine beaches, strong trade winds and the overwhelming presence of vibrant sea life, water sports and activities play a large part of the culture here. There are also excursions on land in 4x4 vehicles and quad bikes available for rental, but one may find that the island itself pales in comparison with what lays just off the coast.

The Bay of Murdeira is a protected area amidst the growing coastal development. The shallow protected waters are filled with corals and diverse marine life.

The saltpans of Salinas are also considered a protected area, though it is possible to enter the crater and explore the area. People arrive every day in droves to examine the remnants of the history of salt extraction, the current extraction and to bathe in the remarkably dense, buoyant water.

Monte Grande, the tallest mountain, and Buracona, "the blue eye," are also considered protected areas, though the amount of trash and visible footsteps of past visitors may lead you to question the latter.

Nearly the entire east coast of Sal is designated a protected area for what many consider to be Sal's most precious natural resource—turtles. Though Sal receives significantly lower number of nesting turtles than neighboring Boa Vista, it is still considered an important location in the preservation of these endangered species. Turtles have always been hunted along the coasts of Cape Verde, but with the increase of population and increase of demand, the slaughter of female turtles also increased, compromising future generations. These future generations of sea turtles are also pushed to the brink with the careless use of quad bikes, crushing vulnerable nests, and mindless acts like litter on the beach, choking and suffocating the turtles, and excessive light from resorts and hotels, leading the turtles astray.

Organizations Making a Difference

Anjos (Angels): *Associação Nós Jovens Santa Maria* (Youth Association of Santa Maria) was started in July of 2008 to combat poverty and its manifestations by offering support through educational programs, youth activities, day care and housing support for families in Santa Maria. The community center is located on Amilcar Cabral Street where they collect and distribute food/clothing donations, offer job and computer training and host community events. *Tel: 242.2091; anjossmaria@cvtelecom.cv*

In Espargos, there are a number of community associations trying to join forces to combat the negative effects of tourism. As the number of visitors has increased, so has crime, drug/alcohol abuse and prostitution. OMCV (*Organização das Mulheres de Cabo Verde* – The Women's Association of Cape Verde), ICCA (*Instituto Cabo-verdiano da Criança e do Adolescente* – The Cape Verdean Institute for Children and Adolescents) and the *Associação Chã de Matias* (Association of Chã Matias) have joined forces to combat domestic violence and child trafficking. They are currently working to create a computer center in Espargos as a vocational training center and a "safe place" for youth and women who suffer from domestic violence. For information on donations or how you can help, please contact the association at Tel: 241.2226 / 241.3846 or achamatias@hotmail.com.

In 2007, a local NGO was established to slow what had grown into a rapid and blind destruction of the turtle population. SOS Tartarugas (www.turtlesos.org; m. 974.5019) was founded by concerned local residents who witnessed the practices destroying nesting areas and have made a strong push to raise awareness throughout the island; for locals, developers and tourists alike. Efforts include informative training for local military and law enforcement officials as well as interested volunteers to participate on supervised night-patrols. Groups head out at night during nesting season to prevent hunting log nesting activity, rescue eggs to a hatchery and offer educational tours of the beach and hatchery for interested visitors.

> For more information about upcoming events and community happenings, visit www.aboutsal.com.

Excursions are organized through SOS Tartarugas (see contact above) during laying/hatching season—July through November (peaking in August). The 3300$ fee goes directly into research and conservation and takes you on a few hour tour of beaches patrolling for mothers and their nests. (Tours start at 10:30).

Excursions

Most excursions and sports are available out of Santa Maria and have been listed with Santa Maria. The following tour operators exclude the centers within resorts. All are located in Santa Maria.

Barracuda Tours Offices in Sal, Boa Vista, São Vicente and Portugal. Offers nearly every activity and excursion, including all-inclusive packages. *Tel: 242.2033 / 241.2452; geral@barracudatours.com; www.barracudatours.com*

Morabitur On the road to Hotel Morabeza, offers a variety of excursions, both on and off island. *Tel: 241.2672; morabitur@cvtelecom.cv*

Unotour A non-profit set up and supported by a number of hotels and agencies, Unotour seeks to promote Cape Verde while assisting its guests in arranging tours and finding their way around. *Tel: 242.1771; unotour@cvtelecom.cv*

Espargos

Right in the heart of Sal, Espargos is named for the wild asparagus stalk that was once common to the area. Now, the only thing that springs up from the soil are the houses that form a starburst around the ASA tower mound.

You may feel like you are walking around in circles while exploring Espargos, and that is largely true. The town itself has grown around the ASA tower mound in the center of town. If at any point you feel lost, walk toward this, the highest point in the city, and you will easily find your way. The commercial area is largely focused on the south side of the mound and is easily covered on foot.

Though most tourists disembark and head directly to Santa Maria—the developed stretch of sand that extends across the southern bay—the effects of tourism can also be noted in Espargos, the business and administrative center for the island. The *Câmara Municipal*, high school, military barracks and a new sports complex are all located in Espargos, so there can be a bit of movement. The *Câmara* is fairly active in promoting cultural and educational events, so it is worth keeping an eye out for upcoming activities, held mostly on weekends.

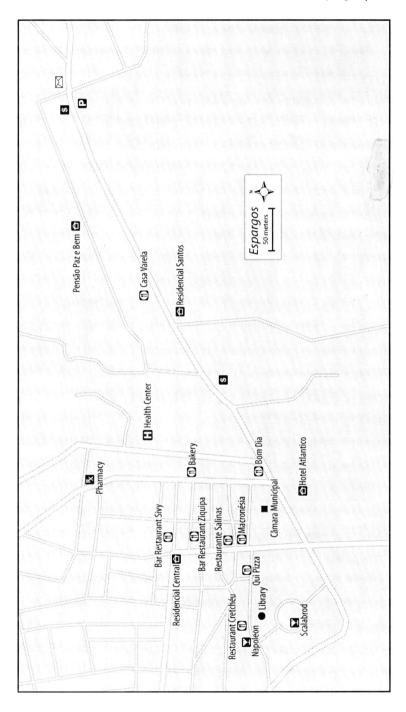

Espargos
50 meters

Sal

Pensão Paz e Bem
Casa Varela
Residencial Santos
Health Center
Pharmacy
Bakery
Bom Dia
Hotel Atlantico
Bar Restaurant Sivy
Restaurant Ziquipa
Restaurante Salinas
Macronésia
Câmara Municipal
Residencial Central
Qui Pizza
Restaurant Cretchéu
Library
Napoleon
Scalabrod

IMPORTANT INFORMATION

Bank The main banks are represented in Espargos: BCA, Banco InterAtlânti-co, Caixa Económica and BCN are scattered throughout the city. All banks are open Monday-Friday from approx 8:00-15:00.

Health Center *Delegação de Saúde* Tel: 241.1130; On Rua Albertino Fortes, until completion of the new hospital currently under construction.

Pharmacy *Farmácia Aliança*; Tel: 241.1109 in Zona Centro

Post Office *Correios* Across from the police station and open Monday-Friday either from 8:00-12:00, 14:00-17:00 or 7:30-15:00

Police *Polícia* Tel: 241.1132; On the corner by the road leading to Pretória.

WIFI WiFi is available in the *praça* by restaurants Sivy and Ziquipa. There are also a number of internet cafés scattered throughout the city. Try the more expensive Info Center or the less expensive yellow café/internet café with beaded curtains just up from the *praça*.

WHERE TO EAT

There are a multitude of little places to eat tucked up and down side streets in Espargos. Those listed are worthy of note, but take your time to explore.

 Restaurant Cretchéu This little pink restaurant is down the street alongside the library. Probably the best place for a Cape Verdean style *prato-do-dia* (plate of the day) lunch and definitely the only place to get *cachupa* at 6:00. Prices are reasonable and portions generous. $-$$

Bom Dia Impossible to miss, this café/restaurant/meeting place is probably popular more because of location than anything else. Prices can be a little steep, but portions are fairly generous. Live music is often performed on Friday nights, closed Sundays. $$

Qui Pizza An extension of Qui Pizza in Santa Maria, it is open for dinner only. Pizza prices vary depending on toppings. $$-$$$ *Tel: 242.2123; quipizzalda@cvtelecom.cv*

Bar Restaurant Sivy In the *praça* across from Residencial Central, just one of many little places in the area. Has a good range of quick bites and portable food behind the counter. The bathroom, however, is deplorable. $$

Bar Restaurant Ziquipa Directly across from Sivy, Ziquipa is a little better maintained. A good stop for a quick coffee. Nice outdoor seating. $$

Restaurante Salinas Up on the top floor, but not much of a view. One of the more sit-down style restaurants in Espargos. $$$ *Tel: 241.1799*

Macronésia Just opposite the *Câmara*, Macronésia is another sit-down style restaurant with a fairly extensive menu and nice outdoor patio. Can be a bit expensive for what is served. There is even a charge for bread and butter. $$$-$$$$

 Casa Varela A well kept secret, this little café is half hidden behind trees across the street from Residencial Santos. There is a nice little veranda, plate-of-the-day and the epitome of a typical Cape Verdean hangout spot. You are likely to find it empty, or with a mixed group sitting around enjoying a beer. $$ *Tel: 241.1765*

NIGHTLIFE

Scalabrod Located in the back of the *praça* opposite Enacol, it is the place to be at night.

Napoleon Tucked away in the Protecção Civil building by the library, this can be a popular spot at night to grab a few beers.

WHERE TO STAY

Hotel Atlantico With a central location, this is probably the nicest place to stay in Espargos. That said, there is nothing special about it. Rooms are fairly standard, clean and all have private bathrooms. Price may vary depending on the season. $$-$$$ *Tel: 241.1210; hotelatlantico@cvtelecom.cv*

Residencial Santos Once a hub for overnight stays and transient visitors to Sal, Residencial Santos is now mainly used to house various employees from other islands visiting Sal for training or other purposes. Because of this, it is frequently occupied. If you manage to get a room, Dona Maria da Monte keeps a clean, simple, comfortable place with all amenities. $$ *Tel: 241.1900 / 241.3599*

Residencial Central Aptly named for its location by the *praça*, a pleasant and affordable place to stay with a beautiful quintal where you can enjoy your breakfast. $$ *Tel: 241.1113 / 241.1366*

Pensão Paz e Bem The 16 fairly modern and well-kept rooms make for a pleasant enough stay up off the main road. All rooms have private bathrooms, some with A/C and balconies. $$ *Tel: 241.1782; pensaopazbem@cvtelecom.cv*

Pedra de Lume

This tiny town of less than 300 is an unexpected hot bed for tourism, but it is not the town itself that brings visitors, it is the massive salt flats just over the hill that bring the crowds. When you arrive in Pedra de Lume, you may wonder why this has become such a tourist destination. The few people that live here mostly fish or work outside of the little town. A quick turn out of Pedra da Lume takes you into Salinas, the famous salt flats of Sal. This volcanic crater has been degraded and fills with a naturally replenishing source of salt water from the ocean that is segmented and slowly dried into varying concentrations of salt.

The road there is long, flat and unbroken, about 5 km from Espargos, marked only by a tiny farm a little over half way. It is possible to walk to Pedra de Lume in about an hour, but it can be unpleasant from the amount of wind and sun and perceived lack of progress that comes from an unvarying landscape. Tourist developments have been underway here for years, but as of yet, none have been completed. Currently, a large part of the road is fenced off under the pretense that a resort will soon be unveiled.

WHERE TO EAT

Salinas Within the crater there is a small café that serves drinks and meals and offers spa treatment to those determined to relax. $$$

Cadamosto Restaurant In contrast to the small, wind-blown town, this upscale restaurant on the coast takes advantage of its monopoly. The food is good, though a bit pricy, but the large terrace and a cold drink can be enticing after time in the sun. $$$-$$$$ *Tel: 241.2210; Open 9:00-18:00 daily*

Salinas of Pedra de Lume

Aside from the beautiful, white sandy beaches, Sal appears to be dry, desolate, and windy. Yet, there are a few other perks to this lonely and barren landscape. One of which is the *salinas*, or salt mines, of Pedra de Lume. Long ago, most of Sal was covered by the Atlantic Ocean. Over time, the ocean water receded but some of it was caught in a large natural volcanic crater. Eventually, the remaining water in the crater dried out and salt formed. Salt exportation was a big commodity in Cape Verde particularly during the 20th century, but ceased in 1985. Small quantities of salt are still mined today which is evident from the machines that continue to grind, clean, and even bag salt.

The salt mines are located about 4 miles east of Espargos near the town of Pedra de Lume. To get there, I recommend taking a taxi since a public car is not likely to be heading in this direction. You can catch a taxi along any of the main roads heading or you can pick one up in front of the *Câmara Municipal* across from Hotel Atlantico and diagonal to the Encol gas station in the center of Espargos.

Upon arriving to Pedra de Lume, have your taxi driver drop you off at the restaurant parking lot or you can ask to be taken directly to the *Salinas* for which you will pay a little extra. It is about a 15 to 20 minute walk along a dirt road which starts behind a small, abandoned looking church with the old wooden towers once used for transporting salt.

The entrance to the salt mines is through a cave beyond the parking lot. Be careful not to slip on the dirt path on your way down to the *salinas* as there is no traction. On your right, you will see a small restaurant/souvenir shop, bathroom, and massage station. Keep in mind that Sal, like the rest of Cape Verde, is hot and sunny throughout the year so make sure you bring sun block, a snack, and a bottle of water or two if you do not plan to purchase any expensive items at the restaurant. Depending on the day of the week, the *salinas* will either be crowded or only a few people will be floating in the warm, bath-like water of the *salinas*. Weekends seem to be the busiest time to visit.

- Caryn Swierzbin

Palmeira

To the east of Espargos is a small village, Palmeira, the port and fishing hub of Espargos. In 1720 the British Captain Roberts stopped in Palmeira in search of supplies for a voyage to the Caribbean. His journal claims that he found small huts, donkeys and birds, but not a single human being. Today, the pleasant little bay is overshadowed by the massive desalinization plant, but this is not the place to come for sightseeing.

On Sunday nights, transportation to and from Espargos is almost non-stop as the small village hosts its weekly party. If you are feeling adventurous and wish to experience a typical Cape Verdean party, this is the place to be. Youth and adults alike crowd the small club to see and be seen. From 20:00-22:00, the music is largely traditional and the crowd is a bit mellow. Shortly after, the music changes to louder, popular music—*zouk*, hip-hop and reggae—and with it, the group shifts to a younger, rowdier bunch. Along the road, women grill chicken and sell simple snacks, but down at the pier, you will find some delicious fried *moreia* (eel).

Regona/Buracona

Before entering Palmeira, you can bear off the road to head to Buracona. Buracona means 'big hole,' but this spot is also known as *odjo azul* (the blue eye). One of the natural gems of Sal, here, the ocean crashes into the dark, lava encrusted shore spraying sea foam and constantly refilling the natural pool.

Regona is part way along the 6 km trek north to Buracona. It is a popular diving site for the winding caverns and tunnels, but the view of pools of brilliant turquoise water in black, lava crevices is nice from above sea level as well.

Santa Maria

The paved road to Santa Maria runs straight down the spine of the island all the way to the southern bay, marked only by a few intersections. While some visitors may venture out on a day trip, many stay, mesmerized by the beautiful bay that has brought the island modern fame.

Along the road south, the landscape is largely flat and barren and the coastline is visible a few kilometers away. You will pass the hydroponic garden center, an effort to utilize desalinated water to reduce food costs inflated due to importation. What you don't see are the clusters of make-shift houses huddled in the low *ribeiras*. Despite the flow of money on this popular tourist destination, many residents live in extreme poverty. At night, cars pick up and drop off workers and musicians, seemingly in the middle of nowhere outside of town to begin the trek to half-built shanties.

As you approach Santa Maria, the signs of growth are visible long before you enter the city grounds. Off in the distance, cranes cut through the skyline like broken arms reaching out to the sky. Vila Verde, a massive complex, has been under construction for years but when complete, will nearly double the size of what was once a pokey little beach town. Even along "resort row," where established hotels pride themselves in exclusive adventures and pristine conditions, there are cinderblock projects sprinkled throughout. Outside town center, houses, hotels and restaurants are built in a haphazard fashion, with little more than dirt tracks to connect.

IMPORTANT INFORMATION

Bank There is no shortage of banks in Santa Maria. BCA even has two branches (try the one on Rua 1 de Julho for shorter lines).

Hospital: *Posto Sanitário* (Health Center) Ask around for location. Tel: 242.1130

Clinitur Mon-Sat 8:00-15:00; A private clinic on the road to the major resorts.

Pharmacy *Farmácia Rama;* Tel: 242.1340; The large green building at the entrance to town.

Post Office *Correios* Open Monday-Friday either from 8:00-12:00, 14:00-17:00 or 7:30-15:00; Located in the eastern side of town.

Police *Polícia* Tel: 242.1132; Up a side road by the school.

WIFI WiFi may be available in the main *praça* by Culture Café.

Internet In addition to WIFI, there are a few internet cafés scattered around the central area. Try Cyber on the road behind CV Telecom (a small building tucked away, but has cheap internet: 200$).

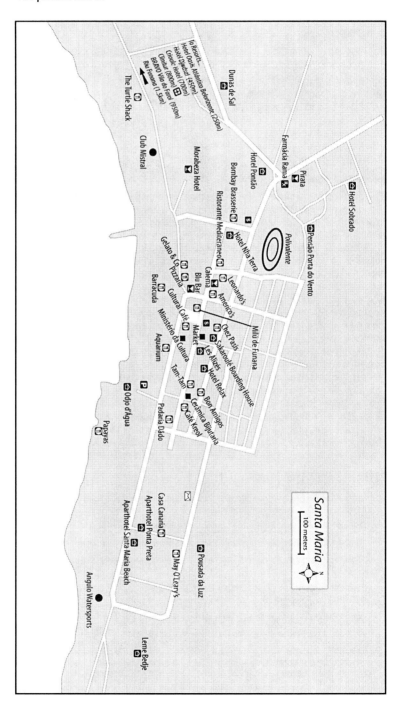

Santa Maria

100 meters

The Turtle Shack

Club Mistral

Dunas de Sal

to Resorts...
Hotel Oasis Atlantico Belorizonte (250m)
Hotel Djadsal (450m)
Crioula Hotel (700m)
Crioula (800m)
Crioula Vila do Farol (950m)
BRAVO Vila do Farol (1.5km)
Rui Funana (1.5km)

Morabeza Hotel

Bombay Brasserie

Hotel Pontão

Farmácia Raná

Pirata

Hotel Sobrado

Ristorante Mediterraneo

Hotel Nha Terra

Polivalente

Pensão Porta do Vento

Gelato & Co.

Pizzaria

Blu Bar

Caleria

Leonardo's

Barracuda

Cultural Café

Américo's

Ministério da Cultura

Aquarium

Market

Chez País

Milú de Funana

Sakaroulé Boarding House

Odjo d'Água

Tam-Tam

Les Alizes

Hotel Relax

Pastelaria Dádo

Cecilmia Bijutaria

Bon Amigos

Café Kreol

Papayas

Casa Canaria

Aparthotel Ponta Preta

May O'Leary's

Pousada da luz

Aparthotel Santa Maria Beach

Angulo Watersports

Leme Bedje

WHAT TO DO

Across from Restaurant Aquarium, the *Ministério da Cultura* (Ministry of Culture, Open 9:00-13:00, 14:00-18:00) has a small exhibit outlining Sal's history and culture as well as a reasonably sized library. Maps and books are available for sale for less than tourist information centers.

Along the boardwalk, the **Turtle Shack**, a local, surf-bum hangout, is a resourceful place for finding out what is happening on the island and how to get involved. Not only are they helpful in arranging excursions or surf lessons, they are also known to host weekend parties.

Located across from Cultural Café and run by the same proprietor, Luciano, **Cape Verde Market** is a new addition to Santa Maria and an effort to offer a central location for souvenirs made strictly in Cape Verde. The first of its kind on Sal, it was started in response to the high population of West Africans selling products from their home countries (Senegal, Guinea Bissau, Mali, etc.) under the pretense of being Cape Verdean. Luciano travels to the different islands and selects a variety of liquors, jewelry, pottery and other *artesanato* products to sell.

Across the street from Café Kreol and adjacent to the *polivalente*, **Cerâmica Bijutaria** sells a variety of artisan products produced locally on Sal. In addition to pottery, there is some simple jewelry and other bits and pieces.

If you're interested in taking home some local music, **Harmonia** is one of a handful music stores in Cape Verde. It's located at the top of the city by Hotel Nha Terra.

More Information Online

Aboutsal.com is a community site for news, events, classifieds, business directory, bar and restaurant guide. A good, comprehensive guide to the happenings on this barren strip of land. www.aboutsal.com

Windsurfing, Surfing and Kite Surfing

With so much coastline and intersecting trade winds, it is no surprise that there is a growing market for these water sports on Sal. World champion windsurfer Josh Angulo has made Sal his mostly permanent residence and has opened a rental and lesson shop for other enthusiasts.

Angulo Watersports Down at the end of the road in the eastern end of town, Tanquinho, Angulo's club is open in the winter and offers wind and kite surfing rentals, private lessons and small island trips to various wind/kite surfing hotspots. *Tel: 242.1899; www.angulocaboverde.com*

Planet Windsurfing Also in Tanquinho, Planet Windsurfing is open in the winter for kite surfing, windsurfing and body boarding. *Tel: 242.1339*

Club Mistral/Sky Riders On the beach along the boardwalk, Club Mistral offers rentals and lessons for windsurfing and Sky Riders for kite surfing. Discount for consecutive days' rentals.

Surf Zone Outside the Morabeza hotel, Surf Zone offers wind, kite and regular surfing instruction and rentals. *m. 997.1062; info@surfcaboverde.com; www.surfcaboverde.com*

Zebra Jet Jet Ski rentals. *m. 994.3646*

Sailing and Boat Trips

Neptunus "The yellow submarine" of Sal, Neptunus takes small groups around to view the rich marine life on a glass bottom boat. Trips during the day and at night cost approximately 3500$ adult, 2000$ children. *m. 999.4200*

Nautica Madrugada Offers day trips to Boa Vista and around the island of Sal for 5000$/day (price may vary depending on group). *Tel: 242.1505; nauticamadrugada@yahoo.com*

Final This 25 meter Turkish Caicco can be booked through hotels or directly for a day trip along the western coast of Sal. Includes a stop in Murdeira for snorkeling and swimming. Prices 6300$+. *m 986.5055; carlo.prevosto@libero.it*

Ilan Voyager Run out of the Morabeza Hotel, offers day trips to Boa Vista, Monday-Saturday, including an island tour and lunch. *Tel: 242.1020; bernard@hotelmorabeza.com*

Diving

If diving is your thing, there is some interesting diving around Sal. There are five wrecks, including a purposefully sunk Cape Verdean ship, creating a man-made reef. There are also caves, inlets and natural reefs. Many of the diving centers are located within a hotel, but are open to everyone.

Scuba Team Cabo Verde Located on the beach right by the pier offering guided dive trips, PADI courses and equipment rental. *m. 991.6543 / 991.1811; scubateamcaboverde@yahoo.fr*

Pro Atlantic Diving Center On the beach in Tanquinho and in Murdeira. NANU and PADI centers with courses for beginners and shore diving around Buracona and Palmeira. *Tel: 241.2621, m. 991.2914; proatlantic@cvtelecom.cv; www.cabo-verde.de*

Manta Diving Center Part of the hotels Belorizonta and Novorizonte, dives around Buracona and Palmeira. *Tel: 242.1540; info@mantadivingcenter.cv; www.mantadivingcenter.com*

Dunas Dive Center A part of the Hotel Dunas de Sal. *m. 982.265; quedesjoao@hotmail.com; www.hoteldunasdesal.com*

Cabo Verde Diving Run out of the Djadsal Hotel. *m. 997.8824; caboverdediving@cvtelecom.cv; www.caboverdediving.net*

Scuba Caribe *Tel: 242.1002 (within Riu resort); Tel: 242.9060 ext 8235 (beach center); www.scubacaribe.com*

Fishing

The territorial waters around Cape Verde are underfished when compared with international standards, creating a prime environment for those looking to get out for some big game fishing. The best time is between July and October.

Club Odissea Operated out of the Hotel Morabeza, Odissea offers big game and bottom fishing as well as spearfishing, snorkeling and assorted water activities. *m. 999.1062; caboverdequasport@hotmail.com; www.salsportfishing.com*

Big Game Fishing/Fishing Dream Right along the pier, Big Game Fishing lives up to its name, but also offers a few other fishing excursions. *Tel: 242.2080, m. 991.5505; info@fishingdream.it; www.fishingdream.it*

Fishing Center *Tel: 242.2050; m. 993.1332; skype: fishingcentercaboverde; caboverdefishingcenter@yahoo.it; www.caboverdefishingcenter.com*

WHERE TO EAT

Santa Maria is littered with restaurants and cafés. There is more variety here than most of the other islands, but you won't necessarily find everything. In addition to independent restaurants, most of the resorts/*residencial*s have a restaurant that is open to non-guests for meals, or have an extension of their restaurant along the boardwalk on the beach. That said, this list is by no means comprehensive, but rather highlights popular, unique and particularly tasty spots.

 Cultural Café Right in the central *praça*, Cultural Café is owned by Luciano, a native of Sal, and offers a mix of Cape Verdean and Portuguese dishes. Emphasis is placed on the use of local products and traditional dishes. Breakfast *cachupa* here is a must. It is a great place to be in the center of the action in town. $$$

Milú de Funana Also in the center of town, Milú de Funana is known for the live music every evening. They also offer a Sunday buffet that is unbeatable. For dinner, try the *atum cebolado* (tuna with onion sauce). $$$

Casa Canaria Down in Tanquinho, Casa Canaria is a Spanish-run Tapas style restaurant. You may have to hunt for a bit as it is hidden on a side street, but there are signs to lead the way. Closes in the mid-afternoon between lunch and dinner. $$-$$$ *Tel: 242.2520*

Leonardo's Off of Rua Amilcar Cabral, Leonardo's is a fairly upscale Italian restaurant. If you are in the mood for eating a full, Italian meal, this is your best bet. Meals include a starter, two courses and desert. $$$$ *m. 981.0057 (reservations recommended)*

Bombay Brasserie Right along the main stretch coming into town across from Residencial Nha Terra, Bombay offers a full menu of Indian dishes with an extensive vegetarian selection. Menu includes regular dishes as well as a less expensive plate-of-the-day. If you like Indian, the smell that wafts from the door is enough to pull you in. $$-$$$

 Café Kreol/Creoulo You will know you've found the spot when you find the restaurant with "Creole" spelled three different ways on the same restaurant. Across from the *polivalente* (soccer field), this is probably one of the best kept secrets in Santa Maria. A variety of traditional dishes and simple meals available, as well as fantastic *iogurte di terra* (homemade yogurt). Not to mention the best cup of coffee in Sal. $$

Aquarium Aquarium is a staple in Santa Maria, but is starting to show its age. Live music most nights and a nice view right on the beach. The cuisine, however, has received mixed reviews. $$$ *Tel: 242.1924*

 Americo's A favorite with tourists, locals and ex-pats alike, Americo's is an all around solid choice for lunch (12:00-15:00) or dinner (18:00-22:00). The menu is extensive, but specialties are definitely from the sea. Chef's choices include *arroz di mariscos* (rice and shellfish mix), *lagosta* (lobster), *atum cebolado* (tuna with onion sauce) and steak Americo's style. Live music most nights. $$$ *Tel: 242.1011; soaresamerico@gmail.com; (dinner reservations recommended)*

Cantinho Bar A small Senegalese run restaurant with typical Senegalese dishes. A great deal for the adventurous eater. $

Ristorante Mediteraneo Right around the corner from Residencial Nha Terra, this small Italian restaurant lists specials of the day outside. Offers a good strong coffee and gnocchi with pesto sauce. $$-$$$

Sal

Angelas If you can find it, this hole in the wall is run by a local Cape Verdean family and serves up a hot, fresh buffet (pay by weight) that is one of the best deals in town. Ask around for directions. $-$$

Tam-Tam This Irish run bar/restaurant has been around for four years serving up a mixed menu with a little bit of everything. There is a page devoted to vegetarian dishes and a good range of simple, inexpensive snacks/meals. They have bread specially made for the famous Tam-Tam burger and fish burgers as well as carrot cake (almost unheard of in Cape Verde). Try the chili con carne. UK football matches broadcasted when available. Closed Sundays. $$-$$$

May O'Leary's Sister of the May O'Leary's on São Vicente, this Irish style pub offers everything you could expect of an Irish style pub in West Africa. $$-$$$

Relax Below the *pensão* of the same name. Relax is something of a typical Cape Verdean snack bar with a more extensive menu. Everything from *tosta mista* (grilled ham & cheese) to fruit smoothies, all at reasonable prices. $-$$

Chez Pasis Reservations are essential for this intimate, hallway restaurant. Open only in the evenings, the six tables are occupied for two, two hour shifts. Italian-run with a French cuisine influence, there have been nothing but good reviews from those lucky enough to try this unique spot. $$$$ *m. 983.7629*

Papayas All the way back past the pool in Port Antigo Hotel, Papayas hangs out over the ocean, sometimes hit with spray from crashing waves. It is well run and managed and offers an extensive menu of mainly western dishes, including a great pizza. $$$ *m. 973.3482*

Bar/Restaurant Bons Amigos Up a side street by the *polivalente* (soccer field), Bons Amigos is a local haunt with an inexpensive *prato-di-dia* (plate of the day). $

Snack Bar/Restaurant Cristal Also around the corner from the *polivalente* (soccer field), Cristal offers up one of the most affordable plates-of-the-day. $

Grijinha This little bar is seamlessly built into the coastline on the far east outside of town. Look around in Santa Maria to see if there are any upcoming events, or call to confirm that it's open. A bit more than 1 km outside of the city, you wouldn't want to show up and find it closed. One of the nicest spots to relax and enjoy the environment. $$-$$$ *m. 996.5212*

Padaria Dâdo On Rua 1 de Julho, the bakery sells fresh bread, but also serves breakfast *cahcupa*, cakes and pastries. $ *Tel: 242.1516*

Pizzaria Fast Food Italian restaurant on the corner on the way to the pier next to Gelato & Co and Blu Bar, this is the best place to get a pizza in Sal and probably serves up the best lasagna in all of Cape Verde. Show up before lunch time if you hope to try the lasagna, it goes quick. $$-$$$

Gelato & Co. Delicious ice cream by the beach. Enough said. $-$$

Restaurante Barracuda Behind Barracuda tours on the beach, this restaurant has a nice, relaxing environment, great view and a fairly extensive (and pricey) menu. $$$

The Turtle Shack Not the classiest restaurant on the beach, but definitely a young, hip environment. Most local surfers make a point of stopping by here on occasion and the staff is working to establish weekly beach parties on Fridays. $$$

NIGHTLIFE

There are a couple of clubs in Santa Maria as well as a growing culture of happy hour. Keep an eye out when walking around for happy hour and performance postings. All happy hours listed are subject to change.

 Blu Bar A totally Western influenced spot, the low, comfy couches and extensive drink menu is easily enjoyed during happy hour (20:00-22:00).

 Morabeza Hotel Not a nightclub, but the second floor bar offers a beautiful view. *Caiparinhas* and beer are inexpensive for happy hour (18:30-19:30). There is also a nightclub within the hotel, Disco Hotel Morabeza, which is open on Saturday nights and tends to draw and more upscale, older crowd than the other nightclubs.

Calema One of two major nightclubs in Santa Maria, starts late and tends to be loud and smokey.

Pirata Second of the two major nightclubs in Santa Maria, Pirata also starts late, though a bit more open (therefore less smoke). Runs in a typical Cape Verdean fashion, you receive a drink card that counts as your cover. But be aware that if you lose the card, you pay the max (6000$).

Ponta Preta

If Santa Maria gets to be too much, Ponta Preta is just about an hour's walk away. One of the kite/windsurfing hotspots, Ponta Preta is also a stunning beach with beautiful breaking turquoise waves. There is a pleasant restaurant (m. 991.8613; Open from 10:00-17:00, Tuesday through Sunday) serving a range of dishes, but seafood is their specialty.

WHERE TO STAY

Four-Star Resorts

Most of the larger resorts are along a road leading out toward Murdeira, parallel to the coast. This list follows them out from the center of town.

Hotel Morabeza Morbeza was the first hotel on Sal built in the 1960s to house South African Airline crews on stopovers. Still run by family of the founding couple, it is considered one of the nicest places to stay in Santa Maria. Close to town, the beach is safer than resorts further out in the bay. The rooms are attractive and comfortable and the resort offers a pool, excursions, massages, Cape Verdean dance and language lessons and a variety of other activities. $$$$$-$$$$$$ *Tel: 242.1020; info@morabeza.com www.hotelmorabeza.com*

Dunas de Sal Though not on the beach, there is an ocean view from this simple, but tasteful hotel. Much smaller than the surrounding resorts, Dunas de Sal was designed for a minimalist effect and incorporation of the environment. The hotel offers all basic amenities, a pool/spa, private balconies for each room and has an in-house diving center. $$$$$ *Tel: 242.9050; geral@hoteldunasdesal.com; www.hoteldunasdesal.com*

Hotel Oasis Atlântico Belorizonte/Novorizonte The Sal extension of the Oasis Atlântico family, the sister hotels stand side-by-side looking out over the beach. The Belorizonte was recently refurbished, touching up aging rooms and bungalows. There are both adult's and children's pools and a variety of packages with activities included. $$$$$-$$$$$$ *Tel: 242.1045; hborizonte@cvtelecom.cv; www.oasisatlantico.com*

Sal

Hotel Djadsal (Djadsal Holiday Club) Despite recent renovations, some rooms still feel a bit old. Overall, it is a nice, all-inclusive resort, but it has received mixed reviews. $$$$ *Tel: 242.1170*

Crioula Hotel The 242 rooms of Crioula Hotel are split in two levels, ground floor with a veranda and first floor with a balcony and 20 bungalows by the beach. The resort offers a variety of sports and leisure activities, excursions and an on-site spa (fee charged). Pleasantly styled architecture frames the large fresh water pool. All-inclusive. $$$$$$ *Tel: 242.1615; crioulahotel@cvtelecom.cv; www.crioula-clubhoTel:com*

BRAVO Vila do Farol (Villaggi Bravo) Around the corner from Crioula Hotel, Bravo Farol is brightly colored, funky and welcoming. An extension of the Italian franchise, the hotel is essentially a small village with a massive pool, theater, sports complex, water sports center and anything else you can imagine. $$$$$$ *Tel: 242.1725; farol.recep@hotels.alpitourworld.it; www.villaggibravo.it*

Riu Funana/Riu Garopa These twin five-star all-inclusive 24 hour package resorts are a part of the Spanish empire of Riu resorts. About 1.5 km outside of Santa Maria, the Moorish architecture and massive walls are visible from a distance, keeping those with a wristband in and those without out. $$$$$$ *www.riu.com; Funana: Tel: 242.9060, clubhotelfunana@riu.com; Garopa: Tel: 242.9040, clubhotelgaropa@riu.com*

In Town

 Hotel Sobrado Off to the left on the way into town, Hotel Sobrado is a quaint, flowering little place to stay. It is far enough from the town to escape the bustle, but close enough to be easily reached. There are 25 double rooms and 7 smaller rooms with less amenities. $$$ *Tel: 242.1720; hotelsobrado@cvtelecom.cv*

Pensão Porta do Vento Open in 2007, this small *pensão* is a few roads back from the beach, but made and kept with care and attention to detail. For those looking to enjoy all that Sal has to offer, but avoid the crowds and constant movement, this is a nice place to escape. $$-$$$ *Tel: 242.2121; ciotti@terra.es; www.portadovento.com*

Hotel Pontão This 36 room hotel is right on the corner opposite Pirata as you enter town. Toted as a Bed & Breakfast with all amenities (including a tiny pool), it is in a great location. Mendes & Mendes Rent-A-Car is run out of the same building and has the same contacts (mendesemendes@cvtelecom.cv). $$$ *Tel: 242.8060/8063; ctpontao@cvtelecom.cv*

Hotel Nha Terra Right at the entrance to downtown, from the outside, Nha Terra doesn't appear much. For what it is, it is very nice. The twelve rooms and terraces were recently refurbished and the small pool outside is slowly growing a garden to hide bathers from passersby in the street. $$$ *Tel: 242.1109 / 1311; nhaterra@cvtelecom.cv / nhaterra@hotmail.com*

Rental Agencies

In addition to hotels, aparthotels and *pensões*, there are many agencies to assist you in buying and renting property in Sal. Below is a list of some of the agencies as of 2009.

www.theirishconnection.org	www.salvistaltd.co.uk
www.capeverdeproperty.co.uk	www.capeverdeexperience.co.uk
www.sal4rent.com	

Les Alizés Located in the heart of town, this French run *pensão* was built in a traditional colonial style house. Rooms have access to the encircling balcony and breakfast is served on a rooftop terrace. $$$ *tel 242.1446; lesalizes@cvtelecom.cv; www.pensao-les-alizes.com*

Hotel Relax Also in the center of town, Relax does not look like much from the outside, but it has been around for years, serving travelers on a budget with consistency and convenience. The restaurant and *pastelaria* of the same name also serves some of the best "budget" food around. $$ *Tel: 242.1680; majoduarte@cvtelecom.cv*

Odjo d'Água Midway through town, Odjo d'Água sits on the shore with the restaurant balcony hanging out over the ocean. Designed and run by a native of Sal, the 36 rooms and 12 suites are built comfortably around one another with a feeling of both privacy and familiarity. The small swimming pool is graced by a surrounding garden. $$$-$$$$ *Tel: 242.1414; reservas@odjodagua.net; www.odjodagua.net*

Sakaroulé Boarding House A funky little B&B in the center of town, Sakaroulé was started by an Italian/French couple in an effort to provide unique, attractive, simple and comfortable rooms at an affordable price. In this, they have succeeded. Happy to offer assistance in arranging tours, excursions or other island activities. $$$ *Tel: 242.1682, m. 992.6820; sakaroule@cvtelecom.cv*

Aparthotel Santa Maria Beach Located down the way in Tanquinho, this smallish B&B is a great find for those traveling on a budget. Basic amenities included (A/C, hot water, TV), but no restaurant for lunch or dinner. The rooms are impeccably clean. Eight small apartments with kitchen available. $$-$$$ *Tel: 242.1450, m. 994.3410*

Pousada da Luz Definitely not a luxury resort, Da Luz can at times feel a bit cramped, but overall it is pleasant and simple. A small pool is available to cool off in the afternoon and the rooms are comfortable. $$-$$$ *Tel: 242.1138 / 242.1286; pousadadaluz@cvtelecom.cv*

Sab Sab Sal Hotel This spacious hotel spreads out in the far east of Santa Maria, where small developments are slowly springing up. A bit older than most hotels, Sab Sab has declined a bit in age, but still offers a relaxing escape fully equipped with gardens, a pool, gym and water sports facilities. $$$-$$$$ *Tel: 242.1301; reservations@hotelsabsab.com; www.hotelsabsab.com*

Sleeping on the Beach

So I recommend, even when it is hot and sweaty all day long, not to sleep on the beach without a blanket. And a *pano* (a thin shawl alternatively used as a head wrap if you are in Africa) does not count as a blanket, though satisfies as protection from the sand.

Jacky and I went on a *passeo*, a.k.a. a big sleepover at the beach with everyone from the community center. It was wild, as most of these family folks didn't sleep a wink and kept the music blaring (to the chagrin of the turtles – and yes, we sadly saw a cut fin and turtle belly, remains of hunters who eat the "tastes like chicken" meat for extra mojo, despite their endangered status) until 7 a.m. Jacky and I attempted to sleep in the sand, were joined by a crab, and mostly just attempted various methods of burying ourselves in the sand to get damper but avoid the winds. Swell.

- Leah Tai

Apartments

In addition to hotels and *pensões*, there are a growing number of apartments available for short term rental.

 Aparthotel Ponta Preta Attractive set of buildings housing 21 apartments for 2-7 guests, the apartments are simply decorated, but bright, new and comfortable. Down in Tnaquinho (a five minute walk from the center of town) the apartments are popular with water sports enthusiasts. Management can offer assistance in arranging water sports (surfing, kite/wind surfing, fishing and diving). Rent for apartments is charged by the day (10% surcharge for sea view). $$$-$$$$ *Tel: 242.9020; m. 991.3385; info@pontapreta.info; www.pontapreta.*

Leme Bedje One of the many newer developments, this apartment complex offers a large group of apartments for sale and for rent. Restaurants, swimming pool and a variety of excursions/information are on sight. At the far east of Santa Maria before the Sab Sab Hotel. $$$$ *info@lemebedje.com; www.lemebedje.com*

Murdeira

North of Ponta Preta and about 8 km north of Santa Maria is the protected cove of Baía de Murdeira. There is a closed community of holiday homes and plans for further construction, though it seems to be muddled by the areas status as a wildlife reservation. The natural reef protects the bay making it a gentler alternative to Santa Maria. Because of this, there is a diverse population of marine wildlife that enjoy shallower waters. Overlooked by Monte Leão, it is a great place to dive and snorkel.

WHERE TO STAY & EAT:

Murdeira Village The rooms here are frequently booked up by tour packages, though it is sometimes possible to make reservations through the website. The resort itself is of high quality and offers a pool, restaurant, gym and car rental. $$$$-$$$$$ *Tel: 241.1604 / 241.2308; reservas@murdeiravillage.com; www.murdeiravillage.com*

Festivals on Sal

March 19 – Palmeira, São Jose

May 3 – Espargos, Santa Cruz

June 9 – Espargos, Santo Antonia

June 24 – Espargos, São João

June 29 – Hortela and Espargos, São Pedro

July (last week) – Fontona, Santa Ana

August 15 – Pedra de Lume, Nossa Senhora de Lume

September 15 – Santa Maria, Nossa Senhora das Dores (kick off for the three day music festival in Santa Maria)

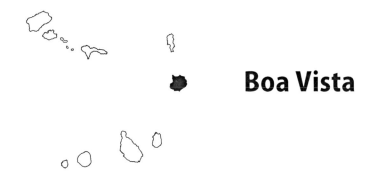

Boa Vista

As you approach the island, by sea or by air, it is impossible to miss the glistening white coastline. The ocean sparkles in blues and greens to accent the flowing sand dunes, and the nearly complete lack of habitation is thrilling and exhilarating.

Prior to the airport being upgraded to international standards, the island of Boa Vista was only accessible from Sal, where it was advertised as a daytrip. Boa Vista, however, is worth a more leisurely exploration. Unlike its bustling neighbor, Boa Vista is in the early stages of development and still exists in relative peace. For the visitor looking for non-stop action and activities, Sal is certainly a better bet. But if you are just looking to absorb and be absorbed by a peaceful, desert island or spend the day catching a wave, Boa Vista is your destination.

GEOGRAPHY

At 240 sq miles (620 sq km), Boa Vista is the third largest island in Cape Verde. Despite this claim, it is quite different than its two larger neighboring islands. Unlike the mountains and valleys that bring Santo Antão and Santiago fame, Boa Vista is known largely for its miles of pristine beaches—at least 34 miles (55 km). As far as staggering heights are concerned, Boa Vista again falls short of its larger counterparts with Pico Estância, the highest point, reaching only1,280 feet (390 m).

Boa Vista is also one of the least populous islands in the archipelago, with a current population estimated at just over 6,000 residents. This number, however, may not take into account the increasing number of immigrants from West Africa and other islands in search of employment. Behind the neat city streets in Sal Rei there is a mass of half built houses of cement block, flattened barrels and card board piled on top of one another.

Outside of town there are a few scattered villages spread across the island, though they are slowly becoming outnumbered by abandoned villages. Agriculture has become nearly impossible as the island is too dry and the sandy, sun soaked soil does not offer residents much chance for survival.

HISTORY

Boa Vista was discovered on May 14, 1460 and originally named São Cristovão. It is alleged that the name "Boa Vista" was unknowingly endowed on the island by a sea-weary sailor who shouted out "*boa vista*" (a good view/sight) upon spotting the island through stormy waters. Though the name is fitting, Boa Vista could use more "*boa sorte*" (good luck) than anything else.

Ringed by reefs and iron-rich soil deposits, Boa Vista may have been a sight for sore eyes for many sailors, but also led many to a watery grave. It is estimated that upwards of 40 shipwrecks are attributed to this sandy oasis. Strong winds and currents, a largely flat surface and inaccurate mapping are all partially to blame in the many wrecks, so despite the natural bay in Sal Rei, Boa Vista was slow to develop.

Christopher Columbus stopped on the island briefly in 1498, but was entirely unimpressed. Like many of the other islands, it was first home to goats before it was to people. There were always a few hopefuls, trying to subsist on the meager offerings of limited plant life, goats and the occasional shipwreck. It was also used briefly as a leper colony.

It wasn't until 1620 when the English discovered and claimed the use of the saltpans that Boa Vista surged to any importance. In previous years the number of residents totaled between 50 and 100, but the introduction of industry and trade brought enough people to establish a small village in Povoação Velha.

The population eventually moved to Sal Rei, the current municipal seat, as production and sale of salt increased. Despite the sometimes dangerous waters, Boa Vista was not immune to pirate attacks and the island was repeatedly made a target until a fort was built on Ilhéu do Sal Rei after the town was plundered and destroyed in 1818.

The increased security allowed for a brief period of peace and prosperity, but it was not meant to last. In 1834, Boa Vista made a push to become the "capital of the north," but the development and success of the Mindelo bay set forth a rapid decline on the larger, less populous island. The economy picked up in the 1940s with the introduction of a tuna preservation factory, but it was not enough to revive the former prosperity.

Today, Boa Vista still seems to struggle to find its place in the archipelago. The development of Sal as a tourist destination has left Boa Vista as an afterthought or daytrip for vacationers. The new international airport is slowly changing this fact, but to mixed reviews. The same endless shores that have enticed visitors and drawn so many ships to a terrible fate have also helped guarantee the survival of many different species of sea turtles. Today, they are threatened by the increasing number of visitors, hunters and development projects that are slowly swallowing the coast.

Fearful of the same fate as neighboring Sal, the governments of Maio and Boa Vista have joined forces to create *Sociedade de Desenvolviments Turístico das Ilhas de Boa Vista e Maio* (Boa Vista and Maio Islands Development Corporation). The organization's mission is to oversee the development of Boa Vista while protecting the environment (see www.sdtibm.cv for more information).

GETTING THERE

It is possible to fly into Boa Vista (airport code BVC) directly from Italy and northern Europe. Initially, the airport only accepted flights from Italy, but it is now listed as taking flights from London (Gatwick), Frankfurt, Hanover, Dusseldorf, Munich and Lisbon in addition to Malpensa and Verona, Italy.

Within Cape Verde, both TACV (Tel: 251.1186) and Halcyon Air (Tel: 241.2324 / 241.2374) make regular flights to/from Boa Vista. Common stops are Praia, Mindelo and Sal—flight times are subject to frequent change due to underbooking.

GETTING AROUND

There will always be public cars to meet incoming planes. Try to get in a full car or else you will be stuck paying 1000$ for a "chartered" ride from the airport to Sal Rei. There are taxis that run within the city limits (400$) and between Sal Rei and Rabil, but Sal Rei is walkable and there are public cars out

Warning: Most cars beyond Rabil only head in and out once, so be sure you can get a ride back if you take a public car out of town.

of town if you ask around. If you are trying to get to a different part of the island without an excursion, ask around in front of the municipal market for drivers heading out.

Car Rental

There are not many places where you can rent a car on Boa Visa as the preferred method of transportation seems to be quad. It is possible to charter a car for a day with a driver to take you around the island and that may be your best bet as most roads are sand blown and in pretty rough condition.

Alucar *Tel 251.1445, m. 991.9204; ~8000$/day*

Olitur *Tel: 251.1743, m. 992.3884 / 998.7150; olitur-bv@cvtelecom.cv; ~7000$/day*

Quad Rentals

Throughout the day, the sound of quad bikes rips through the air. They are a convenient way to get around, but come with some responsibility. Use on the beach and sand dunes is prohibited for its negative impact on the environment and potential destruction of turtle nests.

Quadland/ATC Scooter Right on the corner in the center of town, Quad Land offers a variety of rental packages and guided quad excursions. *Tel: 251.1872 m. 992.7306; atcinfo@sapo.cv; www.quadland-boavista.com*

Quad Aventuras Guided rides and excursions. Some variation in packages. *m. 989.9184; www.caboverdequad.com*

WHAT TO DO

Despite the large size and biodiversity of Boa Vista, there can be surprisingly little to do on land. There are organized trips around the island to the few other inhabited areas, but a large percentage of activities here are based in or on the ocean.

There are a number of species of birds, especially visible by the lagoon by Chaves Beach. During turtle season, there is a bustle of activity as researchers, activists and wildlife rescue proponents head to the beaches on turtle rescue missions.

The following agencies are located in Sal Rei (unless otherwise noted) and offer some of the variety of activities available here. The more exclusive resorts on Chaves Beach may offer excursions and activities of their own. There are also a number of local cars that will happily forgo a day of fighting for fares in exchange for taking you around the island. To get a deal, price excursions at the agencies and keep an eye out for trucks advertising excursions. They will try to up the price for tourists, but if you pick a price and stay firm, you may get your way.

Barracuda Tours Also run on the island of Sal, Barracuda offers a variety of island tours by land as well as day trips to other islands—Sal, São Vicente, Fogo. *Tel: 251.1907; geral@barracudatours.com www.barracudatours.com*

ATC Scooter Popular for quad rentals, ATC Scooter also offers guided excursions around the island. *Tel: 251.1872, m. 992.7306; atcinfo@sapo.cv; www.quadland-boavista.com*

Naturalia Part of the EU effort to concentrate on the affect of tourism on eco-system restoration and the realities of ecotourism, Naturalia offers a variety of ecotours that include whale and turtle watching, bird watching trips and snorkeling in the corals around the popular fishing bay, Baía das Gatas. *Tel: 251.1558, m. 994.1070; curral_velho@hotmail.com; gattgabriella@libero.it*

Morena Tourist Agency Offers a variety of excursions and services to tour-ists, included horseback riding. *Tel: 251.1445; boavistapoint@cvtelecom.cv*

Windsurfing, Surfing and Kite Surfing

Reputed as one of the best sites in the world for windsurfing, there are many great spots for catching a wave along the seemingly endless coas-tline of Boa Vista. It is recommended to stay within the bay of Sal Rei because of the potential damage to ecosystems and lack of rescue/support.

 Boa Vista Wind Club On the south side of Estoril Beach outside of town, Boa Vista Wind Club is a standby for wind and kite surfing. Owned by François—so-called for his nationality—a famed windsurfer, the local guys that run the shop have experience teaching and enjoying the sport that is slowly bringing Boa Vista fame. A variety of rentals and lessons available; windsurfing, kite surfing, surfing, kayaking and excursions. *boavista012@yahoo.com; www.boavistawindclub.com*

Fruits of Cabo Verde (surf school) Offers surf lessons (private and group) and rentals for long and short boards. Along the beach beyond Estoril.

Planet All Sports Along the beach next to Tortuga Club Beach Bar, offers lessons and rentals for wind and kite surfing for a day, half-day or week.

Boat Trips and Fishing

Naturalia Offers boat trips for bird and whale watching. It is also always poss-ible to speak with a fisherman and offer a price to head out to one of the islets around the island or to go along fishing for the day. *Tel: 251.1558, m. 994.1070; curral_velho@hotmail.com; gattgabriella@libero.it*

Boapesca Deep sea fishing. *m. 994.1060 / 991.8778; info@boavista2000.com; www.boavista2000.com; Skype: boapesca (Italian)*

Charterpesca *m. 982.7761; info@sampeifish.com*

Morena Tourist Agency *Tel: 251.1445; boavistapoint@cvtelecom.cv*

Boa Vista

Loggerhead Turtles (*Caretta caretta*)

The expanse of sandy beach in Boa Vista drew Loggerhead Turtles long before it drew the increasing number of tourists. Form the West African headquarters in Senegal, the WWF (World Wildlife Fund) has established a post on Boa Vista in an attempt to protect the second largest nesting site of Loggerhead turtles in the Atlantic Ocean. It is estimated that more than 3,000 of this species head to the beaches of Boa Vista each year in August leaving the seeds of the next generation. Though laws have been put in place to regulate building and travel across the sand, the increasing number of visitors and touristic development is a threat to this and the future generations of many other species of turtles. For more information contact rmonteiro@wwfcaboverde.org.

Diving

Dive School Submarine Center With two qualified instructors, this is a small and intimate PADI-NANU school. Despite the small staff, there are a number of possible activities and Atila and Rose are more than happy to make sure you enjoy your experience. *m. 992.4865; atilros@hotmail.com*

Sal Rei

Though the planes touch down closer to Rabil, most cars automatically head to Sal Rei. Driving into town, you will pass desert land and a series of signs designating hot wind surf points. Beyond the signs, massive dunes block the view of the shore. Buildings suddenly appear on the horizon and the town begins as abruptly as is ends on the northern side. Organized around the central *praça*, the town consists of a few concentric rectangles and the beginnings of sprawl heading toward a small northern beach and the Marine Club Resort

It is here that the majority of the population resides, and most visitors stay. There is not much on Boa Vista and what little there is centrally located in Sal Rei. There are a few all-inclusive resorts outside of town, but their location necessitates "all-inclusive." A few kilometers outside of the Sal Rei, these resorts are surrounded only by sand, sea and sun. Despite being the central town, there is a sleepy feel to Sal Rei. The town itself can easily be walked in just a couple of hours. Depending on the time of day, different groups of people populate the central *praça*. Market days general-ly mean extra bustle as women and men come from all over the island to buy, sell and trade. Groups of tourists walk around while vendors try to entice them to spend some of their holiday money.

Walking around Sal Rei, it is impossible to ignore the Italian influence. Buildings and streets are named after Italians and pizza is as easy to come by as french fries. There is no denying that development of the tourist industry brings jobs in Cape Verde, but it also brings with it opportunists and hassle. Shops with African art line the streets and West Africans will approach you in all languages with a determination that can only be overcome by completely ignoring the advances. "Cabo Verde" is written discretely beneath images that depict a life distinctly continental. The mix of populations seem to coexist tranquilly, but life is not always what meets the eye.

IMPORTANT INFORMATION

Bank BCA, BCN, Banco InterAtlântico and Caixa Económica are all located in Sal Rei. Banks are open from approximately 8:00-15:30.

Hospital (Health Center) Tel: 251.1167 Off the main square in Sal Rei, up the hill toward the port. Monday-Friday.

Pharmacy *Drogaria Rodrigues*

Post Office Correios Open Monday-Friday either from 8:00-12:00, 14:00-17:00 or 7:30-15:00; Located in the eastern side of town.

Police Polícia Tel: 251.1132; Behind Residencial A Paz.

WIFI WiFi may be available in the main *praça.*

Internet There are a couple of internet places right around the main *praça*. Beware, the one across from Hotel Boa Vista will charge every 15 minutes, but the time is automatically renewed and there is no timer. There is also an internet café at the CEJ (Youth Center; 240$/hour) around the corner from Hotel Boa Vista.

WHAT TO DO

There is little to do in Sal Rei beyond laze on the beach or try the multitude of water activities. Some points of interest are the **Igreja Nossa Senhora de Fatima**, a short walk from the Marine Club or a longer walk from Sal Rei. Take the path to the left of the vehicle barrier and around the coast to what remains of this church.

It is possible to walk to the **ship wreck of the** *Santa Maria*—beyond the Marine Club—but it is not recommended as there is an increasing number of desperate locals hiding out waiting to mug tourists. If you choose to walk, perhaps go with a guide, but certainly do not go alone.

From town, the **Ilheu of Sal Rei** is visible just across the bay. Humpback whales are often visible beyond the islet between December and April. You will also find what remains of the **fort of Duque de Bragança**. Scattered cannons and a low wall are all that still stand of the fortress that allowed for a brief period of prosperity in Sal Rei. For an experienced swimmer, you can swim the 1000m or pay a local fisherman (1500-2000) to escort you to and from the islet.

WHERE TO EAT

The number of restaurants has increased with the number of international flights, but they are plagued with inconsistency. Reservations are recommended as the consistently popular places are consistently busy. The restaurants in the *praça* are a bit expensive, but are always open and have fairly quick service in a pinch.

 Blue Marlin (Ca' Sandtinha) This local favorite is probably the most popular place in Sal Rei, with tourists, expats and locals alike. Dinner reservations are a must as there are only a few tables crammed along the wall, but despite the tattooed walls and haphazard decoration, the seafood here is some of the best available. There is also a good wine selection and, during the day, quick sandwiches and snacks ready to go for a picnic. $$$ *Tel: 251.1099, m.992.3877*

Bar/Restaurant Alísios Along Estoril beach between the surfshops, the panoramic view of the ocean is unbeatable. A bit of a hike, walking alone at night is not recommended. May or may not be open depending on the season. $$$ *m. 987.7881*

Restaurant Grill Luar Up the hill north of the *praça*, Grill Luar offers a panoramic view of the bay and the houses that have been built up in between. Prices for meals are reasonable and specialties include seafood and lobster. Watch your head on the very irregular steps. Live music Fridays (reservations recommended). $$$ *m. 995.3653 / 992.9976*

Kanta Morna Café In the entry to the Migrante Guesthouse, this bar is a great place for a quick snack or drink. You may be able to make dinner reservations within the beautiful hotel courtyard which entails an intimate meal of your choosing (depending on availability). $$$ *Tel: 251.1143, m.995.3655*

Restaurant Maresias Consistently open, consistently full and consistently good. Great view over the bay where you can watch as fishermen pull in their boats or strain to see over Ilheu Sal Rei. Seafood is the specialty here, but they also offer a surprisingly pleasant salad. $$$ *Tel: 251.1341*

Boa Vista

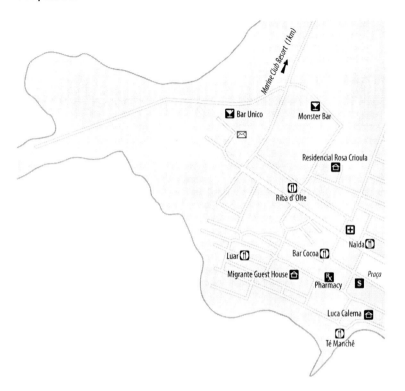

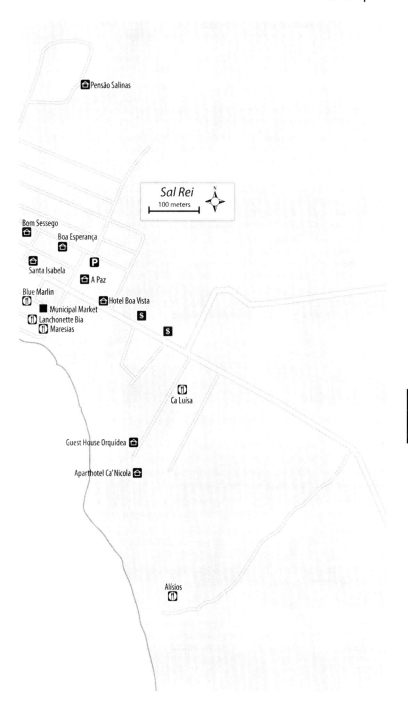

Pensão Salinas

Sal Rei
100 meters
N

Bom Sessego

Boa Esperança

P

Santa Isabela

A Paz

Blue Marlin

Municipal Market

Hotel Boa Vista

S

Lanchonette Bia

Maresias

S

Ca Luísa

Guest House Orquídea

Aparthotel Ca' Nicola

Boa Vista

Alísios

Bar Lanchonette Bia Below Maresias, this little bar doesn't claim to be a restaurant, but fills the role in a pinch. It doesn't appear much from the outside, but you can grab a cheap plate-of-the-day for lunch here and a sit down dinner of whatever is available. There are also quick snacks and sandwiches made locally for sale at the counter. A popular local hangout. $$ *Tel: 251.1340*

Bar Cocoa At night this place turns off the kitchen and turns up the music, but during the day it is a great place to grab a cheap pizza. Right on the main *praça*, it is also a good choice to sit and watch as people come from all over town to fill the square in the evening. $$

Restaurant Naida Serving a mix of simple Cape Verdean cuisine, Naida is popular for the simple reason that it has an established reputation for good food. The courtyard restaurant generally fills up, so call ahead or go early. $$-$$$ *Tel: 251.1173*

Té Manchê Meaning "until the sun comes up," Té Manchê is a popular spot during the day to escape the sun on the pier and at night for a snack/drink. Built out of an old container, it is not known for high class service but for its character (and characters) and good, simple local dishes. $-$$

 Restaurant Tambreira Despite the simple decoration, this restaurant that is attached to Hotel Boa Vista can be counted on for exemplary service and delicious meals. Chef specialties include lobster and the catch of the day. Ask for specials. Live music sometimes on weekends. $$$ *Tel: 251.1145*

 Ca Luísa On the road toward Estoril across from the Shell station, Ca Luísa is a little Italian restaurant with a variety of different pizzas and meals. Open only for dinner, call ahead to guarantee seating. Vegetarian friendly. $$$ *Tel: 251.1532*

Riba d' Olte At the top of town looking out in either direction, Riba d' Olte is Portuguese owned and offers some variety from the largely Italian and Cape Verdean dishes available. Call ahead as it is not always open. $$$ *Tel: 251.1015, m. 992.4292*

NIGHTLIFE

Sal Rei is not known for nightlife. There are a few bars that spill out into the street with a raucous crowd, but it mostly closes up early. That said, on any given night you are guaranteed to encounter a crowd mingling in the *praça*. During times of festivity, the streets fill with music, drinking and activity, but if you want to head out on a Saturday, you are more likely to find the action in Rabil or Estâncio Baixo.

Té Manchê Doubling as a restaurant and spot for nightlife, it is by no means a night club, but it is one of the few places that sees consistent action at night.

Monster Bar Along the backstreets of the north of the city, Monster Bar is a hole in the wall that had gained local acclaim. Can be hit or miss, but generally more consistently busy than some other options.

Unico Bar/Café Up at the top of the hill overlooking to the beach, ask around if there is anything happening that night.

WHERE TO STAY

Aparthotel Ca' Nicola In a quiet corner between the town and the stretch of Estoril beach, Ca' Nicola offers an attractive, peaceful and intimate retreat. Breakfast and snack service available, and all apartments are equipped with kitchens. $$$-$$$$ *Tel: 251.1793; info@canicola.com; www.canicola.com*

Hotel Boa Vista Right on the main road as you enter town, Hotel Boa Vista offers 34 rooms of varying size and quality. The staff here is extremely friendly and helpful and the chef in the restaurant is one of the best around. Communal terraces in the front overlook the sea. $$$ *Tel: 251.1145*

Marine Club Resort To the north of town, Marine Club used to be an isolated resort, but is now being encroached upon by the numerous buildings that spring from the lifeless soil. The oldest resort in Boa Vista, Marine Club has lost none of its charm. Includes chalets and small villas, the pool and playground protected by a beautiful, mature planted area. Buffet style restaurant and facilities are open to non-guests for a fee. $$$$ *Tel: 251.1285; marineclub@cvtelecom.cv*

 Guest House Orquídea Neighboring Ca' Nicola, Guest House Orquídea welcomes you with an overflowing veranda of plants and flowers. More of a family home, this is a pleasant and tranquil place to stay. $$$ *Tel: 251.1041*

Luca Calema Along the coast by the pier, Luca Calema is a pleasant escape right in the center of town. You will not be able to swim right out front, but the beach is not far from anywhere. Tasteful and simple decoration. $$$ *Tel: 251.1225*

 Migrante Guest House West of the square, Migrante Guesthouse is a beautifully renovated colonial house that offers five tastefully decorated and intimate rooms looking out over the planted courtyard. The work done renovating this house has been praised throughout Cape Verde for the efforts at maintaining "authenticity." Dinner and excursions available. $$$-$$$$ *Tel: 251.1143, m. 995.3655; info@migrante-guesthouse.com; www.migrante-guesthouse.com*

Cabo Santa Maria

Sunday, I went for a long hike up north. I went past Marine Club, but instead of exploring the first little valley, I continued to where a dried up ribeira has carved a much larger canyon and bay. I climbed up a tall hill, mostly on all fours, and then skirted the edge of the valley, still heading north. The view from up on top was pretty damn good, though a small mountain was blocking my view of Sal Rei. Unfortunately, there is an access road leading to the top of the hills from another direction and it looks like a lot of people have chosen to get tanked and smash their bottles up there. Lame. Nonetheless, my goal was to get a view of the northern coast, so I kept going. After I got to the top of another rise, I found that I could see Cabo Santa Maria, which is a huge sweeping beach that covers about half the north shore of Boa Vista. I could also see the famous shipwreck that is there. Who knows how old it is, but it is a huge rusty cargo ship that wrecked itself right on the beach. For whatever reason, no one ever cleaned it up, and now it is an icon of Boa Vista, appearing on post cards and paintings. It was probably 5 miles away, but it's a pretty big boat, so I had no trouble seeing it. I also got for the first time a solid view of just how small my island is. Standing on the hill, I could see both the north and west coasts, as well as the long oasis that stretches from Vila to Rabil, not to mention the Deserto do Viana beyond, and the mountains off in the distance. In all, I probably had a full quarter of the island in my field of vision. I guess it helps that it is mostly flat. On top of my small mountain, there was nothing but brown dirt and volcanic rocks everywhere. There are also dry river beds everywhere, and you can see how perhaps once upon a time, there might have been more water here.

- Leland Smith

Boa Vista

Pensão Santa Isabela Located at the top of the central *praça*, you won't miss any of the action from here. Of the budget places to stay, it offers some of the nicer rooms available. Recently renovated. $$ *Tel: 251.1252, m. 992.7990*

Pensão Salinas Far back behind Pensão Roas Crioula, Salinas is named for the proximity to the saltpans, not the beach. $$ *Tel: 251.1563*

Residencial Boa Esperança The names means "good hope," but don't get your hopes up for Boa Esperança. The rooms are the least expensive, but you often get what you pay for. Some shared bathrooms, the stale smell of smoke lingers in the stuffy rooms. Simple breakfast included. $$ *Tel: 251.1170*

 Residencial A Paz Undergoing renovation and changing hands at time of visit, Residencial A Paz is a quaint Bed & Breakfast with a variety of rooms (some with private bathrooms, some shared). Simple, but pleasant décor, this is a good choice for relaxation on a budget. $$-$$ *Tel: 251.1078*

Residencial Bom Sessego Another budget place to rest your head, Bom Sossego will leave you close to the local action. Back behind the police station, you will have easy access to the local bars and crowd. $$ *Tel: 251.1155*

Residencial Rosa Crioula Behind the center of town in what is becoming the sprawl of Sal Rei, Rosa Crioula is relatively new, simple and pleasant. $$ *Tel: 251.1786*

Beyond Sal Rei

The road that leads into Sal Rei goes as far as the Marine Club, but not beyond. In the opposite direction, you can access the few paved roads and number of varying paths that will take you around the island. The best way to truly see and experience the island is to take a trip around. Because it is large, it is wise to break the trip into two days to give you an opportunity to explore. There are few places to stay outside of Sal Rei; they may be a good option for the sake of sanity and relaxation.

NORTHERN CIRCUIT

From the lighthouse at Ponta do Sol, head north along the coast to Baía da Boa Esperança. It is along this coast that you will encounter the wreck of the Santa Maria, stranded on the beach and slowly decaying since September of 1988. If you continue along, you will find the villages of Espingueira and Bofareira.

EASTERN CIRCUIT

In the far east of Boa Vista, are the villages of João Galego, Fundo de Figueiras and Cabeça dos Tarafes. The three villages are comprised of only a few hundred people, but they are responsible for much of the agricultural production. From these villages, it is possible to visit the fishing outpost of Baia das Gatas (Bay of the Sharks), the lighthouse at Morro Negro as well as Odjo de Mar, a natural pool of volcanic rock that fills during the rainy season and stands during the dry.

SOUTHERN CIRCUIT

Povoação Velha is located in the southern part of the island. The first settlement of Boa Vista, this tiny village has declined a bit over the years.

To say that it is overshadowed by Pico Estância would be an overstatement, but the mountain is nearby. There is a picturesque chapel off in the distance at Praia de Curralinho, also known as Santa Monica for its resemblance to the beautiful Californian beach. Also, for a taste of desolation, head to Curral Velho, an abandoned village that has been taken over by birds.

WESTERN CIRCUIT

The church of São Roque, built in 1801, still stands in the center of Rabil. You will also find the ceramics factory/*artesanato* center, established in 1850 for the manufacturing of tiles, today it is largely responsible for small souvenirs. You can continue inland to the Viana Desert, or head to the coast to check out Chaves Beach, home to a growing number of resorts and the diminishing remains of a brick factory.

Chaves Beach

As you pass the airport on the way out of town, you can bear right to head to Chaves Beach. The site of a former brick factory and one of many stretches of beautiful sand, Chaves Beach is slowly turning into a stretch of resorts. The Riu Karamboa is visible from Sal Rei, a massive fortress-like structure that sprawls symmetrically across the sand. It is possible to walk along the shore from Sal Rei to reach Chaves Beach.

From here, you can walk to the Rabil Lagoon, a protected area for birds in Cape Verde. The lagoon is visible when flying in and is crossed by a bridge along the road, but the best area is down by the beach.

WHERE TO STAY

Riu Karamboa Part of the Spanish Riu chain of all-inclusive resorts, Riu Karamboa has hardly opened their doors and is already entering the construction phase of a second, larger resort on an otherwise untouched beach in the southern corner of the island (Praia de Lacação). For what it is, Riu is one of the best, but it is hard to like from the outside as the fortress-like walls keep some out and others in. Check website for details on packages and prices. $$$$$$ www.riu.com

Boa Vista

Morna

Though popularized by Eugenio Tavares of Brava and Cesária Évora of São Vicente, the musical genre of *morna* is said to have originated in Boa Vista. When the enchanting melodies are heard echoing in the street, it is certainly believable that the sad and haunting sounds came from this, the siren of the islands. The slow, steady rhythm is said to channel the constant pound of the fisherman's oars in the oarlocks. In the dead of night and *madrugada* (early morning), this sad sound that has taken so many lives while providing so many with a livelihood makes its way through the bones and into the soul.

On many islands, *morna* has lost its popularity and has been replaced with more modern, international music. But on Boa Vista, it is the enchanting melodies of *morna* that you will often hear.

Parque das Dunas Village Though the chalets lack some amenities (like A/C, TV, fridge), the atmosphere south of the brick factory is one of wild beauty and abandonment. There is a bar and restaurant (open to the public), a welcoming pool and much needed shade provided by the plated trees. Swimming is not recommended because of the tide, but ask at the resort for information on current conditions. Free shuttle to and from Sal Rei at scheduled times and internet access also available. $$$$$ *Tel: 251.1283 / 251.1288; info@parquedasdunas.com; www.parquedasdunas.com*

Rabil

If you head left at the rotary (or straight from Chaves Beach) you will enter Rabil. Here, the sounds of Morna echo in the empty streets on a sunny afternoon. The low growl of air transport blows across empty land and blasts the neat rows of houses. This is a slow place, sand swept and wind-blown with an echo of children's street noises rising into the air. There is generally not much happening here, but has a reputation of getting pretty busy on weekends.

It is here that you will find the famous shop where so many of the terra cotta pots and souvenirs sold in Cape Verde are produced. The *artesanato* shop is found at the top of town before heading through (there is a sign to point you in the direction) and is open from 8:30-15:30. It was originally used to manufacture tiles for rooftops, but has since switched operations to large planters and decorative items.

WHERE TO EAT

Restaurant Sodade di Nha Terra Specializes in local dishes. A good place to try out some of the Boa Vista goat cheese and have a few drinks with a mixed local crowd. $ *Tel: 251.1048*

Residencial/Restaurant Souvenir D'Europa The *residencial* is in somewhat questionable condition and the restaurant may or may not be open depending on the owner's availability. $ *Tel 251.1107*

Estância Baixo

Beyond Rabil, Estância Baixo is a bit smaller than the former capital and, if possible, a bit quieter. The major drawing point may be access to the Desert Viana, an expanse of dunes that covers almost a quarter of the island. There are date palms and coconut palms growing from an oasis and it truly is a sight to marvel.

Bofareira

There is currently a project to connect Sal Rei with Bofareira directly, but until that happens, the road passes through Rabil and beyond then loops back around toward Sal Rei. Bofareira itself is tiny and there is not much happening. Beyond Boafareira along the coast is the abandoned village of Espingueira that is half renovated into the resort **Spinguera** ($$$$ m. 997.8943 / 999.1021; info@spinguera.com; www.spinguera.com*). Unlike the jam-packed resorts along Chave Beach, Spinguera's approach is one of simplicity and solidarity with the environment. Twelve small cottages are built in harmony with the landscape and offer a remote escape on a remote island. A variety of activities are offered (with advance notice) including guided hikes, boating and snorkeling, turtle watching and surfing. There is, however, no TV, telephone or internet (and electricity is only available at night), allowing visitors to truly escape the outside world.

João Galego, Fundo das Figueiras, Cabeço das Tarafes

If you return to Rabil but head in the opposite direction, follow the signs to Fundo das Figueiras. It is difficult to separate these three towns, though they are physically set apart from one another, each is equally as quiet and equally as tiny. The residents survive off of what meager crops they are able to coax from the land, and many work as fishermen out of nearby Baía das Gatas. Known for shark and dolphin sightings, there is a permanent camp with a rotating group of fishermen and lobster divers.

It is also possible to get to Odjo de Mar (eye of the ocean), a natural pool in a rock formation, one of Boa Vista's natural wonders, from Cabeço das Tarafes. Ask around for directions.

WHERE TO STAY & EAT

Casa de Dona Maria Celeste Owner of the restaurant Nha Terra in Fundo das Figueiras, Dona Maria Celeste also rents a room in her house to visitors. The upstairs room is decorated in a way typical to Cape Verdean homes (a hodge-podge of imported items) and is quite quaint and comfortable. One room available for two, breakfast included. This is a good option for those who want to experience the life of the people of Boa Vista. Located in Fundo das Figueiras. Single $, double $$. *Tel: 252.1103*

Restaurant Nha Terra If you choose not to stay, grab lunch or dinner at the restaurant of Dona Maria Celeste. Call ahead with reservations/requests. Located in Fundo das Figueiras. $-$$ *Tel: 252.1114*

Tiéta Restaurant Similar style to Nha Terra, Gracinda serves typical Cape Verdean meals. Call ahead with requests. Located in Fundo das Figueiras. $-$$ *Tel: 252.1111*

Boa Vista

Desert Viana

Well, this past weekend was another to go down in the annals of history (or at least the annals of this month). My co-worker invited us to Estância de Baixo again, only this time for a *grelha* in the desert. We put together a few coolers of food and drinks and walked about 25 minutes out of town to where the desert begins. The Deserto da Viana is weird: it starts and ends suddenly, and it's pretty small. One minute you're walking through fields of brown dirt and lava rocks, and then all of a sudden, there are huge sand dunes that go for a few miles.

We set up camp underneath a big tree that gave us shade from the sun. Someone had set up a grilling pit there, but we had to find it under the sand first and dig it up. We grilled fish and some chicken legs that Beti had marinated in something close to liquid heaven because good goddamn they were delicious. After the meal, we struck off into the desert to enjoy it. I don't know what the original goal was, but it turned into a romp in the sand dunes. In the end, we made it home just after sunset, exhausted and covered in sand.

- Leland Smith

Povoação Velha

The first settlement on Boa Vista, Povoação Velha has declined over time. The town itself is comprised of a few streets lined with houses in varying states of decay. You will be able to practice the steadfast Cape Verdean tradition of sitting along a wall while you watch others do the same. During the day, chickens, donkeys and a dwindling number of children haunt the streets. From this quiet town, it is possible to climb nearby Pico Santo António (1,243 feet/379 m) and Rocha Estância (1,161 feet/354m) or head to Praia de Curralinho or Verandinha Beach.

PRAIA DE CURRALINHO

Perhaps one of the most famous beaches on Boa Vista, Praia de Curralinho is better known as "Santa Mónica" for the resemblance to the famous California beach. On Boa Vista, it is about 6 km from Povoação Velha and far less populous than its Californian twin. If you decide to make the trek, bring your own supplies—water, snacks and shade—as you will not be finding beach kiosks and ice cream trucks. The stretch of sand is almost painfully beautiful in its arid silence and peace and, unlike many of the other beautiful beaches, it is possible to swim here.

PRAIA DE LACAÇÃO

The proposed site of a new Riu hotel, construction is now underway. This southern beach is not much different from the many beaches on Boa Vista, an impossibly beautiful stretch of sand kissed by turquoise sea. As a southern beach, it is possible to swim here, and it is also an important site for turtles.

Festivals on Boa Vista

January 6th – João Galego, Twelfth Night

May 3rd – Rabil, Santa Cruz

May 4th – Rabil, Pidrona

May 8th – Povoação Velha, São Roque

Last weekend of May – Estância Baixo, Cruz Nhô Lolo

June 13th – Santo António

June 24th – João Galego, São João Baptista

July 4th – Sal Rei, Santa Isabel (the patron saint of the conselho, this festival draws a large crowd)

August 15th - João Galego, Nossa Senhora de Piedade

August 16th – Rabil, São Roque (Praia da Cruz music festival)

December 8th - Povoação Velha, Imaculada Conceição

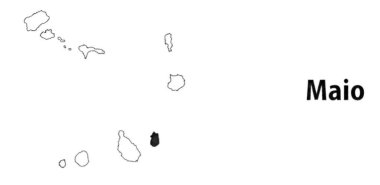

Maio

With only 7,000 inhabitants scattered in various isolated villages and large parts of Maio entirely unpopulated, it sometimes seems to truly embody the term "deserted island." Roads stretch for miles between inhabited areas, changing from cobblestone to dirt to a brief paved passage cutting through the barren middle of the island connecting two equally lonely towns. As quickly as you enter a small cluster of houses, you find yourself exiting on the other side. Though you will not encounter a lot of movement or tourist attractions, Maio boasts stunning beaches and an ideal opportunity for relaxation.

Leaving Praia, the capital of Santiago and Cape Verde, by boat, it is possible to see Vila (Porto Inglês), the "capital" of Maio. A few stacked streets of houses, schools and the well-kept church are a small mark of civilization on the otherwise pristine and welcoming coastline. The pier in Maio is a mere 15 minute walk from the outskirts of town and seems to be dropped randomly on an endless stretch of welcoming white sand. A few brightly colored boats are dragged up on the sand and throughout the day it is possible to find a mix of fishermen, children and tourists scattered along the beach.

Of Cape Verde's three "beach islands," Maio is the least developed and, because of this, is often overlooked. With international airports on Sal and Boa Vista, many visitors travel no further, making these larger islands their holiday destination. Maio can be more difficult to get to because it is necessary to go through Praia and transportation can be less reliable. However, if you are looking for isolation and escape, Maio affords an opportunity to experience the peaceful tranquility and *morabeza* of Cape Verde while soaking up the natural beauty that draws so many to Sal and Boa Vista.

Maio

GEOGRAPHY

One of the flattest islands, Maio is also one of the smaller islands in the archipelago. At 103 sq miles (268 sq km), most of this land is rocky and windswept. The exceptions are the salt flats, sandy dunes and beaches and a few rounded peaks with Monte Penoso being the highest at 1,434 feet (437m).

Like the other islands, Maio was formed by volcanic eruptions millions of years ago. Rocks and sediment have been found dating back more than 100 million years causing debate over the actual age of the island, but it is believed that these rocks are deposits from the ocean floor. Regardless, the age of Maio is undeniable when examining the level of erosion and deterioration. Once a mountain growing out of the sea, Maio has been reduced to a largely flat, desolate blip on the ocean's surface.

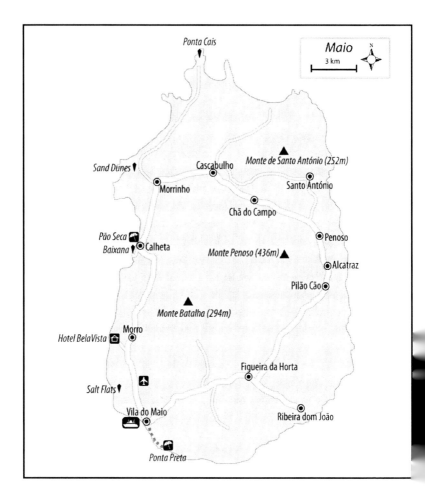

HISTORY

The name Maio was given for its discovery on the first day of May *maio*. Like Brava, Maio was initially overlooked by the Portuguese settlers. Goats were left to roam the barren surface and consume what vegetation they could find, but the land was largely left alone. It was the English that came to Maio and discovered the wealth in salt exportation. The port town is now known as Vila do Maio, the name Porto Inglês is a remnant of this period that lasted for over one hundred years. Between the 16th and 19th centuries, the English used a primitive, but intricate system exploiting donkeys and the few locals to extract the salt, transport it to the bay and from smaller ships to the large ships anchored beyond the lashing winds and breaking tides.

The salt was brought to Europe, Africa and the West Indies and sold as a product or used to salt fish and meats. For the English, it was a lucrative business as they essentially stole the salt from the few locals, paying them for their services with cheap goods and trinkets such as hats and household items. It worked well for them until the 19th century when trade shifted to Brazil and collapsed after the introduction of tariffs on trade.

Despite being largely controlled by the English and relatively quiet, Maio was not immune to pirate attacks. A fort was built in Vila looking out over the bay, inspired by attacks in 1818 and 1827. The deteriorated walls still stand and scattered cannons lay on the sand like forlorn sunbathers, a scattered reminder of times past.

GETTING THERE

When everything is running smoothly, it is possible to travel by plane or by boat. The easiest way is to take the fairly regular three hour boat ride from Praia. For 1200-2000, it is also an affordable option. Planes fly two to three times a week, but for twelve minutes in the air, it may be the most you will ever pay for distance covered on a flight. Unfortunately, with any transportation to and from Maio, regularity is not guaranteed and schedules are always subject to change.

By Sea

Cape Verde Navalis The ferry "Marina Princess" has been running since late 2009 and makes the Praia-Fogo-Brava circuit four days a week. Slightly faster than the older boats, the trip from Praia to Fogo takes just over four hours and from Praia to Brava just under five hours. The agency is located on the corner across the street from Sucupira (see pg 178) in Praia. *Tel: 262.1023 Cost: 2000-4000*

By Air

TACV It is possible to get tickets at the airport, the main TACV building on Rua Serpa Pinto or at any agency on any island. Flights are generally only a couple of times a week, but may increase during the summer and around the time of festivals: the first weekend of May and the music festival in September.

Halcyon Air May or may not be running to Maio, but check for competitive rates. Schedule will reflect that of TACV.

GETTING AROUND

It is possible to either charter a driver or rent a car and explore on your own. A chartered driver will take you anywhere you wish and around the island for about 6000$. There are public cars that run in and out of the city once or twice daily bringing men, women and children to shop, sell and socialize. The most reliable public transport are the student buses that bring the students to Vila to attend the only high school on the island. They make the trip to and from the remote villages three times a day, but are generally overflowing with students. Arguably the best way to get around is by bike because the island is small and largely flat.

MaioCar Rent-A-Car cars are relatively inexpensive to rent (4000-5000/ day) *Tel: 255.1700*

Bicycle Rentals

When you enter Vila from the port, you will come up a slight incline to a corner where, almost unfailingly, you will find a group of young men sitting under the billboards waiting to see who passes by. If you turn to the right, you will pass a nightclub and bar that doesn't seem to have a set schedule for opening. The IMO Maio building, where an ex-pat French man rents bicycles, is located toward the end of the street surrounded by a variety of construction.

Vila do Maio (Porto Inglês)

For a short visit, it is possible to enjoy the "best" of Maio without leaving Vila. From wherever you are staying, the beach is no more than a 20 minute walk. BitchaRotcha, the main beach, stretches from the end of Vila for what seems like miles, walk beyond the port and you will find yourself in complete isolation. On the beach below the wall, the fishermen bring in their boats and there are two small restaurants where you can sit, relax and watch the waves lap at the shore.

The town itself is charming and quaint. The streets are lined with houses, shops, restaurants and bars and culminates at the top of a hill with a well kept church. On the north end of Vila, the *polivalente* (sports complex) is often the focal point for activities. There are a few bars clustered around the area and the c*ooperativa* (food cooperative) is impossible to miss at the end of the road with beehive-like spears and painted walls.

Vila offers the largest variety of places to eat and to stay. Because the island is small, it is a nice place to spend the evening as you wander and explore during the day. Despite being the "capital" of Maio, it is only really rowdy during times of festivity. On a typical day, the village is quiet and you will likely find people sort of milling around and watching to see who else is milling around.

IMPORTANT INFORMATION

Bank BCA, BCN; Open Monday-Friday. Will likely have Euros for exchange.

Health Post *Posto Sanitário* There are not facilities for serious health issues, but the health post can provide bandages or other small services. Tel: 255.1130

Pharmacy *Farmácia Forte;* Tel: 255.1370

Police *Polícia* Station is located at the far end of the main street. You will also likely easily encounter police patrolling the small village. Tel: 255.1132

TACV Maio On the road to Figueira da Horta; Tel: 255.1256

WHAT TO DO

The miles of beautiful beaches also offer hours of discovery with scuba diving expeditions and various ocean excursions. Alain, the coordinator of **PescaMaio** (Tel: 991.4424), will take people on guided scuba tours after an introductory class. He speaks Kriolu, Portuguese, French and English.

You can also hunt down Wally (Tel: 992.5944), a Senegalese/Cape Verdean lobster diver who is also willing to give tours along the main beach.

Be sure to check out the reef about 1 km out of Ponta Preta. Underwater life abounds off the coast of this enchanting beach. In addition to the creatures around the reef, there have been a number of whale spottings further off the coast.

WHERE TO EAT

If you are staying at Ana Rita's, Bom Sossego or Marilú, it will be possible to arrange for meals to be taken in the hotel's restaurant. If you are not staying at these places, you will still be welcomed for a meal. If you have an itinerary, be sure to plan and ask for meals in advance as food is prepared fresh and often ingredients are not immediately available.

In addition to the following restaurants, keep an eye out for open doors with grills. In the area of the post office, there are a number of people and places that prepare grilled fish and chicken. You can also stop in one of the shops to pick up supplies. For variety, your best options for selection in Vila are the Cooperativa or Pick N' Pay.

Bom Sossego In the hotel of the same name, the restaurant is a bit upscale, but the "arroz mariscos" (rice and shellfish medley) is superb. Prices begin around 850$, but are served generously. $$-$$$ *Tel: 255.1365*

Tutti Frutti On the main road toward the airport, Tutti Frutti offers excellent Italian cuisine and some simple plates for slightly elevated prices. The price reflects the availability and quality of food. Homemade dough makes the pizza hard to pass up. Try one with local goat cheese. $$-$$$ *Tel: 255 1575*

Restaurant Bea This brown house on Rua 3 de Maio is not advertised as a restaurant, but Dona Bea is known as one of the best cooks in Maio. She caters many of the official meetings and functions and will likely be happy to have you sit down in her kitchen. Stop by in advance to confirm availability. $$

General BenBow's On the same strip as Tutti Frutti, General BenBow's is run by an English man and his Cape Verdean wife. The food is good and can be a little less expensive than other restaurants. $$.

Kulor Café Owned and run by the French ex-pat Sebastian, the quaint restaurant is well decorated and offers indoor and outdoor dining (add 20%). Meals are made with locally available products but are given a French twist. The caramel and curried pork dishes are excellent, but if you're looking for something lighter, try a *brochet* (grilled fish kebob style). Whatever you do, don't leave Maio without trying his homemade *ponche*. Plates begin around 1000$, but are well worth it. Always open for dinner, lunch by request. $$$ *m. 9811303*

 KabanaBar Located on the beach, the little round hut offers a break from the shade, reasonably priced and various dishes, cold drinks and pleasant service. Here you can get anything from a hamburger to fresh lobster. A wonderful place to sit and watch the fisherman bring in their catch and allow time to melt around you. $-$$$

Bar Tropical Next to KabanaBar on the beach. On a windy day, the transparent walls will protect you from the wind, but separate you from the environment. $$

Culinaria Newly opened, this small restaurant is located off the main strip. Owned and operated by Sauzinha and her husband Chite, the varying menu is typical of availability at many Cape Verdean restaurants. Here you will find the best buzio south of Calheta, also swing by in the evening to check out the soccer match of the day. Plates start at $$. *Tel: 985.1518*

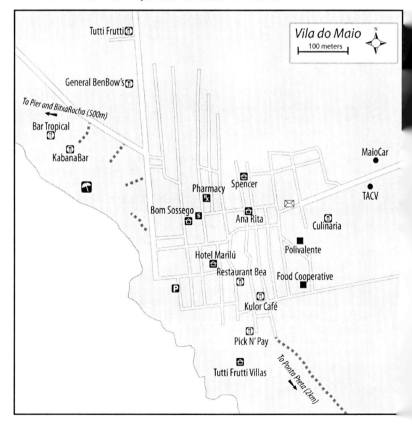

WHERE TO STAY

Bom Sossego Owned and run by a Senegalese couple, Bom Sossego is located in the center of town in the *praça* in front of the church. This is a popular choice with groups of travelers. Breakfast is included in price, but the price may vary depending on number of people and amenities (hot/cold water, A/C). $$ *Tel: 2551365*

Hotel Marilú Located a short walk from the central *praça*, Hotel Marilú is one of the tallest buildings in Vila. There are currently eight rooms available with plans for four more. $$ *Tel: 2851198*

Spencer A small house next to Electra. Spencer rents rooms at a reasonable price, though breakfast is not included, the house has facilities to prepare your own. $ *m. 991.7438*

Restaurant/Pensão Ana Rita Behind the church in the same area as Electra and Spencer's rooms. The restaurant here is popular for the upstairs/outdoors view and ambient. Dona Ana Rita can be found when the boat comes in handing out cards. Prices range depending on accommodation. Breakfast included.$-$$ *Tel: 255.1660 / 994.8561*

Tutti Frutti Villas The proprietors of Tutti Frutti, Marco and Francesca, rent villas along the outcropping toward Ponta Preta. More pricey than a hotel visit, the villas offer a nice view and the opportunity to prepare your own meals if you are on Maio for an extended stay. $$$ *Tel: 255.1575 / 997.9195*

Ponta Preta

If you walk about 15 minutes South of Vila, the beach at Ponta Preta offers a stunning alternative to BitxaRocha. The beach itself is beautiful, but it is also appealing because of the isolation from town. Despite the feeling of isolation, beware of leaving items unattended. Because of the strong current, swimming is not recommended, but a walk along the shore away from the city will bring you to a rare spot of black sand, a reminder of the islands' distant volcanic origins.

North of Vila

If you choose to venture out of the city, Maio offers many isolated beaches and coves that are stunning and incredibly peaceful. It is possible to *pedi boleia* (hitchhike) or get a ride on public transportation, but it can be irregular and there are long stretches where you may not encounter a ride. There will be more traffic during the school year as the only high school on the island is located in Vila and students from the whole island travel to and from in the morning, mid-day and evening—the cars do get quite full. Biking (rentals available from IMO Maio along the main road near the police station, see pg 158 for more information) is arguably the best option. If you choose to walk or bike around, be sure to bring plenty of water as there are long stretches without towns and *lojas* (stores) are not well stocked.

As you head out of Vila toward the airport along Rua Frontera, (commonly referred to as Rua Principal) you will pass some of the more prominent restaurants—Restaurant Frontera, Tutti Frutti, General BenBow's—several travel agencies and the general store Drogaria Ramos.

Maio

A few kilometers out of Vila you will pass a stretch of saltpans on the left and the airport on the right. The massive saltpans stretch for almost four miles and are at least a mile across at the widest point. Low vegetation circles the saltpans and looking out across the expanse, it becomes clear why the island was historically known for its natural salt reserves.

Continuing along the windswept land, you will quickly come across the turn to Morro. It is possible to see the outline of the BelaVista hotel from the road, but the hidden beach beyond is said to be the most beautiful on the island. Though the hotel looks out over the water, the beach is open to the public and, usually, swimmable. Use caution if you decide to head in as the tide can be extremely strong.

WHERE TO STAY

Hotel BelaVista Though it was closed temporarily during research, it is proclaimed that Hotel BelaVista offers the best views (hence the name) and a peaceful escape. Additionally, there is a tennis facility and pool for guest use. Prices run from 5000$ upward depending on number of guests, but contact for current prices and availability. *Tel: 256.1388, m. 995.2087*

Calheta

The road continues on from Morro with Monte Batalha, one of Maio's low peaks, off to the right. The landscape changes just a little as you enter the limits of the planted forest of Maio, the largest in Cape Verde.

In the distance, the outer limits of Calheta, the second largest village in Maio, will be visible. Primarily a fishing village, the people of Calheta struggle to exist on the arid soil and meager natural resources. Tourists and residents alike will tell you that Calheta maintains an essence of Cape Verde that has virtually disappeared in Vila due to exposure to the various immigrants and tourists. Calheta is comprised of four virtually indistinguishable areas. Head towards the coast and you will pass the recently

Artesanto

Calheta is known as the artistic center of Maio. There are currently plans to establish a micro-enterprise enabling the artists of Calheta, Morro and Vila to finance and display their work, but like many things in Cape Verde, there is no established timeline, limited funding and no rush on behalf of those involved. However, even without an established center, the artists continue to produce.

Ask around in Calheta to meet Isidora and Djubabo at the Centro Comunitario to see their loom and weaving. Pam, a carpenter, is hard to miss as his house is painted as the flag of Cape Verde. He is involved in the development of the artisan project and contributes by creating miniatures of fishing boats and noteworthy landmarks of Calheta and Maio. Santoso also works with miniatures and carvings and forms beautiful animals out a variety of available resources. If you can, try to meet Fogo, one of the resident artists. He is a nationally renowned painter who has left his mark on more than just Maio. All will be happy to display their work for you and even happier to sell some.

- Rachelle Faroul

inaugurated statue recognizing women's *trabadja duru* (hard work). The short bay, Baixana, is endearingly called "the swimming pool of Maio" as the shallow bay is protected on both sides and boats are pulled ashore outside of bar Porto Kural.

At 6:00 and 18:00, the fishermen pull into Baixana with the catch of the day. The less fortunate of Calheta flock around, waiting in hopes that the remainders will be given out. Knowing the situation of their neighbors, the fishermen often comply.

Despite the pressures of poverty in Calheta, there is a strong solidarity and sense of culture. Neighbors work with neighbors in the fields and on various projects and food is shared generously, leaving no mouth hungry.

Music is extremely popular as many youth spend their days trying to live up to the famous Tó Alves, Calheta's guitar prodigy who now owns and runs the music school in Praia. If you are lucky, you will catch a performance of Lugi and Pedro. Lugi works as a carpenter and boat maker by day, but can often be found in the afternoon and evening around Calheta playing his violin.

WHERE TO EAT

If you decide to spend some time in Calheta, contact or ask around for **Sylvia** (aka Cheena $-$$; m. 987.9700). If you contact her in advance, she will happily purchase fish, lobster or buzio from the fishermen and prepare a meal. She also keeps a good stock of cold beer and is always happy to entertain. If you haven't had luck finding Lugi for an impromptu performance, Sylvia might be able to help.

Moving On

As you leave Calheta and make your way toward Morrinho, there is a virtually indistinguishable left turn marked only by a fence. From there, you can travel out to the coast to Pão Seco, a rocky cove with a little isolated beach that looks across the bay toward Calheta.

Morrinho

Continuing along the road, you will come across another tiny village of hardly 30 houses. The road comes to an end and splits here in the center of Morrinho. Take the left turn toward the coast and you will head across an expanse of dirt, pig sties and the occasional cow to the sand dunes of Maio. It is possible to climb the soft white sand and trek across to the coast. Along the coast at the northern most point of the island, Ponta Cais, is a weather-beaten lighthouse, a prominent feature looking out over the Atlantic.

Turn right in Morrinho to continue around the island. Just out of town, the road turns from cobblestone to a maze of criss-crossing dirt paths. Be sure to have people point you in the right direction and use Monte de Santo António to guide you east across the island into Cascabulho. There is a small rotary at the top of town where you can continue on to the right or venture to the left to the north coast of Maio.

North Coast

The dirt road to the left takes you up and down across valleys to an expanse of isolated beaches in the area of Ponta Cais. The water is tempting, but watch the tide carefully before heading in.

CASCABULHO

There is not much of note in this small village beyond the rotary leading out. This area tends to be more green and fertile than the southern half of the island, but it is fairly evident that subsistence farming would not be possible here. If you turn right at the rotary, you will continue toward the east coast and will soon be faced with the decision to continue on the worn path or veer off in Chã do Campo on the newly paved road that winds through the center of the island, dropping you just outside of Figueira da Horta.

East Coast

A few small villages—Penoso, Alcatraz, Pilão Cão and Ribeira dom João— are sprinkled along the east coast. From each, it is possible to reach practically abandoned coastline and some hidden beaches that are a stunning contrast to the barren landscape.

RIBEIRA DOM JOÃO

After entering the town, turn right into the ribeira and follow the dirt path beyond the *polivalente* (sports complex) and up the other side. Once on the plateau, it is possible to descend to a myriad of isolated beaches (depending on how far you wish to venture). Be sure to bring plenty of water and beware of the steep descent. Like so many paths in Cape Verde, it consists mostly of loose soil sprinkled with rocks that can serve as footholds or deceptive foes.

FIGUEIRA DA HORTA

Upon entering and leaving the town, you immediately get the sense that this is a town frequently entered and left. Its proximity to Vila helps it to maintain a more substantial population than many of the other villages, but despite that fact, there doesn't seem to be much to do beyond watching passing cars.

The Enchanted Forest of Maio

Aside from the beaches and salt, Maio also boasts Cape Verde's largest forest. Though it is not enchanted, on first glimpse, it doesn't appear to be much of a forest either. As a part of the reforestation effort, the acacia trees are neatly planted and spread for miles along the road between Morro and Morrinho on the West side of the island. Wind swept, neatly placed and standing at just 20-40 feet tall, the trees are an interesting take on the word forest. They were planted to encourage water retention, use as firewood and for the production of charcoal, one of Maio's few exports.

Festivals on Maio

Santa Cruz – May 3

Nossa Senhora da Graça – August 15

Nosso Senhor da Luz   – September 8 (the big festa)

Santa Flumeno – January 11

Nossa Senhora de Fatima – May 13 (Morro's big festa)

Nossa Senhora de Lordes – February

Coração de Jesus – June

São Jose – March 19 (Calheta's big festa)

Nha Santana – July 26

Dia does Reis – January 6

San Pedro – June 29

Nosso Senora do Rossario – February 8

Santa Antonio – July 13

Alcatraz – February 19

San João da Paz – June 24

Christo Rey – November 21

Sagrada Familia – December 28

- Compiled by Julia Kramer

Maio

Santiago

It is possible to spend an entire vacation exploring the reaches of Santiago, though many find themselves enticed by the promises of adventure that await on other islands. Whether or not you decide to move on, don't overlook the potential on this, the largest and most diverse island.

Flying into Praia, the sprawl of houses is visible pouring through valleys and spreading far inland from the coast, a daunting mess of half-planned urban growth. The mountains of the range of Pico de Antónia are visible beyond the city limits, but what is not visible is the varying landscape and lifestyles perched high in the mountains— Rui Vaz, Serra Malagueta, Porto Madeira—tucked away in verdant valleys—São Domingos, São Jorge, Assomada, Hortelão—and hugging the coast—Cidade Velha, Ribeira da Barca, Calheta, Pedra Badejo. There are also a handful of white sand beaches sprinkled along the coast—Tarrafal, São Francisco/São Tomé and Praia Baixo.

Many would argue that Santiago *is* Cape Verde. It was the first island to be populated and is today the most populous. With this population density, you will find a bit of everything in the city and around the island.

Santiago has long been the center for commerce and trade, drawing Cape Verdeans from other islands and West Africans looking for a better life through education or and employment. International Aid has brought Europeans and Americans, and Chinese immigrants run hundreds of Chinese *lojas* (shops) carrying an array of products on a vast spectrum of quality and price. This already diverse mix is agitated by the presence of tourists who are seen as a source of money, both by resorts and by the many homeless, unemployed and poverty-stricken residents. Of all the islands, Santiago has the loudest and most abrasive culture and white skin is irrevocably tied to the idea of money. Though it is less violent outside of the city, you will undoubtedly be asked for *dinheiro* (money), a *caneta* (pen) or some other item of value.

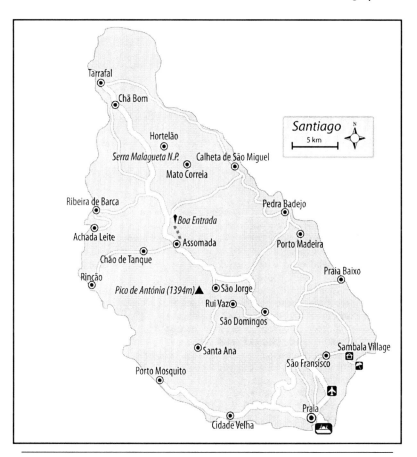

What's in a Name?

Most Cape Verdeans from other islands refer to the island of Santiago as "Praia." This may be because it is the capital and administrative center, it is home to nearly a quarter of the population or because many people from other islands have either never been to the capital, or never traveled beyond the city limits. However, Cape Verdeans from Praia refer to Plateau as Praia, and to each other neighborhood by its proper name.

GEOGRAPHY

At 382 sq miles (991 sq km), Santiago is the largest and most diverse island. A few nice beaches are sprinkled along the coasts—São Francisco, Tarrafal, Praia Baixo—and two mountain ranges, Serra Malagueta and Serra do Pico de Antónia, rise above the clouds. Close to half of the country's population resides on Santiago and nearly half of the 265,000 people of Santiago live in Praia, the capital and administrative center. Not far out of the city, however, many still live an agricultural lifestyle, virtually untouched by modern amenities—some areas yet to be connected to the electric grid.

Estimated to be between four and five million years old, the once active range now lies dormant. The landscape varies between dry, stony deserts and moist, rich microclimates hidden up in the clouds. Santiago has the most groundwater and fresh water resources. This combined with the amount of arable land available makes Santiago the top agricultural producer of the nation. The main crops are corn and beans and in select areas, sugar cane, but there are also fruit plantations—bananas, mangoes, papaya—and many root and seasonal vegetables—principally potatoes, manioc (cassava root), carrots, tomatoes, cucumber and squash.

HISTORY

Santiago was the first island to be settled by Diogo Gomes and António de Noli in 1462. Throughout the island are sites of historic significance, most notably Ribeira Grande (Cidade Velha), Espinho Branco and Tarrafal, and Praia that has a small collection of museums and statues marking important periods and events (see each section for more detailed explanation of history).

It was in Ribeira Grande that the first city was established and populated, and an act whose global significance was recognized in July of 2009 by its naming as a UNESCO World Heritage Site. The city was recognized for the expansion of European colonialism and domination and as the pivot point of trans-Atlantic shipping and trade.

As with any colony, Cape Verde was originally established to make money for the Portuguese crown. Settlers were offered fair rewards for their willingness to go abroad and work in trade and the various agricultural exploits. Though history reports that at the time the island was much more verdant, there was little that Santiago, and Cape Verde in general, had to offer besides a prime location in the burgeoning trade industry.

The history of Santiago continues to be written as the city grows and expands. The slave trade no longer exists, but there is undoubtedly questionable trading taking place in the largely unregulated bays. With the expansion of the port and increase of international flights, there has also been an increase of external influences. Cape Verde always has been, and likely always will be, a place where many countries meet.

LOGISTICS

As Praia is home to one of the increasing number of international airports, you may fly into the capital directly.

If flying from the United States, TACV offers direct flights from Boston to Praia for half the price of connecting flights through Portugal. There is a rumor that Delta will soon offer flights from Atlanta, but this has yet to be confirmed.

TAP Portugal also offers direct flights into Praia from Portugal and other connecting airports.

Praia

Arriving in Praia, you descend upon the city and almost immediately find yourself in the heart of the action. During the dry season, you will cross a water bed that is not filled with water, but rather trash. Plateau, or "Praia" for those who live here, rises up above the city and looks out on the bay. As you drive along the coast, the hospital looms large on the edge of Plateau and around the other side, you pass Sucupira, the massive outdoor marketplace. The streets are a constant bustle of activity, packed with taxis, Hiaces, buses and an ever increasing number of private cars.

Just a few short years ago, the trash and traffic were a much larger problem. Since the elections in 2008, the new government has been making a push to beautify and regulate the city. Efforts include replanting trees that had been removed to pave the streets, installing traffic lights, cleaning the litter that dances along in the wind, fencing off the barrier between the busy streets and the sand stripped beaches (a prime mugging location) and reducing the disproportionate street dog population. The main streets are now well maintained and are more pleasing to the eye.

Up on Plateau you enter the commercial and administrative center of the city. During the day, it is nearly impossible to pass through the busy streets as well-dressed professionals walk the same paths as weather-beaten women and men that come from the *fora* (outside the city, the interior of the island) to sell their produce and wares. Cars double and triple park along the main stretch and traffic sputters along in jerks and waves. Beggars and homeless persons hang around in the *praças* or outside of restaurants and hotels as the upper echelon of residents, foreign investors, municipal and embassy employees, and successful business owners sit down for a *café* (coffee). This contrast of status is a fairly new concept in Cape Verde as up until recently, people were always reliant on family.

Within the *conselho* of Praia, there exist many subcities. Between each orderly and developed *plateau* (Plateau, Achada Santo Antonio, Palmarejo) there are piles of unfinished houses crammed on top of one another filling the empty land, a visual reminder of the rifts between wealth and poverty. Under many of these illegally constructed buildings, it is possible to see the foundation peeking out of the eroding soil and the trash that is cleaned from the main roads fills the pathways that wind between houses. In the forgotten *ribeiras* and more distant subcities, there are many people living without water or electricity. This is Cape Verde.

Santiago

IMPORTANT INFORMATION

Bank There are a variety of banks in Praia—BCA, BCN, Banco Interâtlantico, Caixa Económica—and there are branches in the prominent areas of the many neighborhoods. The lines can be excruciatingly long at all branches. For simple transactions, try a smaller branch in Achada Santo António or Palmarejo. All banks are open Monday-Friday from approx 8:00-15:00.

Western Union There is a branch on Plateau as well as in Fazenda. Money can also be sent/received through the post office.

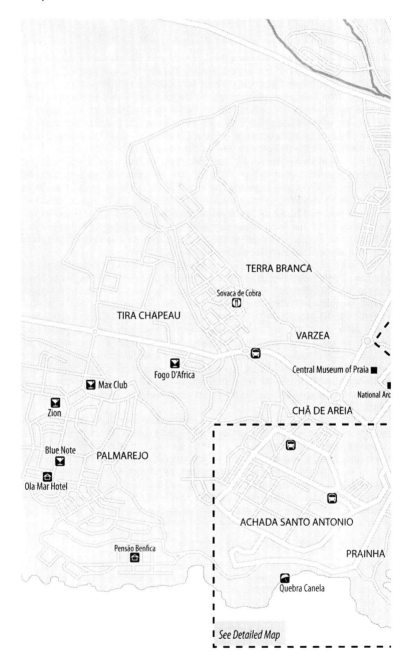

TERRA BRANCA

Sovaca de Cobra

TIRA CHAPEAU

VARZEA

Fogo D'Africa

Central Museum of Praia

Max Club

National Arc

Zion

CHÃ DE AREIA

Blue Note

PALMAREJO

Ola Mar Hotel

ACHADA SANTO ANTONIO

PRAINHA

Pensão Benfica

Quebra Canela

See Detailed Map

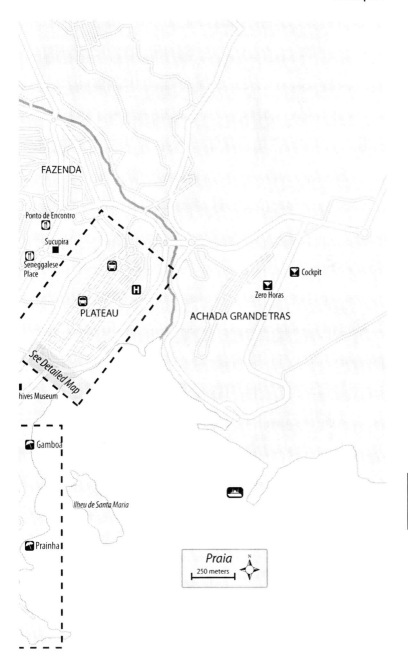

FAZENDA

Ponto de Encontro

Sucupira

Senegalese Place

PLATEAU

See Detailed Map

hives Museum

Cockpit

Zero Horas

ACHADA GRANDE TRAS

Gamboa

Ilheu de Santa Maria

Prainha

Praia
250 meters
N

Santiago

Hospital Agostinho Neto Perched on Plateau looking over the bay, this is the main hospital for the Sotavento and often for patients from the Barlavento as well. Because of this, it is often overbooked and understaffed. For a non-emergency or mild emergency, one may want to consult one of the many private doctors available. Tel: 261.2462

Pharmacy There are pharmacies in most areas of Praia, on Plateau, try *Farmácia Africana* (Tel: 261.2776) or *Central* (Tel: 261.1167).

Post Office *Correios* On Plateau it overlooks the bay at the opposite end of plateau as the hospital behind the *Palâcia de Justica* (court house). There are also branches in Fazenda and Achada Santo António. Open Monday-Friday either from 8:00-12:00, 14:00-17:00 or 7:30-15:00 (the government has been experimenting with working hours).

DHL Shipping Located in Achada Santo António. Tel: 262.3124; dhl_praia@cvtelecom.cv

Police *Polícia* Polica headquarters are on Plateau. There are also police stations in Palmarejo and Achada Santo António. Tel: 261.1328, 261.1600, 261, 6158

TACV On Plateau up Rua Serpa Pinto open 8:00-12:00, 14:00-17:00. You can book flights through any agency as well. Tel: 260.8241, 260.8400; www.flytacv.com

Halcyon Air On Rua Andrade Corvo around the corner from the Café Sofia *praça*. Tickets available through Morabitur at the airport. Tel: 263.4823

TAP By the rotary in Chã d' Áreia. Tel: 261.5836; www.flytap.com

WIFI: WiFi is available in the *praça* by the *Câmara*. There are also a number of internet cafés scattered throughout the different neighborhoods.

CRIME

Because of the drastic discrepancy of wealth, there have been increasing problems with crime. Literally no place outdoors is safe at night. Muggings and robbery are significantly less frequent during the day, but still occur. The presence of violent crime has increased over the past few years as well. If venturing out at night, it is highly recommended that you take one of the many easily accessible taxis. Most hotels should have numbers for a reliable taxi driver.

GETTING AROUND

Taxis are easily recognized and readily available throughout the city. A few years ago the government mandated that all taxis be painted a cream color and labeled "Taxi." You may still be propositioned by a private vehicle for a taxi ride, but as they are not regulated, it is not recommended. Within the city, a taxi should cost anywhere from 150-300 depending on distance (after 22:00, price increases 50-100).

Alternatively, it is possible to take the bus to most destinations. From Plateau, buses stop on either side (depending on where one is heading) of Avenida Amilcar Cabral and Avenida 5 de Julho. Each bus is labeled with a number and list of destinations in the front window. If you get on the wrong bus, they all eventually return to Plateau, though you may have to pay an additional fare. Buses run from around 7:00-21:30 and currently cost 35$.

If heading to Achada Santo António, wait across the street from the *Câmara Municipal* (a large blue building on Avenida Amilcar Cabral) for number 4 or number 6. Further down the street toward Calú and Angela, you can catch the number 10 to head to Palmarejo.

Despite the recently paved roads and increase in traffic, it is quite possible to enjoy the sunset walking along the road above Quebra Canela (see the following *Beaches* section). The sound of revelry carries up softly from the beach below and the low hum of cars does nothing to disturb the peacefulness of the expanse of ocean. If you continue on past Quebra Canela, you can take a sundowner at The Alkemist or the slightly higher priced (and better decorated) Kappa (see *Nightlife* on pg 180).

BEACHES

Swimming is generally fairly safe during the dry season—the tides can be strong, but the water itself is not too polluted. Avoid swimming during the rainy season as the water runoff from the city is quite polluted. Quebra Canela and Prainha are fairly naturally sheltered and there is no direct dumping happening in these areas. Gamboa beach is a wide open area in the main bay, although swimming here is not recommended.

Quebra Canela (literally meaning "break shin") is aptly named for all the rocks hidden under the sometimes turbulent waters. The cove is

Public Transportation

I took the bus twice today. The first time, I walked to the furthest bus stop in Achada because I did not want to wait. Sometimes, impatience is a virtue. Rather than stand by the fetid dumpsters, I walked for 10 minutes and arrived at the same time as the bus. I climbed aboard, happy to escape the mid-day sun. I sat as a mix of people climbed aboard, young professionals, uniformed students and a few elderly. Outside, the same woman sits everyday with brightly colored buckets overflowing with fruit for sale. Her tattered umbrella provides her with meager shade, but the fruit sits out in the harsh sun.

The last of the passengers had long since boarded and the bus driver was finishing his cell phone conversation when a woman in a shrink-wrapped purple shirt with matching earrings called for the bus to stop, leaned out the window and returned with a *freshquinha* (homemade popsicle, crucial for beating the heat). This caused a chain reaction on the right side of the bus and I could only smile and think "Only in Cape Verde."

Later that day, I once again found myself waiting for the bus. The oldest bus in Praia went rattling past, took a long U-turn in the middle of a busy intersection and pulled up to the stop. Luck! Behind the library, there is a pile of bus skeletons that I have dubbed the "bus graveyard." Though this bus has yet to make its way there, I have a feeling it will be the next added to the heap. Despite its "rustic" appearance, I have taken a liking to this ancient remnant and its smiling driver. Too old for a radio and practically gutted already, the aisles are wide and the seats have been worn by years of use. As I pay my fare, I see the camera in his hand, one similar to my own. A group of men gather by the door, also noting the camera, and an impromptu photo shoot begins. Though I am once again delayed, I can't help but smile.

slightly protected from the open ocean, but don't be fooled. The tide, even in calm waters, can be quite strong. As the tide comes in and out, different flocks of people will speckle the shore. Early risers will find a quiet and athletic crowd. Later in the day, you are likely to come across a strange mix of youth, "rastas" and a handful of tourists. Afternoons and early evenings are generally quite loud and rambunctious, the limited sand filled with enthusiastic soccer games, flocks of youth and an exciting time. If you are visiting by yourself or wish to enter the water, it is highly recommend that you find someone to watch your things. During the summer and the weekend, it can be a madhouse.

Prainha (little beach) is also appropriately named. Nestled between two high class hotels, this little beach doesn't leave much room for spreading out. The water can be much calmer due to the enclosed nature, but it doesn't take long to get crowded. In the morning and afternoon there are frequently exercise groups doing aerobics in the sand. Don't assume that because the beach itself is more intimate that your possessions will be safe. Check out the bar by the street as it was recently renovated and reopened.

Home of the famous Gamboa music festival (the weekend around May 19th), **Gamboa** is a giant sandless beach stretching the length of road connecting Plateau with Chã de Areia. The maritime police are located about midway, but that doesn't mean the beach is well monitored. It is common to see a group of youth jumping off the pier and for a while there was a soccer field set up in the area by Plateau. The beach may be nice for "a long walk on the beach," but it tends to be dirty and the secluded areas may not be safe. Recent efforts to clean the streets have resulted in a reduction of the number of street dogs that would lounge on the sand, but, festivals excluded, it is not recommended (especially for swimming).

MUSEUMS

The *Museu Etnógrafico* (Ethnographic Museum, Rua 5 de Julho in Plateau; Open Mon-Fri 9:30-12:00, 14:30-17:00), located in a converted house, stores a variety of artifacts from all the islands. Some are distinctly of European influence and some show a Cape Verdean ingenuity in adapting to the environment. Most plaques are in Portuguese.

Directly across from the Maritime Police, the *Instituto do Arquivo Histórico Nacional* (The National Archives Museum, Open Mon-Fri 9:00-13:00) can be a bit stiff about some resources, but you should be able to enter and have a look around.

The *Núcleu Museológico da Praia* (The Central Museum of Praia, Tel: 261.8870, nmuseológico_praia@yahoo.com; Open Mon-Fri 9:30-12:00, 14:30-17:00) is located behind the National Archives down a back alley, walking here can feel a little sketchy, but it is worth a visit. Expositions don't change frequently, but are meant to embrace and present Cape Verdean culture.

Tucked away with the Central Museum, *Centro de Resturação e Museologia* (Center for Museums and Restoration, Tel: 261.1528; crm@arq.de) displays an array of treasure painstakingly retrieved and restored from shipwrecks around the archipelago.

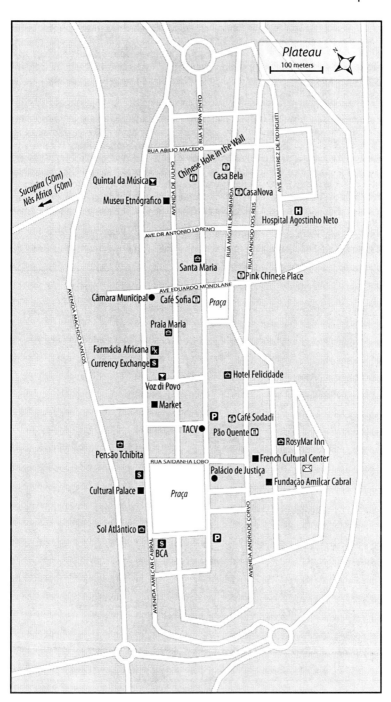

Praia | Plateau

100 meters

Sucupira (50m)
Nòs Africa (50m)

RUA SERPA PINTO

RUA ABILIO MACEDO

AVENIDA DE JULHO

AVE MARTIREZ DE PID JIGUITI

Quintal da Música

Chinese Hole in the Wall

Casa Bela

CasaNova

Museu Etnográfico

RUA MIGUEL BOMBARDA

RUA CANDIDO DOS REIS

Hospital Agostinho Neto

AVE DR ANTONIO LORENO

Santa Maria

Pink Chinese Place

AVE EDUARDO MONDLANE

Câmara Municipal ● Café Sofia

Praça

AVENIDA MACHCO SANTOS

Praia Maria

Farmácia Africana
Currency Exchange

Voz di Povo

Hotel Felicidade

Market

TACV ●

P

Café Sodadi

Pão Quente

Pensão Tchibita

RosyMar Inn

RUA SAIDANHA LOBO

French Cultural Center

Palácio de Justiça

Cultural Palace ■

Praça

Fundação Amilcar Cabral

Sol Atlântico

P

AVENIDA AMILCAR CABRAL

AVENIDA ANDRADE CORVO

BCA

Santiago

Up on Plateau by the main *praça*, **Palácio da Cultura: Ildo Lobo** (Cultural Palace, Open Mon-Fri 9:00-13:00, 15:00-18:00) holds some pieces of art and crafts and occasionally hosts exhibitions and concerts (check the sign at the entrance for upcoming events). Next door there is an underground bookstore that sells various crafts and *artesanto* as well as a collection of books, music and postcards.

Celebrating the efforts of Amilcar Cabral, one of the leaders of the independence movement (see pg 21 for more information on Cabral), the **Fundação Amilcar Cabral** (open approximately 10:00-19:00) is emerging as a cultural hot spot for young Cape Verdeans. Tucked away behind the *Palácio de* Justiça and around the corner from the French Cultural Center, the *Fundação* has a great little café, historical information and the building hosts everything from English and French lessons to music and drama rehearsals. There are frequently events at the *Fundação* or in surrounding venues. Keep an eye out for event postings or check them out on Facebook (Fundação Amilcar Cabral).

Located on Avenida Andrade Corvo on Plateau, the **French Cultural Center (**Tel: 261.1196; www.ccfcv.org) is one of the most active entities in

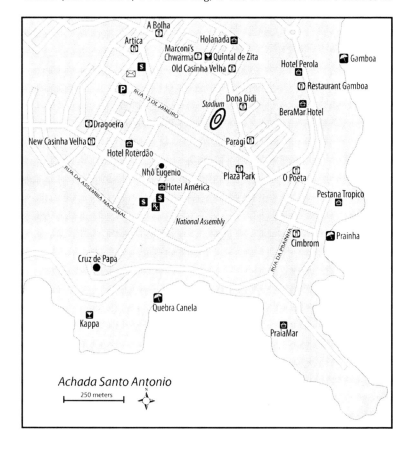

organizing cultural events in Praia. There is a monthly program put out with times, dates and locations of events and a perpetually changing art exhibit in the front room. The library is open from 9:00-12:30, 15:00-18:30 Monday-Friday and the center stays open during lunch hours to serve a fantastic buffet with a variety and mix of Cape Verdean and French cuisinet.

MUSIC/CULTURAL EVENTS

There are a number of music festivals that occur in Praia, most notably Gamboa festival in mid-May and the Jazz Festival in April (dates vary). You can also find live music at a few of the nightclubs. During the summer months (July–September) there are frequently unannounced concerts and activities held in the main *praça* on Plateau and sporadic festivals on the beach (Quebra Canela). They are generally announced on the radio, posted on fliers and publicized by trucks driving around with large speakers. A popular and inexpensive weekend activity is to go to a soccer match at Varzea stadium or pull up a chair in a bar and watch a game.

Cruz de Papa

This park was inaugurated a few years ago in honor of Pope John Paul II's visit in 1990 and is popular in the evenings and during the weekend, especially during the summer. One of the first children's parks to be built in Cape Verde, it is fully equipped with colorful playground equipment, a statue of the pope and young palm trees. Even if you're not a child or don't have children, it is often the place to see or be seen. It is also a stopping point for beach goers as it looks out over Quebra Canela and the small platform that was built for the Pope's visit.

WHERE TO EAT

PLATEAU

 Casa Bela At the far end of Plateau around the corner from the American Embassy (#29), this little hole in the wall is a great find. During the week there is a great, inexpensive plate of the day posted outside the door. The wooden tables and benches are a rarity and framed photos of musicians decorate the walls. $

 Panorama Literally, the "high life" of Praia. The restaurant at the top of Hotel Felicidade offers catered dinners and a pay-by-weight buffet for lunch. A good option for vegetarians as there are salad items and the opportunity to pick sides without meat. It can get a bit expensive, but the upstairs dining is nice, looking out over the city. $$-$$$

Café Sofia The full name of this outdoor café is "Fashion Café Sofia" and it is accurate considering the clientele. One of the few places where it is possible to sit outside and watch life go by, there is a constant flow of Cape Verdeans, tourists and ex-pats. If you are looking for a quiet afternoon coffee, there are better options, but if you are looking to socialize and mingle, see and be seen, this is your best bet. Prices are a bit inflated and the service is terrible, but with a monopoly on location, anything goes. $$-$$$

Pão Quente This Portuguese bakery/café has expanded and is now open in Varzea as well. There are a variety of breads and a lunch menu that varies each day of the week. Prices are reasonable, the food is good and the service is upper mediocre. $$

Santiago

French Cultural Center Management of the café has changed hands multiple times for various reasons, but the excellent lunch buffet providing a variety of French and Cape Verdean dishes has been consistent throughout. $$$

 Café Sodadi Across the street from Pão Quente, this hole in the wall has quick snacks as well as a plate of the day (or two). Prices are far more reasonable than some of the foreign owned operations and you will avoid the group of beggars and vendors that have set up in front of the neighboring café. $

CasaNova The plate of the day will be listed on a chalk board outside the door. Price varies depending on the plate, but it is also possible to get more simple options, i.e. sandwiches, fruit juice or whatever happens to be available. $$-$$$

Chinese Hole in the Wall Located on Rua Serpa Pinto up the street from Residencial Santa Maria, you will have to look in the doors to find this little place. There is a short menu including dumplings, fried noodle dishes, soups and possibly the only place in Cape Verde to get tofu (*nika*). $$

Pink Chinese Place (May now be called Plateau Restaurant.) Offers a full menu of Chinese food with various soups, noodle and rice dishes and a variety of meats. Right by the *praça* by Café Sofia and bright pink, it is impossible to miss. $$

Sucupira

In the back of Sucupira, there are rows of stalls that offer a variety of plates for 150-200. The food is cooked in traditional Cape Verdean or Senegalese style and if you don't like the menu, just head to the next stall. Outside of Sucupira on the main street are a row of converted trailers that also serve lunch. The green trolley run by Mariza serves up a heaping delicious plate-of-the-day for 150$.

Varzea

Nôs Africa At the top of the shopping center in Sucupira, the menu here is comprehensive including dishes native to Cape Verde, Senegal and other African delicacies. The full menu may not always be available, but with all the options, you will not run out of choices. There is frequently live music and the view is unbeatable. $$$

Senegalese Place For a handful of change, get the Senegalese plate-of-the-day that won't let you down. Be prepared for some serious flavor. Eat at your own risk. $

Ponto de Encontro Marketed as a high-end Italian style eatery, the list of pizzas is a mile long and probably the best choice for variety. The pasta dishes are delicious, but quite pricy for small servings. $$$-$$$$

Achada Santo Antonio

Dona Didi Dona Didi (Senhora/Mrs. Didi) grills fish on the side of the road in Achada. Pull up a rusty chair and mingle with the hoards of taxi drivers that come for dinner. The fish comes with a heaping pile of rice, cooked vegetable salad and a mouth-watering salsa loaded with fresh cilantro. Soup and sandwiches stuffed with a seafood medley are also sometimes available. Open Monday-Friday from about 18:00 until she runs out of food. $

Artica Known for the ice cream, Artica also offers a full menu. Prices are a little steep but the plates are extremely generous and are more than sufficient for two. Don't leave without trying at least one flavor of ice cream, though you can get two flavors in one scoop! $$

A Bolha Across from the bus stop in Achada, this place is owned by a promi-nent Cape Verdean family. The service is lacking, but there is a full menu and a nice covered patio. Good for a quick *cafézinho*. $$

Marconi's Chwarma Spelled chwarma or shwarma depending on who made the sign, anywhere you see this famous word means an adaptation of the Middle Eastern treat. Marconi's in Achada is popular and offers a variety of other quick snacks. The wrapped delight generally consists of goat meat, french fries, tomatoes and a mystery sauce. $

Paragi A colorful little restaurant on the edge of Achada and Brasil. The neighborhood itself is one of the most colorful, but the walled in porch and fresh breeze are a great accompaniment to the fragrant Cape Verdean dish-es. Lunch is inexpensive, the flavor is great and the portions are perfect. $

Cometa The little round restaurant tucked away in the heart of Achada Santo António is a popular spot for young people and the occasional cultur-al/weekend activity. The food is fairly inexpensive and they cook up a variety of dishes—including decent pizza. $$

 Dragoeira Dragoeira and Benfica are owned and operated in exactly the same manner with the same menu around the corner from one another, yet both are extremely successful. They may offer other items, but your best bet is to choose between a grilled half-chicken or *pinchu* (pork skewers)—the best is Praia. Both are staple street foods during festivals, but if you can't wait for a festival to relish in the grilled delicacies, either restaurant won't let you down. On Saturdays, Benfica serves *feijoada* (a pork and bean mix with vege-tables served over rice). Pay close attention to your bill as they have been known to short change foreigners. $$

Casinha Velha Down the street from the blue chapel in Achada, it used to be known as the "best place for fish." Although The former owner has moved to the other side of Achada (see below), locals say that Dona Didi cooks up an equally delicious fish for a third of the price. The only thing she lacks is a menu and variety. $$$

The Owner of Casinha Velha...

The new restaurant for this French restaurant proprietor does have a name, but it is not visible from the outside. Instead, cross the street from Dragoeira, walk to the right and look up side streets on the left for the glowing red soccer ball. Here you can get delicious skewers of *barriga de atum* (meat from the tuna stomach) served with simple potatoes and the best salsa around. $$$

O Poeta Famous for the view, the food is fairly mediocre and the prices are a little steep. The first building on the left when you climb the hill to Achada. O Poeta sits on the hillside overlooking the bay. There is generally live music on Friday and Saturday. $$$-$$$$

Plaza Park Tucked in the dirt lot near the *Assembleia Nacional* (National As-sembly), this unlikely location guards one of the best kept secrets in Praia. The food and service here are excellent with a variety in the menu that is al-most unheard of elsewhere. Reportedly the best meat dishes in Praia. $$$$

Gamboa

BeraMar Famous for the grilled fish, the restaurant at the hotel of the same name is a nice place to sit outside, smell your dinner cooking and watch the city flow by. $$$

Santiago

Restaurant Gamboa One of the most expensive and upscale restaurants around, the quality of the food is reflected by the price. The menu is expansive and offers a good selection. $$$$

 Sovaca de Cobra The name means "armpit of the snake," and the restaurant is about as out of place as an armpit on a snake. Located up the hill in Terra Branca (not the nicest neighborhood, take a cab at night), there is a fairly comprehensive menu, but the specialty here is crêpes of any combination you could imagine. Also home of one of the best caiparinhas in Praia. $$

 Cimbrom Located under what used to be the Solimar Hotel, Cimbrom is a well executed small restaurant. Intimate indoor and outdoor seating available and the service is excellent. One of the few restaurants where you can find vegetarian dishes, and delicious ones at that! $$$

NIGHTLIFE

Most nightclubs in Praia operate with a strange cover charge. There is an obligatory fee, but it is paid at the end of the night based on your number of drinks. You will be given a card on entering and the number and price of beverages consumed is added to the card. Be careful not to lose it or you will have problems leaving. Also, be aware of when you are getting tired/fed up because the line to get out is generally longer than the line to get in.

In smaller venues, women can expect unwanted attention. Men are likely to grab your arm or try some method of coercing you to dance with them—be warned, persistence is considered key to getting what you want. The level of hassle goes down as the cover charge in the club goes up. There are a range of places to visit, some offering an intimate bar setting (Quintal de Zita, Zion), some have a more sophisticated environment (Kappa), and some boast live music (Fogo D' Africa, Quintal de Música).

 Quintal de Zita (So Sabi) For a relaxing bar experience, head to Quintal de Zita in Achada Santo António (near the Escola Tecnica around the corner from Marconi's Schwarma). A large rubber tree fills the quintal and, during the dry season, protects the wicker patio furniture. Can be a bit bleak during the rainy season as everything of value is removed for protection from the rain. The décor is the charm of this little watering hole.

Zion New to Palmarejo, this club run partially by Cape Verdean musician Vadu, Zion has quickly gained popularity. Up from the main *praça*, the cover charge is reasonable and drink prices are acceptable. A nice environment.. Status update: The club operation is unknown as Vadu was killed in a tragic car accident on January 13, 2010.

Blue Note A new jazz club in Praia, the popularity and success have yet to be determined. Located down the hill from the pharmacy in Palmarejo.

Voz di Povo This bar is also new to Praia. It was opened in the summer of 2009 on the bottom floor of the building of the old newspaper of the same name. *Voz di Povo* (the voice of the people) has quickly gained popularity and sometimes has film nights in partnership with the Fundação Amilcar Cabral and Language Link (see pg 237).

 Quintal da Música Located on Plateau, a weekly schedule of live, local music is posted outside the door. You can regularly find music and a quiet mix of clientele, drinks are obligatory, but the cover is easily surpassed.

Fogo D' Africa Off the main road in Tira Chapeau, you will find a mix of the best and worst of Cape Verde. A little grubbier than Quintal d' Musica, the music rivals its upscale counterpart without the expensive menu and classy crowd. The neighborhood is not the best and unaccompanied women can expect to be harassed, but it is unbeatable for a traditional *tocatinho* (jam session) and a taste of the reality of Cape Verde.

Kappa Down by the beach Quebra Canela, the restaurant is a popular upscale place, but the bar is a Friday night standby for many of the Praia elite. The atmosphere and crowd can be hit or miss. The upstairs bar has billiards. Kappa is often closed from August to September.

Zero Horas On the outskirts of the city in Achada Grande Tras, this club is aptly named as the party doesn't start until 00:00 (midnight). The open air club is a maze of balconies with a massive dance floor. You can expect to encounter a mixed crowd and probably a bit of claustrophobia.

Cockpit Practically across the street from Zero Horas, Cockpit caters to a slightly more upscale crowd. Considerably smaller and mildly more expensive, women will be treated with more respect here and, unless you are looking for attention, you will generally be left alone.

Max Club Often the location of CD release parties and live performances, Max Club is the more upscale of the clubs in Palmarejo. Thursday night is Reggae Night. Further up the hill is Cachoeira, easily recognized by the outdoor decoration (false trees on the pillars).

WHERE TO STAY

Being the capital, there are a multitude of places to stay in Praia. The best options for each price range are listed here.

Plateau

Sol Atlântico On the left as you climb into Plateau, the dingy rooms are certainly the most affordable on Plateau. Breakfast can be skimpy, but the rooms are more than acceptable for the low price. $ *Tel: 261.2872*

Hotel Felicidade Located centrally in Praia, the biggest appeal of Felicidade (also a chain of supermarkets in Praia) is Restaurant Panorama perched on the 6th floor of the building. The hotel boasts some 25 rooms and 2 suites. All amenities included (except elevators). Single $$, double $$$, suite $$$$ *Tel: 261.5584; www.hotelfelicidade.com*

 RosyMar Inn A gem in the heart of Plateau. Hidden on a side street behind the French Cultural Center, this *pensão* is worth finding. One of the oldest hotels in Praia (originally established in 1983) the entire building was updated, modernized and beautifully decorated with style and taste. Rosalina, the proprietor, lived in the U.S. for many years, is fluent in English and pays close attention to detail (sometimes a rarity with accommodations). All amenities and breakfast included. $$-$$$. *Tel: 261.6345; www.rosymarinn.com*

 Residencial Santa Maria & Residencial Praia Maria These hotels are on opposite streets and are perpetually confused by taxi drivers. Prices are the same at both hotels with a variety of rooms, single, double and suite (small extra beds also available) and both are impeccably clean. The layout and décor in Praia Maria is more appealing with an open sitting area and two floors of rooms on the perimeter. Santa Maria has a lot of floors and a lot of stairs. Breakfast is served at the very top. Single $$, double $$, suite $$$$, extra bed $ *Santa Maria, Tel: 261.8581; Praia Maria, Tel: Tel:261.4337*

Pensão Tchibita Located off the main road behind *Banco de Cabe Verde* (the Central Bank), Tchibita offers rooms with private and shared bathrooms. Sometimes there is hot water. $-$$ *Tel: 261.3491*

Santiago

Prainha

This short strip of land between Achada Santo António and the ocean is considered the "posh" neighborhood of Praia. There are a number of embassies, wealthy residents and the two four-star hotels. Aside from the beach, there is not much happening here.

 Hotel Pestana Tropico This former prison has been converted into the nicest hotel in Praia. Pleasant rooms look out into the courtyard over the pool. There is a fitness center and a great public bar on the edge of the pool. Breakfast is included at Restaurant Alex, arguably one of the best restaurants in Praia. $$$$-$$$$$ *Tel: 261.4200; www.pestana.com*

Hotel PraiaMar The "resort" of Praia, the grand yellow expanse offers everything from a pool/hot tub/outdoor café to tennis courts, fitness center and beyond. The dive center is headquartered on the grounds and the service meets/exceeds international standards. A standard single starts fairly low and the price increases with special requests (i.e. garden or ocean view). Singles, doubles and a variety of suites available. $$$$$-$$$$$$ *Tel: 261.4153; r eservas@oasisatlantico.com; www.oasisatlantico.com*

Chã d'Áreia

More commercial than residential, Chã d'Áreia connects Plateau with Achada Santo António and extends in the opposite direction to Sucupira and Fazenda.

BeraMar Hotel BeraMar has been under renovation to add another floor for guests. The rooms are open, clean and fresh. The restaurant is probably more famous for the grilled fish than the hotel. $$-$$$ *Tel: 261.6400; beramar@cvtelecom.cv*

 Hotel Perola Between BeraMar and the Shell station in Chã d' Áreia, Perola is fairly new and well-kept. The rooms are bright and spacious and the staff is welcoming. $$-$$$ *Tel: 260.1440; perola@cvtelecom.cv*

Bed & Breakfast

There is a new bed and breakfast above the Pão Quente across from the *Assemblea Nacional* and the *Biblioteca Nacional* (National Assembly and Library) that was opening at the time of research. May be worth checking out for modern, simple accommodations.

Achada Santo Antonio

Achada Santo António looks out over the coast and across expanse of city stretching off to the north. 'Chada (as referred to by those from Praia) is relatively quiet compared to the center of the city, offering more of a chance to wander freely during the day. There are a few cafés and popular restaurants that offer respite from the sun. There is also a lovely bookstore, Nhô Eugenio.

Pensão Holanda A little off the beaten path, you may encounter some unsavory company at night, but caution at night is always recommended. Holanda has been known for a while for the live music and familial feel toward residents. $$

Hotel América Located in the commercial heart of Achada Sto. António, Hotel América offers a quiet respite close to the beaches and only a few minutes away from Plateau. All amenities included and rooms range from single to suite, extra beds are available. $$$ *Tel: 262.1431; hotelamerica@cvtelecom.cv*

Hotel Roterdão Opened in the fall of 2009, Roterdão has yet to establish a reputation for itself. However, the bar/restaurant is quickly becoming known for happy hour and chicken wings, an influence from the owner's years abroad. $$

Palmarejo

Palmarejo sometimes has the feel of a ghost town. Built rapidly without full understanding of the market, it has been left with hundreds of apartments begging for sale under retail price. The boutiques and cafés rotate ownership and appearance around the already deteriorating central *praça*. It does have its appeal in certain respects. Many foreign investment programs are located in Palmarejo (Bournefonden for example) so the high number of expats draws some high-end establishments. Go to **HiperCompra** for food you won't find elsewhere—assorted fresh fruits and vegetables and imported grocery items—for a considerable price. *Padaria Palmarejo* (bakery of Palmarejo) has some delicacies, like chocolate stuffed loaves and the best whole wheat bread around.

Ola Mar Hotel This recently renovated hotel is an example of modernity. There are 30 rooms available in various sizes from single to suite. The hotel includes a beauty salon and restaurant and offers laundry, bar and island tours. $$$-$$$$ *Tel: 260.4540 / 4541; www.olamarhotel.com*

Pensão Benfica Is nice for what it is, a small scale family run hotel down by the coast. The restaurant is one of the better restaurants in Praia, but can seem a bit expensive. A major downside is the increasing crime in Palmarejo and the relative isolation of the *pensão*. Walking alone is not recommended. $$$-$$$$ *Tel: 262.7226*

Leaving Praia

To catch a car out of Praia, head to Sucupira. Behind the market there is a rank of cars that travel to the different parts of the island. Drivers will spot you as a tourist and try to get you in the car, some more aggressively than others. Be sure to hold onto your possessions and stand your ground if you don't want to go with a particular car—conditions of cars and drivers vary greatly. General price is 300$ to Assomada, 500-600 to Tarrafal. (Prices fluctuate greatly with the cost of gas, learn your numbers and pay attention to how much other passengers are paying.)

To save time, walk beyond Sucupira market and stand by the church on the opposite side of the street from Enacol. Most cars that start in the rank end up driving around in circles (*volta*) until the car is full. Alternately, if you are willing to pay, you can take a taxi—Assomada is roughly 2500$, Tarrafal 4000$-5000$ (one way).

Santiago

Cidade Velha

The road that leads along the west coast takes you to the birthplace of Cape Verde, Cidade Velha (old city) and beyond. If you are spending more than a day on Santiago, Cidade Velha is probably obligatory. Though it is close to the city, it is a nice, quiet escape that offers a bit of everything.

Special thanks to Konstantin Richter who contributed extensively to this section.

Heading along the coast on your way to this historic village, the road offers glimpses of the city below. The **Fortress of São Filipe** stands watch over the city—turn right before the descent to visit. Below, houses in various states of repair are scattered around the sites of historic significance. There is something uncanny about the contrast of old and new in the city square and as you walk around the small village, the tourist shops and restaurants contrast with the faded paint of old houses standing under the deteriorating cathedral ruins. The deeper into the *ribeira* you walk, the further removed from present time you become. It is almost as if the city simultaneously exists in different time periods.

GETTING THERE

Catch a Hiace from Sucupira or take the bus (#10 or #3) to the traffic circle where Terra Branca and Achada Sto. Antonio meet. On the right hand side of the road you will find MiniMercado Cidade Velha where Hiaces line up to cart passengers to and from the city. You should pay no more than 80-100$. To get back to Praia, hang out in the center of town waiting for a car to leave. Alternatively, you can take a taxi for 2000$ round trip.

HISTORY

On June 26, 2009, Cidade Velha (the old city), originally named Ribeira Grande, was granted status as a World Heritage Site by UNESCO. This title was granted for the city's role as the first European established city in the tropics. During the height of its reign as capital, Cidade Velha played an integral role in the transatlantic trade. People were brought from continental West Africa to Ribeira Grande in preparation for a life of slavery. They were used in the then lush fruit and sugar cane plantations deep in the *ribeira* (river bed) and shipped off to Europe and the Americas. From the few existing records, it is estimated that more than 28,000 slaves passed through Cape Verde from 1601 to 1700. The *pelourinho* (pillory), a monument to the cruelty of slavery and the punishment of slaves, still stands in the town's central square, now surrounded by West African vendors hawking cheap, mass produced wares.

Over the past few years the historical significance of the city and the idea of tourism have taken grasp. Just recently Proimtur, a tour company run jointly by the Cape Verdean government and the Spanish Cooperation, has taken responsibility for the historic sites and opened a restaurant and small bed & breakfast is gently hidden from the bustle a few moments walk

Fortaleza Real de São Filipe

Built between 1587 and 1593, the fort continues to stand watch over Cidade Velha and Ribeira Grande today. King Filipe I of Portugal ordered its construction after repeated pirate attacks, the most notable was Sir Francis Drake who took the city twice in 1578 and 1585. João Nunes of Portugal and Filipe Terzio of Italy worked together to design and build the Renaissance style structure. The walls jut out in a slightly stellar formation to allow for a full range of visibility and are angled for durability in the case of cannon attacks. Despite the efforts, Cidade Velha continued to be attacked and was finally defeated in 1712 when Jacques Cassard attacked the city from behind, coming over land from Praia.

into the *ribeira*. The restaurants of Cidade Velha are a popular spot on weekends as the Praia elite escape the city for a day.

Proimtur Excursions

To experience all the historic sites, Proimtur (Tel: 267.1618; proimtur@proimtur.com; www.proimtur.com) offers tours that begin at the fort and head down into the *ribeira* to the hidden historic underbelly of the city. Call in advance for a guaranteed guide. Groups are limited to 5 or 6 for 500$/person (250$ for Cape Verdeans).

WHAT TO DO: SELF GUIDED TOUR

If going by foot, it is a good idea to start at the fort and head down. Take the right turn before the descent to the city to arrive at **Foraleza Real de São Filipe**. A small tourist shop is built into the hillside opposite the entrance where you can pay 500$, watch a video about the history of Cidade Velha, have a cold drink (additional cost) and test your Portuguese and Spanish skills on the bilingual information plaques. There are a few limited souvenirs in the underground shop and many more in the city below.

The fort has been superficially restored and there are empty plaques denoting places of historical interest without the complimentary information; one can assume they will eventually be filled with information.

Caboverdeanity

In addition to the significance of Ribeira Grande in the Portuguese transatlantic trade route, it is also the birth place of "caboverdeanity," the essence of Cape Verdean creole culture. The origins of caboverdeanity are hotly debated even today as many disagree over whether the roots lie in Europe or in West Africa. Upon inspection and consideration, it is undeniable that these roots mixed and met before the culture came to fruition.

The Kriolu spoken today is a clear mix of Portuguese vocabulary and basic structure with a thick African flavor. The skin tone of Cape Verdeans range from the darkest dark to the lightest light. Blue and green eyes peek out of dark skin and hair tone and texture covers the entire spectrum.

Aside from physical appearances, the base of culture is also equally a European and African mix. The islands and towns are named after Catholic saints. Each town has a patron saint whose holy day is cause for mass celebration. Despite this distinctly European influence, day-to-day, one passes women with their heads wrapped and a child strapped to their back in an unarguably African manner. The traditional agricultural methods practices today can also be traced to Africa.

Though the influence from both sides exist – today it is appropriate to add the United States and Brazil to the already rich mix – what truly stands out is the fact that regardless of the influences, Cape Verde is uniquely Cape Verde. In his pursuit of caboverdeanity in *Compreensão de Cabo Verde*, author Manuel Ferreira concludes *"Afinal: Africa? Europa?: Cabo Verde."* (All things considerd: Africa? Europe?: Cape Verde.)

Santiago

From above, the *ribeira* appears as a vibrant green scar cut through the dusty brown landscape. Climate change and increasing drought have stopped the once flowing river, but water still trickles down to a small pool where it is not uncommon to find women bathing and washing piles of laundry.

On the opposite side of the fort, there is a path that leads down into the city. From here, you will be able to see the ruins of the **Cathedral.** The once ambitious project of Frei Francisco da Cruz, bishop for the Diocese of West Africa began around 1556, but was suspended during the 1590s for almost a century. It was not completed until 1699 through the enthusiasm of Bishop Vitoriano and the over 150 years of toil and labor were brought down after just 13 years when Jacques Cassard conquered the city. Not much is left but jagged remnants of the thick walls, the faded tomb and doorways that lead to nowhere. If you are lucky, Senhor TchoTcho will be playing the harmonica across the street.

As you head down the road into the center of the city, it is not unlikely that some houses you pass will have been constructed with the broken pieces of the Cathedral walls. There are a few small shops along the road where it is possible to purchase a cold drink or quick snack, but all the restaurants are clustered together in the center of town. Some tourist shops have sprung up amongst the remnants of times past. As you walk toward the *ribeira*, you will pass the *pelourinho* in the central *praça*. A few kiosks have been set up along the road and the two restaurants are set back along the coast. There is a little **beach** protected by a rock outcropping where it is possible to swim, watch the fishermen come in with the catch of the day and often find children caught up in a game of soccer.

Beyond the *praça*, turn left to head into the *ribeira* via Rua Banana, one of the oldest European built streets in Sub-Saharan West Africa. Along the street is Nos Origem, probably the most upscale restaurant in Cidade Velha, but not with the nicest staff.

Continue along the path and follow the signs to the **Igreja Nossa Senhora do Rosário**, the church of Our Lady of the Rosary, patron saint of the blacks of Cidade Velha. Built in 1495, it is one of the oldest buildings in Cidade Velha. Nearby, the **Convento de São Francisco** was built around 1640 and, despite attempts in 1712 during the Cassard invasion to destroy the monastery and educational center, the remains that stand today are a credit to its quality of construction.

If you continue into the heart of the *ribeira*, you will pass **Pousada Nacional de São Pedro** built by Proimtur. Where the trees thin, the path forks and climbs a hill to the right where the sugar cane is transformed into the national drink of choice, *grogue* (sugarcane rum). The factory of Fortaleza *grogue* is open to visitors, though there is no formal tour. You will be able to smell the cooking sugar cane as you climb the hill. A pile of crushed sugar cane towers over the little hut where barrels of the potent liquid are stored. Across the way, a fire is kept burning to steam the liquid. Inside, drops of *grogue* pour constantly from the narrow pipes. If you are feeling adventurous, take a sip!

Beyond the factory, the path continues on through the mango and banana trees. The occasional Baobab tree stands head and shoulders above the rest and a series of dykes leave algae filled pools. Water becomes more abundant the further you travel until you reach the pool at the end where water trickles from the massive rock wall. At a casual pace, you can reach the end of the *ribeira* in about an hour.

WHERE TO EAT

Restaurant Pelourinho Part of the Proimtur group, the dark furniture and outdoor seating is immediately visible. The food is nice and there is an extensive menu that may or may not be available depending on supply. Beware of the posts as the cheap varnish gets sticky in the heat and humidity and rubs off easily on skin and clothing. $$$-$$$$

 Local Restaurant Next door to Pelourinho there is a smaller, slightly less glossy and less expensive locally owned restaurant. The menu is not as extensive, but it is still possible to get the basics; chicken and fries, grilled fish and assorted other seafood. Fried *moreia* (moray eel) is always a popular snack. $$-$$$

 Real Turis As you enter the bay area in the center of town, you will see a yellow building of the same name. Advertised as a sort of cultural center, this entirely Cape Verdean owned operation offers a wide range of souvenirs made on the various islands. On Saturdays, they host information sessions, cultural events, films and a traditional lunch. Lunch is only available on Saturdays. $$$$

Casa Velha Opposite of Real Turis is a tastefully decorated restaurant, Casa Velha. It is generally ignored by the escapees of Praia because of location and price. It would be more popular if it was on the beach, but it is nice for a sit down meal. $$$

WHERE TO STAY

Real Turis The souvnir shop/cultural center has converted an old house into a Bed & Breakfast. Arguably one of the most beautiful and well put together hotels on Praia, the three rooms are immaculate and tastefully decorated. From the minute you walk through the door, it is evident that a lot of time was spent putting the various artifacts and rooms together to make the house feel like home. Breakfast is prepared in the cozy kitchen and the three rooms are a single, double and "suite." $$-$$$

Pousada Nacional São Pedro Built in 2005, the five rooms are hidden away in a lush area. There is an outdoor patio set up to enjoy the cool, fresh air. The rooms are simply furnished and well kept. $-$$ *Tel: 267.1618; proimtur@proimtur.com; www.proimtur.com*

Residencial Pôr do Sol If you continue down the road leading away from Praia, in a short while you will come upon Por do Sol. The patio practically hangs over the coastline and a built in pool and tables with umbrellas make it an ideal location to watch the sunset (por-do-sol = sunset). The rooms are nice, if a little expensive and meals are pleasant as well. $$-$$$. *Tel: 267.1622; m. 9912136*

Artesanato

As you pass through the center and enter the mouth of the *ribeira*, the Proimtur headquarters is adjacent to Sulada, a souvenir/*artesenato* shop established and run entirely by the local women's association (ACCVE). The products available are made in neighboring São João Baptista and the money made from sales directly impacts the lives of many otherwise unemployed women.

Santiago

West Coast

Beyond Cidade Velha, the road continues on to **Porto Mosquito**. The airport in Praia boasts an image of Porto Mosquito that is enticing and enchanting. Though the small port is both of the above, there is a reality there that is carefully removed from the touched up photography. As is generally the case, fishing villages tend to suffer more poverty than other villages due to their isolation and source of survival. In mainly agricultural villages, there is more of a sense of respect for the land from which sustenance is cultivated. The very meticulous and deliberate nature of agriculture leads to a more careful and calculated existence. The very nature of fishing villages is quite the opposite. There is still limited agriculture and breeding of livestock but here, the ocean is king.

The fishermen are subject to the changing moods of the vast expanse of Atlantic and the unpredictability of each days catch makes every day a gamble. Standing above the small cove in Porto Mosquito, pigs and dogs run wild in the dirty streets. A dilapidated house stands directly behind you, but the boats are beautifully painted and maintained, each with a creative, though sometimes inappropriate, name. Each day, as the boats come in, the children flock down to the water to help pull in the boat and examine the day's catch. Fishing is arguably one of the most dangerous professions in the world, and is certainly at least one of the top three in Cape Verde. In villages like Porto Mosquito, the men head out each day in tiny boats to try their luck on the open seas. There is an abrasive quality in the way the men shout over one another in competition, but the laughter that reigns supreme is thick and rich like no other.

From Porto Mosquito it is possible to hire a boat for a day (roughly 5000$) to take you to the **Santa Clara cliffs,** about 5 km up the coastline. The journey includes the varying geography of the Santiago coastline, including non-volcanic buttes pushed up from tectonic shift, the crisp blue ocean and a few species of coastal birds not readily visible elsewhere. After about 40 minutes, the boat rounds an outcropping and the dizzying cliffs come into view. Their immensity is indescribable and hardly recognizable until a lone fisherman is spotted in a small crevice, dwarfed by his surroundings.

The water in this protected cove is incredibly pure and blue and it is possible to see various types of fish playing amongst the rocks from above. Bring a snorkel and swimming goggles and swim amongst schools of flitting silver fish while larger and more colorful fish meander below. Your guide will be more than happy to take you for a little fishing excursion within the cove, and the relatively untouched waters will reap nothing but success.

The pristine location of the cliffs is a stark contrast to the reality of the village. To climb into the boats, it is necessary to climb up and over a giant rock that doubles as a public toilet. Watch your step, hold your nose and remember the destination is well worth it. The excursion is fairly inexpensive and that money will make a significant difference for at least one family.

East Coast

The new road system on Santiago has been largely funded by the Millennium Challenge Corporation and while the future of the asphalt remains to be seen, it has increased accessibility to many once isolated communities and the pace of life in increasingly less remote areas. Hiaces scream around corners, packed with people and their purchases along the smoothly paved roads at speeds that don't seem wise for the varying terrain.

> One small place that is growing exponentially from this venture is São Fransisco.

SÃO FRANCISCO

São Fransisco was once a quiet village just inside the *conselho* of Praia. A few years ago, it was almost entirely isolated and people were outnumbered by livestock. The road there was in terrible condition and many students stopped going to school after grade school for want of transportation. Today, it is a rapidly growing suburb of Praia. As of May 2009, it became possible to travel to this remote village on a newly paved road. The motivation of paving the road did not come from the desire to create opportunities for the isolated inhabitants, but rather to connect Praia with the beach that exists just beyond the small village. The new road has dropped the price of taxi rides to 500-1000 and during the summer months, buses run on a set schedule for 150$ (see advertisements in bus windows for scheduling). If spending a few days in Praia, it is an excellent way to get out of the city and enjoy the sun and sand.

As you approach the village, there is a traffic circle connecting the paved road from the airport, the half-paved road from Paiol, the paved road to the beach and the unpaved road into São Francisco. The village itself is quite small (300-400 people) and at certain times of day, you are more likely to encounter goats in the streets than people. Within the past year, a central *praça* was built, a *polivalente* is being constructed and computers have been donated to the once neglected school. From almost everywhere in São Francisco it is possible to see the portentous buildings of Sambala looking out from the opposite plateau. The recent development of São Francisco can likely be accredited to the emergence of this tourism giant trying to claim the beach of São Francisco as its own. The beach is itself quite nice, though it can be windy.

On the weekends, the beach can be busy, the sand packed with people fleeing the city. There is a rock outcropping that separates the beach into two distinct parts and it generally also separates the local crowd from visitors. Venture over to the far beach for a more colorful crowd, more enthusiastic drinking, talking and games of soccer. You will also find less wind and calmer waters. For men, if you stand around the bar and try out your burgeoning Kriolu skills, you will find an enthusiastic audience (and teachers). Women will find an enthusiastic group of admirers.

For a different perspective, visit German ex-pat Thomas and his mother. They live tucked away in the verdant *ribeira* and work hard to maintain a hydroponic farm that supplies many local restaurants with vegetables during the barren dry season. He is always up for conversation if you catch him during some down time and will tell you all about the challenges of agricultural life in Cape Verde trying to coax life from the dry soil while keeping the crops safe from the occasional flood during the rainy season and herds of drunk beach goers in the summer months. Bring cigarettes and you'll have a friend for life.

Where to Stay

Sambala The self proclaimed leading luxury development of Santiago, Sambala is currently in the second phase of a proposed eleven phases. The 20 sq km of land that surround the village are privately owned and will eventually be transformed into an island oasis–including displacing an entire village in favor of a golf course. Currently, there is a cluster of buildings around a tennis court and pool. Every weekend, there is a barbeque around the pool for 1500$ (three drinks included). It is possible to rent one of the many empty townhouses for a weekend stay. $$$$ *Tel: 264.8000; m. 987.4089* *www.sambaladevelopments.com*

Where to Eat

For now, there is one lonely restaurant looking out over the water, but the food is well worth the wait. The fish is always fresh and well-prepared, and be sure to try the *arroz mariscos* (shell-fish rice). Open during the weekend and sometimes on weekdays in the summer. There are also a number or restaurants scheduled to open in Sambala.

The Road North

If you are only on Santiago for a few days, the best way to get the full-bodied flavor of Santiago is to take a trip around the island. There is a road that runs along the spine of the island, climbing to impossible heights and winding around tight, treacherous bends that eventually lead all the way to the northern bay of Tarrafal. On a clear day, the road offers spectacular views of the interior of the island, but even on a cloudy day, the few visible houses clinging to cliff-sides and the steep terracing are a sight of wonder.

SÃO DOMINGOS

São Domingos is the seat of the *conselho* and in the past few years, a hospital has been built, the high school expanded with a whole new wing and an athletic facility, and the road has been paved. As you approach the town, a new road forks to bypass São Domingos, a project that has greatly reduced the number of accidents and pedestrian deaths on the narrow winding roads. Take the left turn to enter São Domingos and you will find a vital and active little community..

Continuing on, the turn up to Rui Vaz will be on the left after the *correios* (post office) and *Câmara Municipal.* For a quick snack, stop in the bakery at the corner and get some bread or grab some fruit from the ladies who set up shop on the corner. You will almost immediately hit an intersection where you will turn right to head up to Rui Vaz. Be sure to stop in **Bar 7 Estrelas** and try Cheena's homemade *ponche* , which she makes in her house and sells it by the bottle or shot. Try the coconut *ponche*, or for a lighter, less sweet flavor, *tambarina* is always a good bet. Empty wine bottles are welcomed as they are reused.

Exposisão Artesanto

Almost immediately upon passing the school, there will be a sign on the left of the road pointing to the Artesanato Shop, off the road to the right. This small building displays pottery, painting, various cloths and recycled art produced in São Domingos. Neusa Riberio and her father make bags and other assorted items from juice and water bottles. May be a good idea to call ahead because posted hours are merely a suggestion. *Tel: 268.1211; Open Mon-Sat 8:30-12:00, 14:00-18:00*

RUI VAZ

From São Domingos, the road climbs steeply up to the peaceful, sleepy village of Rui Vaz. Hidden up in the mountains, the only sign of life from below is the outcropping of television and radio towers. However, this mystical little village has much more to offer. From here, it is possible to climb **Pico de Antónia**. At 4573 feet (1394m), it is the highest peak of Santiago. A guide is highly recommended for this hike and it is not for the faint of heart.

If you climb to the towers, there is a little trail that will take you to the adjacent peak of Monta Xota. From that peak, you can look out over the ocean and, on a clear day, gaze out on distant Fogo. It is also possible to hike down into neighboring São Jorge and spend some time in the flourishing Botanical Gardens. On Sunday all of these highlights are overshadowed by the Sunday lunch buffet at Quinta da Montanha, the local hotel. There are a few small stores scattered around the hotel and throughout the village, but Quinta da Montanha has a monopoly on food service. Speak with Lindorfo to arrange a local guide for any of the hikes.

Where to Stay & Eat

Quinta da Montanha The project of Lindorfo, this once small hotel had grown quite a bit and, in turn, made a large impact on the community. It employs many young people from Rui Vaz and São Domingos and uses locally grown vegetables for the famous Sunday lunch buffet (1400$, drinks extra). There is a conference room that can be rented for business or personal events and now has 28 rooms. Guides can be arranged through the hotel for hikes to Pico. Breakfast and hot water included with room; lunch and dinner available for 1200$. Single $$, double $$$ *Tel: 268.5002 / 5003, m. 992.4013; quintamontanha@cvtelecom.cv*

MOVING ON

After São Domingos, there will be a left hand turn off the main road where to you can access São Jorge, the botanical gardens and the INIDA (*Instituto Nacional de Investigação e Desenvolvimento Agrário*—National Institute of Investigation and Development of Agriculture) agricultural projects there. Stay straight to continue north.

SÃO LOURENÇO DOS ÓRGÃOS

You will know you have arrived when you reach the rotary in front of the brand new school with a poorly covered crack running straight through the middle. Not to be confused with São Jorge, São Lourenço is a fairly new *conselho* on Santiago.

Santiago

Botanical Garden Loop

Before you reach Quinta da Montanha, there is an unmarked trail that leads down to the Botanical Garden Loop. It begins with a fifteen minute steep and rocky descent. When you reach the sign, you can either continue straight ahead for a more casual walk through the roads leading gradually down to São Jorge dos Orgãos. If you bear right, the steep rocky descent continues through the *ribeira* until you reach the Botanical Gardens. In São Jorge, you will pass through the INIDA agricultural research center that has introduced new farming techniques and provides employment for cultivation of land. They are also responsible for the Botanical Garden that protects and displays endemic species.

The trail was established as a protected area and marked by the French Corporation. Though there are occasional chipped green posts marking the trail, it has not been well maintain and it is easy to wander off on one of the many intersecting paths. Be sure to keep an eye out for the posts and ask people as you go.

Established in 2005, São Lourenço's claim to fame is as the home to the Polião dam, the first dam built in the country. The dam was funded by the Chinese and cost 38 million CVE. This site is currently part of a project funded by USADF through the local association in Bom Pão to more effectively regulate the use of water from the dam and introduce more sustainable practices for agriculture and irrigation.

During the dry season, the lingering water of the dam is a welcome sight. Little patches of green encircle the dirty water, breaking up the seemingly endless rocky, brown lands and birds flock from throughout the island to revel in the water.

Bear right at the rotary to head towards Pedra Badejo and the Polião Dam, or left to continue on towards Assomada.

Assomada of Santa Cantarina

The *conselho* (district) of Santa Catarina is nestled between the two mountain ranges of Santiago—the Serra de Pico Antónia and Serra Malgueta. Only in this once sleepy metropolis is it possible to forget that beyond the distant mountains, you are surrounded by water.

The center of Assomada is fairly small and contained, but its fingers stretch across a great expanse of land leading all the way to the western coastline. Recently upgraded to "city" status, it is home to two large high schools, the well equipped and modern Escola Tecnica and the public high school, which is overflowing with more than 6,000 students—a number that rivals the populations of Boa Vista, Maio and Brava.

The city itself is worth visiting on market days, Wednesdays and Saturdays. The large dirt field at the end of the *avenida* fills with livestock for sale and trade and the streets in the center of town fill to twice the capacity with women and men trying to sell anything you could imagine. The rest of the week you

This land was first settled by slaves fleeing indentured labor and violence in the increasingly dangerous port of Cidade Velha.

will find a few vendors in the vast market place. The municipal fruit and vegetable market is always bustling, and is possibly livelier than that of Praia.

If you are looking to experience Santiago, Assomada is an ideal central location. The city itself is not on the coast, but there are outlets to the ocean within Santa Catarina that are more interesting and less hectic than those of Praia. From Praia, a trip to Tarrafal, Calheta or Serra Malgueta can be long and exhausting, but from Assomada, everything is just a quick ride away. Tourism in Assomada has developed in the past few years, but is still lacking in some areas. Where there was once no place to stay and hardly any places to eat, there is now an array of choices. Fortunately, there is something for every budget.

> Amilcar Cabral was raised in a small house in Assomada, off the main road heading north. The house is not marked, nor is it open to the public.

GETTING THERE

It is possible to take a Hiace from Sucupira to Assomada for around 200$. You can catch the Hiace at the mouth of the road to Sucupira, but you may be better off walking up to the intersection at the Enacol station and waiting on the road by the church on the corner. It is still likely that you will end up turning back to fill the car, but chances are you will make less *voltas* (circuits around the city searching for passengers).

If you are already between Praia and Assomada or Assomada and Tarrafal, wave down any car passing and ask to be dropped in Assomada. Alternatively, it is possible to take a taxi for 2500$ one way.

IMPORTANT INFORMATION

Bank There are a variety of banks in Assomada—BCA, BCN, Caixa Económica— mostly along the Avendia or the main road. All banks are open Monday-Friday from approximately 8:00-15:00.

Hospital Tel: 265.1130

Pharmacy: *Farmácia Santa Catarina;* Tel: 265.2121

Police Polícia Near the *Palácio de Justiça*; Tel: 265.1132 / 265.1212

TACV Tel: 265.1122

WHAT TO DO

Museu da Tabanka

Located across the main *praça* of the *Camâra Municipal* and above the market, the Tabanka Museum is impossible to miss. The building is a pleasantly renovated *sobrado* that holds a variety of historic items. There is an open theatre space and the museum frequently hosts exhibits, concerts and local theatre groups. Check for advertisements outside or speak with one of the employees for upcoming events. *Tel: 265.5122, Mon-Fri 9:00-13:00, 15:00-18:00; Sat 9:00-16:00; Cost: 500$*

Santiago

Boa Entrada

A short hike from the geometrically intriguing *praça* by the BCA, the sometimes slippery path takes you down into the *ribeira* where you will find an entirely different life from the one you left moments ago. You can feel the air changing as you enter an eternally moist haven of green. An intricate system of irrigation makes it possible to continue agricultural practice throughout the year. During the months of May and June, the path and trees are overflowing with mangoes. The culmination of the short hike is the giant Boabab tree that is rumored to have existed before the Portuguese discovery of the islands.

Águas Belas

This beautiful and intriguing Grotto on the coast can be reached by a variety of methods. For the hiker, begin in Achada Leite (shorter) or Chão de Tanque (longer) and walk toward the coast. (If at any point you are unsure, ask a passerby.) It is also possible to charter a boat from Rincão or Ribeira de Barca (around 2000$).

Fonte Lima

During market days, you will find the production of pottery expressing life in Cape Verde and on Santiago. This pottery is locally produced in the zone of Fonte Lima (down the *ribeira* on the left as you enter Assomada).

Artesenato Terra Terra

If you can't make it to Fonte Lima, be sure to peruse the crafts in this shop located up the street from Café Central. The hours say it is open 9:00-18:00, but beware of extended lunch breaks. *Tel: 265.2668, m. 992.4954*

Rincon

This small fishing village is in the process of being connected to the main drag by a newly paved road. The long trip west is probably only worth it if you have time and are looking to pass the day in a leisurely, isolated spot. Rincon has been in a somewhat static state, heavily reliant on fishing and small scale agriculture and livestock ventures, it was/is truly a place untouched by the modern world. Time will change this, but in many ways, the village will remain a small coastal village with a stunning view of Fogo.

The Boabab Tree

The Boabab is awe inspiring for its sheer size, but also the astonishing way in which it grows, roots pouring out the sides like many searching arms. Holes and crevices are entangled in the trunk and branches pour out into the sky in all directions. In continental Africa, the Boabab is considered a sacred tree and serves many purposes. In Central Africa, when women give birth, the placenta is buried at the roots of the Boabab, eternally tying the child to home. The sinewy bark is commonly used to make rope and the tree also produces the chalky *calabaceira* fruit that is used in Cape Verde as a flavoring for *frescinhas* and *ponche*.

Ribeira de Barca

This fishing village is nestled in the *ribeira* and is the birthplace of the emerging musician, Tcheka. There is a little bit of everything here with fruits and vegetables in the verdant ribeira, a constant supply of fresh fish, small restaurants and a hit-or-miss nightclub. It is possible to swim where the village meets the sea (though it may be a little dirty), or ask around for the hike/boat ride to a isolated beach up the coast.

Hiking Around Rincon

Take a day hike to Selada (pronounced, Say-Lah-Duh) by following the main riverbed which separates the upper and lower sections of town. At the first fork, veer to the right. After 3 km you'll come upon many irrigated fields. Follow the riverbed another 2 km and you'll come to a spring fed creek with running water year round. A risky devil climber might be able to get past it and reach the source.

WHERE TO EAT

The restaurants listed are in central Assomada. Though there are restaurants in some of the smaller villages, they may be irregular. When out hiking, bring a supply of water, fruit or bread (available in all markets) and ask around for a *prato de dia* or the closest *loja* (shop).

 Pingo Pingo (Casa Lesa) Around the corner from the Lamfil supermarket, Pingo Pingo is an old reliable in Assomada. The meals take a while to be prepared, but there are no surprises. The plate of the day is generally a safe bet and so is the *frango* (half a grilled or fried chicken) or *bife de atun* (tuna steak). $$. *Tel: 265.3517*

Festivals of Santa Catarina

Municipal Festivals	Tabanka Festivals
February 11 – Figueira das Naus	May 15 – Chão de Tanque
15 days after Easter – São Salvador do Mundo	June 13 – Achada Grande,
May 1 – Serra Malagueta	Charco, Lém Cabral
May 13 – Assomada	June 24 – Boca de Mato,
May 30 – Achada Leitão,	Mato Sancho
Mato Baixo	June 29 – Ribeira Manuel
May 31 – Ribeira de Barca	
June 29 – Rincão	
July 5 – Palha Carga	
July 26 – Achada Lém	
August 5 – Chão de Tanque	
October 1 – Ribeira Manuel	
November 25 – Assomada	
November 30 – Santo André	

Restaurant Asa Branca Across from the *correios*, Asa Branca has an extensive menu and most of the items are usually available. The price varies depending on the plate, but the food is generally of good quality. A nice place to sit with a cold beer and watch the traffic go by. $$-$$$

Lamafil A little kiosk in the market/praça area, not to be confused with the grocery store of the same name. Plates here are simple: chicken and french fries, maybe *pinchu* (pork skewers) and cold beer. The number of clientele drastically increases when there is a soccer game on television. $-$$

 Lanchonette Tribo Brasil Across from Pingo Pingo. It is rumored that this little watering hole has changed management, but it used to be the best place to get a capirinha. Also a good place to simple meals, pizza, hamburgers, pastries, etc. $$-$$$ *Tel: 265.2011*

Cozinha de Avo (Grandma's Kitchen) One of the three buildings sharing the street name with Hotel Prestige, this restaurant has earned its name. A favorite with locals that have spare change to spend, the price can be higher than the hole in the wall restaurants, but definitely worth it. $$$

Nova Alegria Has been dubbed "the blue bar" for the strange blue mood lighting. It may not seem like much, but the menu is fairly extensive and a nice touch is the choice between a full plate and a half-plate. Full plates can be more than enough food for two, so if you are fed up with being fed, try the half-plate (it is also less expensive!). $-$$

Restaurant Silvina One of the nicer restaurants in Assomada, located across the street from the BCA. Simple plates start at 700$ and range to 1500$ (seafood). The food is all well made and served in generous proportions. $$$ *Tel: 265.1019 / 265.3789*

Mercado Municipal Along the edge of the market there are women who make a variety of food to serve up a quick lunch.. You are guaranteed a heaping plate of rice, beans and the chosen meat of the day. You typically won't find traditional style meals (*cachupa*, *feijoada*, etc.), but you will experience typical Cape Verdean cooking. (Warning: There is a chance your stomach may not agree with your delicious meal...) $

Café Central Aptly named for its central location, this place has it all. There are computers with internet access and probably the most appetizing and full menu. Prices are a little higher than other smaller restaurants, but, like everywhere, portions are generous and appetizing. $$-$$$

Cachoeira Padaria/Pastelaria From the outside it looks like a corporate business center, but inside you will find an array of delicious baked goods. Perfect for a quick coffee and snack. $$

 Hotel Avenida Has a buffet style lunch with pay-by-pound including a mix of traditional plates and Cape Verdean homestyle cooking. 100 grams for 90$. $$-$$$

NIGHTLIFE

Tropical is the main nightclub in Assomada, but has become increasingly dangerous over the last few years. Fights are a regular occurrence, as are muggings and pick-pocketing.

> Special thanks to Tina Robbins for contributing to this section.

If you can, go with a local for a loud, sweaty, sexually charged night of dancing. Apparently, it is also the best place for grilled chicken in Cape Verde.

Women are advised not to go into the club alone. Cape Verdean men can be quite aggressive in *asking* for a dance. Females should know that just walking down Main Street at noon is just cause for some Cape Verdean males to propose marriage. They will appear shocked and hurt when you refuse this, totally heart-felt query, but other than being annoying, they are for the most part harmless.

WHERE TO STAY

All places listed below are located in the city of Assomada unless otherwise noted)

 Cosmos This towering modern building stands opposite of the municipal market, giving a stark contrast of two different sides of life. The building boasts office spaces, boutique shopping a hotel and a restaurant at the top with a panoramic view of the cityscape and mountainous region spreading beyond. The only drawback may be the many flights of stairs that stand between the guest and the hotel on the 4th floor. $$$ *Tel: 265.1596; ccomercialcosmos@mail.pt; adsl6551@cvtelecom.cv*

 Prestige Located off the beaten path on Rua Antonio Hopffer Cordeiro Almada (there are possibly more words in the name of the street than buildings located on the street), Prestige offers a quiet escape from the sometimes busy city. The rooms are well kept with all amenities. Rooms range in size and quality from singles to a three person suite. Breakfast is included in cost with an option of adding 1000$/day for lunch, 2000$ for lunch and dinner. It is also possible to arrange excursions to various parts of Assomada and Santiago through the hotel. Price varies depending on the trip. The hotel is entirely Cape Verdean owned and operated. $$$ *Tel: 265.5000; hotelprestige@cvtelecom.cv*

Hotel Avenida Named for its location on the Avenida, this hotel offers 17 clean, fresh and simple rooms with all amenities. Breakfast is included and lunch is self-service buffet (pay by kilo). Add 500$ for A/C. $$ *Tel: 265.3462; hotelavenidaj@hotmail.com*

Hotel Vidalcre This hotel looks over the Shell station as you enter Assomada from Praia. There are 14 rooms, well kept with hot water and private bathrooms. . Breakfast is included and lunch and dinner are available on request. $$ *Tel: 265.4519*

Pensão Monacri This newly renovated *pensão* is located across the street from the Shell station. The staff was not immediately friendly, but everything is neat and well kept. Definitely a safe bet if travelling on a budget. Singles, doubles and triples are available. Rooms are equipped with hot water and private bathrooms and lunch and dinner are available on request (500-700$). $$ *Tel: 265.1932*

Pensão Passagem Located off the main road before the green T-Mais building. There are six double rooms available for hourly or nightly rental. Good for a budget, but you might get what you pay for. $ *Tel: 265.2118*

MOVING ON

From Assomada, it is possible to see the mountains of Serra Malagueta looming large to the north. Between the city and the mountain range, you can bear left and head toward Ribeira da Barca. The *pensão* Cote de France is set on the right side of the road in Achada Lem between the city of Assomada and the mountain range of Serra Malagueta.

Santiago

You will take a step back in time as you continue north and the road switches from asphalt to cobblestone and the surrounding area becomes yet more remote. As the car begins the ascent into the mountains, the sight of Santa Catarina below is something to behold. If you are not careful, you will miss the poorly placed sign welcoming you to the park. The altitude and jagged peaks frequently grab hold of passing clouds and visibility can drop to a few feet on a cloudy day.

Serra Malagueta National Park

Over the past few years, a lot of work has been done with the Parque Natural and within the community of Serra Malagueta to mark trails, identify endemic species of plants and wildlife and to establish this

| Parque Natural de Serra Malagueta |
| Tel: 237.1829; fax. 237.1835 |
| ecotourism.pnsm@gmail.com |

protected area as an up-and-coming spot for ecotourism. The people that live high up in the mountains mostly practice subsistence farming, some of which is sold in the markets of Tarrafal, Assomada and Praia.

The United Nations Development Programme (UNDP) and U.S. Peace Corps have been working to protect natural park areas and endemic species. Part of this effort has included the introduction of a variety of irrigation and farming techniques to help maximize the resources available for an increased yield. Some techniques include the use of nets designed to capture moisture from the fog of the perpetually cloudy slopes. Farmers have also used empty glass bottles stacked in the soil to capture and store moisture.

While these steps have not dramatically altered farming in general, they have taken a step toward new, resource-conscious methods. The introduction of ecotourism to the parks in Cape Verde is also a step. While it will not immediately make any dramatic changes to the way of life of the residents or visitors, it is a step toward preserving what remains of endemic species and reminding everyone how precious and valuable the resources are.

Check out www.ecoserramalagueta.cv for full descriptions about the projects within the park, a complete list of endemic species with photos for identification, a hiking map (available at the *Casa do Ambiente*, the visitors' center along the main road) and descriptions of marked trails and photos. The center can also arrange for guided tours with knowledgeable, trained guides as well as help you arrange a meal or a place to stay at a local home. There is a project to develop a small *pensão* in the area, but as of yet, it is not ready. Because the area is remote, the park requests advance notice for visitors looking for a meal or place to stay.

Tortolho

This unique shrub was originally found on all the islands but Boa Vista, it now flourishes only on the island of São Nicolau and in the mountains of Serra Malagueta on Santiago. Tortolho (*Euphorbia tuckeyana*) is characterized by its pointed leaves grouped in rosette clusters. The waxy leaves encourage the distribution of water onto the dry, rocky soil in which they thrive. The milky latex within the leaves is also mildly toxic and was used for tanning animal hide.

WHERE TO STAY & EAT

Cote de France This four room refuge is a beautiful and quiet base within the heart of Santiago. On the outskirts of Assomada in Achada Lem, it is in an excellent location for access to the mountains, Tarrafal, Ribeira de Barca and Serra Malagueta. Rooms include private bathrooms with hot and cold water, television and simple, tasteful décor. If you don't stay, definitely stop by for lunch or dinner (12:00-15:00 and 19:00-21:00) as the restaurant is excellent. Reservations recommended. $$ *Tel: 235.7431; barbosacorreia3@yahoo.fr*

Homestays Contact the park to see if there are homestays available. The park is in the process of gathering resources to build a small Bed & Breakfast in Serra Malagueta, but this was not complete at the time of research.

Camping Contact the park for approval if you are planning to camp. As of now, there is no organized camping or regulations, though this is something that they are working toward with the current efforts.

HORTELÃO & RIBEIRA PRINCIPAL

One of the more popular hikes from Serra Malagueta leads you down through Ribeira Principal. The village of Hortelão can be difficult to get to and to get out of by car, but it is here that many of the *doces* (jams) sold in the airport, grocery stores and shops around the island are made.

In the past, a *formação* (training) was held for the weaving of *panu di terra* in an effort to revive the dying art form unique to Cape Verde. The training was held for women throughout the area, but centralized in Hotelão. Contact the community center for the status of the project (Tel: 263.6622). The cloth produced is available at the *artesanato* center at the Parque in Serra Malagueta where you can watch girls weaving. Although more expensive than that in Praia, it is hand woven by local women. The more inexpensive cloth can be a cheap imitation either machine woven or a pattern pressed onto mass produced fabric.

What is Eco-Tourism?

As tourism has rapidly developed through advances in transportation and technology, there has been a growing push for responsible tourism. In 1996, the World Conservation Union defined ecotourism as *"Environmentally responsible travel and visitation to natural areas, in order to enjoy and appreciate nature (and accompanying cultural features, both past and present) that promote conservation, have low visitor impact and provide for beneficially active socioeconomic involvement of local peoples."*

Though there are not established excursions in the mountains of Cape Verde, the parks have made efforts to establish responsible practices by aiding and including the population in decision making and employment and making efforts to protect the more than twenty endemic species of plants found within the parks.

One particular species, the Carqueja de Santiago (*Limonium lobinii*), is found only on Santiago. You'll be able to spot the small bush (around a half meter tall) on the face of rocky cliffs by its florescent violet blue coloration. As it only grows between altitudes of 500-800 meters, the species is very rare not only to Cape Verde, but the world. It can only be found on the cliffs of Chã das Figueiras, Chiquinho, Ponta Chada, Ribeira Cuba and on the cliffs NE of Pedra Comprida.

Santiago

Tarrafal

Touted as the must see beach of Santiago, travelers from Praia should be prepared for a long journey. The trip begins smoothly over the paved road past the mountain range of Pico de Antónia and on through Assomada. After you pass through the center of the city, however, the hands on the clock wind back and you find yourself rattling along through the mountains on cobblestone. The sheer drop from the side of the road rivals only those of Santo Antão and the view of Tarrafal when emerging from the mountains is well worth the bumpy ride.

Tarrafal itself is a fairly sleepy town that doubles in population during the summer months. From July to September, people from all over the island flock to this beautiful refuge and the main beach literally crawls with men, women and children. Back away from the coastline, people break out little grills and the smell of smoke and grilled chicken is almost overwhelming. Music blasts from speakers that don't seem to belong on the beach and soccer balls fly. During the week and during the winter (December to March) when the wind and the waves pick up, the beach can be practically deserted. If you are not one for a large crowd, visit during the off season or take a brief hike to one of the less popular, out-of-the-way areas.

HISTORY

In addition to being a relaxing beach destination, there is a bit of interesting history and some cultural strongholds in Tarrafal. Originally established as a *conselho* in June of 1872, Tarrafal was valued for its wide bay as a good port. One of the original landings on Santiago, Tarrafal later became a site of infamy with the building of the Portuguese version of a "concentration camp" in Chã Bom for political prisoners.

First built in the 1930s, the *Campo de Concentração* in Tarrafal was modeled after those of the Nazis as a prison for Portuguese anti-fascists. Despite the name, this camp didn't live up to the horrifying reputation of its Nazi counterparts. Though equipped with torture devices, it was regarded as a place of "slow death." One prisoner, Manuel Francisco Rodrigues, the Portuguese writer and poet, wrote a book while interned entitled *Tarrafal Aldeia da Morte. O diário da B5* (Tarrafal: Town of Death; the diary of B5) saying that "*Tarrafal é o pior dos piores lugares da pior ilha*" (Tarrafal is the worst of the worst places of the worst island).

The first prisoners arrived on April 23, 1936 and population peaked at 261 prisoners in 1942, but declined to a mere 46 in 1950 and was closed down in 1954. Unrest in Portuguese colonies caused the camp to reopen in 1961 to hold independence fighters and conspirators from Angola, Cape Verde, Guinea Bissau and Mozambique, but was closed for good on April 25, 1974. Today, this site is well on its way to becoming a restored and converted museum.

WHAT TO DO

Aside from lounging on the beach, there is not too much that Tarrafal has to offer, but there are a few enticing options that will help you pass the day. The town itself is fairly small and self contained. You could pass a morning walking up and down the few parallel streets, stopping occasionally for coffee. The *praça* in front of the church is a popular place to pass time and on the way out of town, a new municipal market was built a few years ago.

There are some nice beaches outside of the main bay. Check out Ponta de Atum along the coast between Tarrafal and Chã Bom for a breaking tide and a bit of isolation. Snorkeling is popular along the coast.

For the avid hiker, you can walk north from the bay to the lighthouse. Beyond the bungalows of Baía Verde, the path begins uphill and continues on-sometimes more clearly than others-through a low *ribeira*. As this is a common hike for tourists, *banditos* (bandits) often see opportunity for muggings. Be aware or go as a part of a group.

Diving

There are two dive centers based out of the Kingfisher Resort.

> **Divecenter-Santiago** m. 993.6407; divecenter-santiago@email.de; www.divecenter-santiago.de

> **King Bay** Contact Monaya, a resident expert in Cape Verde's marine history and marine biologist. *Tel: 266.1100; hrolfsl@gmx.net*

Surfing

For the serious surfer or someone with interest in windsurfing or kite surfing, Sal or Boa Vista are better options than Santiago, but along the western coast, you can find groups of locals in the early morning looking to catch a wave.

WHERE TO STAY

 King Fisher Resort Large and nicely decorated holiday houses of varying size and amenities, each unique. The cottages are designed as apartments with kitchens. Set up for longer-term visitors, an additional charge for reservations of less than four days may be added to the price. Breakfast and dinner are available. $$$ *Tel: 266.1100; hrolfsl@gmx.net; www.king-fisher.de*

Hotel Baía Verde The obligatory beach bungalows, these 46 apartments would be nice if there was more emphasis placed on maintenance and customer satisfaction. Nestled along the bay, there is a fence and guard dogs to keep unwelcome trespassers out. The rooms are of varying size, but most have more cockroaches than guests. Water is sometimes an issue, but the price is reasonable. $$-$$$ *Tel: 266.1128*

Hotel Tarrafal Reasonable rooms, a small pool (sometimes empty) and a restaurant (sometimes closed). The hotel was closed at time of research. $$$ *Tel: 266.1785; htltarrafal@cvtelecom.cv*

Pensão Mille Nuits Affordable rooms in a large building in the center of town. Price varies according to the quality of the room. Some rooms include private bathrooms. Breakfast included, lunch and dinner are available in the restaurant. $$ *Tel: 266.1463*

Vila Botanico This German couple has recognized the need for comfortable places to stay in Tarrafal and have opened two rooms of their house to guests. There is a minimum three day stay, but guests are welcome to use of the pool and relaxing on the terrace/roof. Breakfast included. $$$$ *Tel: 266.1800; info@villabotanico.de; www.villabotanico.de*

Santiago

WHERE TO EAT

There are a number of small restaurants tucked away on back streets that offer a lunch *prato de dia* for the working population of Tarrafal. There was a Spanish restaurant opening at the time of research, seek and ye shall find.

 Sol e Lua On the far end of the bay by the basketball courts, this small restaurant run by an Italian and his Cape Verdean wife serve up delicious cuisine inspired by their ethnic mix. A great spot to pass the evening. $$$ *Tel: 266.2339, m. 997.9535*

Hotel Baía Verde The restaurant is better run than the bungalows, yet both have a monopoly on the location. The restaurant offers indoor and outdoor seating looking out over the beach. Dishes can be fairly expensive. $$$-$$$$

 Altomira Definitely a dinner hotspot in Tarrafal, it is best to arrive early and expect a bit of a wait. There is a small door leading in, but the restaurant itself is large and quite open. Specialties include pizza and fresh fish. $$$ *Tel: 266.2251; m. 996.3865*

Dia das Mulheres (Women's Day) in São Miguel

Cape Verde's *Dia das Mulheres* (Women's Day) is March 27, and was celebrated in full force in Calheta. Last weekend I went to a *Batuque* festival in Mato Correia, a really beautiful place. It is definitely out in the *fora* (country) and almost seems untouched. Houses sit not only on top of hills, but on sides of mountains. Sometimes I have wondered how people walk home at night. It was an interesting experience all together.

When we first arrived, there were literally hundreds of people eating. At first, I thought that people brought their own food, but then I was asked by an older woman to come into her house and eat. I realized that not only was I going to eat there but *everyone* was eating in this one woman's home. Apparently her house was the designated food place. I ate so much I had to sit down for a few minutes. In Cape Verde, any time there is a big event you can always find traditional foods: *cachupa* (corn, bean stew), *xerem* (Cape Verdean "grits"), *couscous* (cornbread), *batatas* (potatoes), and *arroz* (rice), and even meats such as lamb, goat, beef, and chicken.

After eating, we walked down to where the stage was set up. We watched about five groups perform the traditional dance of *Batuque*. This dance has its origins in slavery and the dance in which they wear the traditional cloth, called *panu de terra* (cloth of the land). They play the beat on their knees, boards, or cloth-filled bags and you can't help but to be enthralled as groups of women sing, cry and dance in ways that look almost unnatural.

Since a lot of people emigrate abroad and outside influences are becoming much stronger, the traditional dances of Cape Verde, at one time were slowly being forgotten. Other Cape Verdeans noticed this and started a huge campaign in the last couple of years to bring it back to the forefront. Now, a lot of the zones have young girl's *Batuque* groups. At the event, we watched as the *Batukadeiras* of Mato Correia became an official group. It was touching to watch the girls get encouragement and support from some of the older women.

- Dannielle Thomas

Calheta de São Miguel

When returning from Tarrafal to Praia, you can take the road that runs along the east coast for stunning ocean views and a glimpse of life in the scattered coastal villages.

The *conselho* of São Miguel is the smallest county of Santiago and is situated on the northeast coast. Despite its small size, it is quite diverse encompassing a chunk of coastline, small city, agricultural areas and lush mountains. Calheta is mainly a fishing town and as early as 6:00, you can hear women calling out to sell the fresh catch of the day. Toward the interior, residents live a mostly agricultural life. A road is being developed from Assomada to the coastal town of Calheta which will increase transportation and opportunities for residents and visitors.

If just passing through, Calheta might be a nice place to stop for a breath of fresh air and a bit to eat, but if you intend to explore the reaches of Santiago, there are a number of hikes to and from Serra Malagueta, Assomada and along the coast that make Calheta an appealing resting place. The location on the coast offers the best of both worlds, access to the mountains and to the ocean, and it can be less hectic than its northern neighbor, Tarrafal. The people here are also very friendly, welcoming and laidback making it a nice place to relax.

WHERE TO STAY & EAT

Mira Maio At the southern end of town, there are rooms of varying size and quality. There is a large roof terrace. Breakfast is included $$ *www.miramaio.com*

Pensão Morgana Around the corner from Mira Maio, this place offers a few affordable rooms. $-$$

Esplanda Sillibell If you are looking for adventure, this German-run restaurant also specializes in excursions around the area. Sibylle and Geraldo will help with information or organizing a guided tour. If you are just looking for a meal, drink and relaxation, it is also the place to come. $$ *Tel: 273.2078; m.996.7930 www.reisetraeume.de; Open Mon-Sat 12:00-22:00*

Loja Casa Tute/Bar Esperança There are a number of small places to get grilled chicken or a plate-of-the-day if you walk around the main area. $-$$

Pedra Badejo

This coastal fishing village is filled with winding side streets and back alleys of stairs climbing gradually toward the cross that stands watch over the town. Pedra Badejo is the municipal seat of Santa Cruz and is famous as the home of the Carlos Martins (aka Katcha), leader of the *funana* musical group Bulimundo popular in the 1980s. Bulimundo incorporated the traditional sounds of Santiago (Tabanka, Funana and Batuko) into modern music that spread these sounds throughout the archipelago. The group split in the late 1980s and was permanently put to rest with the death of Katcha in March of 1988.

There is a coastal hike from the black sand beach in Pedra Badejo to the white sand beach of Praia Baixo. It is easy to lose the path as you cross through the *ribeira*, so be sure to confirm directions as you go.

Santiago

WHERE TO STAY & EAT

Palm Beach Resort A massive structure looking over the more swimmable beach of this small village. The resort seems out of place in the small town as it is much more polished than the surrounding buildings. Rooms are large and comfortable. The restaurant looks out over the beach and excursions are available on request. There are plans for a swimming pool and mini golf that have not yet come to fruition. Double including breakfast $$$, full board $$$$ *Tel: 269.2888; m. 995.6942; palmbeachs.cruz@hotmail.com; www.pedrabadejo.com*

Mariberto 'A La Française This beautiful guest house is along the coast on the way out of Pedra Badejo toward Praia. Turn off at the Restaurant BelaVista and head to Punta Coroa. Run by the French/Russian couple Bernard and Marina, Mariberto was built mindfully and well. There is a ocean water pool and electricity is supplied by solar panels. Breakfast included and restaurant services available for other meals.. Children under 13 and pets are not welcome. $$$$-$$$$$ *Tel: 269.1900; m. 991.2298 bernardlorac@yahoo.fr; www.hotelmariberto.com*

Porto Madeira

The name itself is a preface to the strangeness of this isolated and entirely unique village. Port implies water, but as you turn up the road and head into the mountains, it is clear that you are heading away from the ocean. The road winds for about 1000m before you arrive at the first signs of the colorful village.

Rebelados de Rabo Espinho Branco

For a "cultural" experience, visit the Rabelados in zona Espinho Branco on the coast of Santa Catarina near Calheta. The Rabelados belonged to a separationist sect that refused assimilation to the Portuguese "purification" of religion and ways of life. The Rabelados wished to continue living communally, ignoring land ownership and eliminating the need for an established monetary economy. During the fight for independence, many of the Rabelados were charged as political activists and incarcerated in Tarrafal.

For many years, the Rabelados refused contact with the outside world, but in such unforgiving natural conditions, there is a need for some income in order to survive. Children and adults dress in the same imported clothing and residents of Espinho Branco are now open to outside medical care and some even have a radio playing. Today, two groups of houses stare at each other across the road that passes through. The houses are kept in a traditional manner of woven stalks of sugar cane. Without much rain, the buildings last for years without much need for repair.

To support the settlement, residents produce and sell artwork under the training and supervision of Miza, the director of the project in Porta Madeira. The work is displayed in an exhibit hall where it is currently possible for 1-2 guests to stay. There are plans to build a *pensão* for interested tourists. Contact TcheTcho (the spiritual leader) at Tel: 995.7946 or rabellados@yahoo.com.

In 2008, the community was turned into a living work of art. Misá, a native to Porto Madeira who studied in Switzerland returned to her small village and decided to put her artistic background to use. She gathered a group of artists from various countries and began the transformation of trash into treasure. Various sculpture and paintings are littered along the streets in the same manner that litter decorates most other villages. Be sure to continue through the length of town to the colorful school and *caminho poetica* (poetic path). Misá also works with the Rabelados of Espinho-Branco in an effort to develop a community of artists. Contact Misá at Tel: 991.8197 or misacv@gmail.com / portamadeira2008@gmail.com.

Infrastructure for tourism is currently lacking, but it is currently the developmental focus of the community. There is a well marked restaurant out of one of the houses, an information center and a quaint museum area featuring a house of times passed. If you would like to stop for a bite or a cup of coffee, it is recommended that you order before you continuing on the path. If, however, you are enjoying the peaceful atmosphere and don't mind the wait, stroll up, take a seat and relax.

Praia Baixo

Before returning to the road that runs through the center of the island, there is a left turn that will take you toward Praia Baixo. A part of the *conselho* of São Domingos, Praia Baixo is one of the few white sand beaches on Santiago. The wide bay would make a safe landing spot for small boats, but also makes a great place to swim. During weekends and summer months, people come from all over Santiago bringing grills and carloads of family members to enjoy the sun and sand.

WHERE TO STAY

ApartHotel Praia Baixo There are an assortment of rooms and apartments available here, but apartments are only for rent for a long-term stay. This may be negotiable depending on business. $$$ *Tel: 268.7105; yuba@yubasol.com*

WHERE TO EAT

In addition to the restaurants listed below, there are a number of small kiosks and bars where you can get grilled chicken or fried *moreia* (moray eel) and the obligatory french fries.

ApartHotel Praia Baixo The rooftop hotel here is a weekend escape for residents of Praia. Depending on the season, meals may or may not be available during the week. Call ahead for information and reservations. $$-$$$ *Tel: 268.7105*

Restaurant Praia Baixo There is a restaurant on the beach open only on Sundays. At the time of research, it was in the process of changing hands. May or may not be open at all. $$$

Santiago

Festivals on Santiago

January 15 – Tarrafal; Municipal Day

February 2 – São Domingos, Nhô Fenrero Festival

March 13 – São Domingos, Municipal Day

Two weeks after Easter – Picos, São Salvador do Mundo

April 23 – São Jorge, São Jorge

May 1 – São Jose

May 19 – Praia, Municipal Day

Weekend closest to May 19 – Gamboa Music Festival in Praia

May 8 – Calheta, São Miguel Arcanjo Feast

May 13 – Assomada, Nossa Senhora de Fatima

June – As with all the islands, there are a number of festivals throughout the month of June in various communities. Ask around.

August 13 – Achada Santo António (Praia), Santo António

August 15 – Nossa Senhora do Socorro

September 12 – São Domingos

November 25 – Santa Catarina, Municipal Day

Fogo

Flying into São Filipe, Fogo appears on the horizon, looming and dramatic. Even cloaked in a sea of clouds, the peak pokes through. On a clear day, it is possible to see the aftermath of years of volcanic activity ripping scars of varying shades of black that pour down the steep landscape. Flying around the cone, few houses are visible and it seems miraculous that they can even exist up and down the slopes. São Filipe seems to appear out of nowhere and looks to be both large and small at the same time, a dense cluster of houses surrounded by wild, barren soil.

With around 38,000 inhabitants, Fogo is one of the more populous islands, though you wouldn't know it by the small town feel of the capital, São Filipe. Clusters of houses along the road circling the island are just a small portion of the residences scattered about the steep hillsides. Outside of Fogo, the inhabitants of this island are notorious, referred to as loud, lively and a little bit crazy. Anywhere else in Cape Verde, *"Abo é de Fogo?"* (Are you from Fogo?) is synonymous for "Are you crazy?" Though eccentricity abounds, the residents are nothing short of open and welcoming.

GEOGRAPHY

The most symmetrical island, Fogo is almost entirely round and conical and fills 183 sq miles (476 sq km). The island itself first emerged from the sea a few hundred thousand years ago and has built upon itself since its emergence. The original peak reached well over 11,000 feet (3,500m), but sometime over the last 10,000 years, the instability of the tremulous walls gave way and the peak slid into the Atlantic. What remains today is known as *Chã das Caldeiras* (Floor of the Caldrons), a vast black lava landscape covered by peaks and flows from more recent eruptions, a crater wall stretching around more than half of the floor and Pico do Fogo, the result of an eruption in 1785 that reaches over 9,280 feet (2829m).

The only island in Cape Verde that is still volcanically active, recent eruptions on Fogo are visible throughout the crater and running down slopes on the southeast side. Though these more recent eruption have been less violent and without casualty, they have devastated land previously used for farming.

HISTORY

In Portuguese and Kriolu, *fogo* means fire. Though the origins of the island are evident, it was originally named for the saint's day on which it was discovered, São Filipe. It wasn't until a massive eruption in 1688 that the name was changed to Fogo and São Filipe was relegated to the confines of the capital. This eruption forced many residents to flee to neighboring Brava and let up a burst of flames and cloud of smoke so thick that it was used as a point of navigation for well over 20 years.

Fogo was second to be inhabited after Santiago partially due to proximity and partially to the richness of the volcanic soil. The wealth of Fogo was not overlooked by pirates and, because of the isolation and rough terrain, was considered a hardship post by Portuguese settlers. Slaves were sent from Santiago to neighboring Fogo to cultivate cotton for production of the easily traded *panu* (cloth). Cotton production is no longer promi-

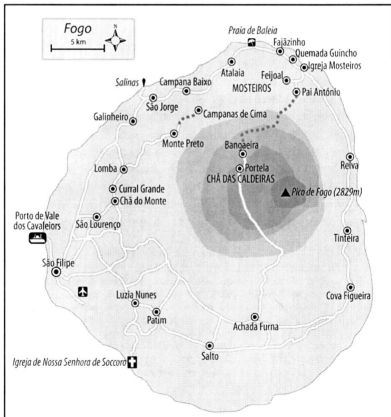

nent on this fertile island, but it remains one of the most dominantly agricultural regions producing corn, grapes for wine production, coffee beans and a variety of fruits grown in Chã das Caldeiras. The rich volcanic soil has been an asset to the many inhabitants reliant on agriculture, but not without difficulty stemming from drought and lack of accessible ground water. German and Italian projects have helped build large *tanques* (water catchment cisterns) in areas of higher elevation, but most—like that of Curral Grande—have been around for years and are not yet utilized by the community in an organized fashion.

Tourism on Fogo is rapidly developing and many hotels have changed hands, are being renovated or are currently being developed in São Filipe. There is much debate about what is being done in the city. Some fear that the conversion of the buildings will destroy the history and feel of the city. Others argue that it is a wonderful way to embrace the past while welcoming the future.

LOGISTICS

Both the airport and the port are a short trip from São Filipe, each costing about 300$. If travelling light, it is possible to walk into the city from the airport (bear left at the fork). It is also possible from the port if you are ready to start climbing from the beginning of your trip.

By Air

TACV makes daily flights to Fogo from Praia and Halcyon air also makes frequent trips. You can make reservations or purchase tickets at any TACV office or tour agency in any of the islands.

Direct flights may or may not be available from Sal and São Vicente depending on time of year and demand. Look around on Sal for advertised day trips through Barracuda Tours and other excursion agencies.

By Sea

In 2008, two of the main ships that made the Praia-Fogo-Brava circuit went under, one off the coast of Santiago and the other off the coast of Fogo. There were no fatalities in these unexplained incidents, except for the boats. The government and some private agencies have been working on bringing new boats to the archipelago to release some of the pressure on the existing system of cargo and passenger transportation, but, like everything in Cape Verde, progress is slow.

Schedules are always subject to change due to weather, boat conditions, festivals and a thousand other causes that you will never be informed of, so try to be flexible. The water can get pretty rough, so if you are unsure of your sealegs, some kind of medication is highly recommended. The aptly named "Vomidrine" is available at all pharmacies for 25-30 per pill.

Cape Verde Navalis "The Marina Princess" has been running since late 2009 and makes the Praia-Fogo-Brava circuit four days a week. Slightly faster than the older the older boats, the trip from Praia to Fogo takes just over four hours and from Praia to Brava just under five. The agency is located on the corner across the street from Sucupira. *Praia; Tel: 282.1023*

Agentur S.T.M. S.T.M. is the main agency in Praia, but the office has been moved off of Plateau. This agency sells tickets for the *Praia Aguada*, which runs the Praia-Brava-Fogo circuit twice a week. Not to be confused with the *Praia D'Agua* which strictly runs between Fogo and Brava. The *Praia Aguada* is also a cargo ship and you can expect delays in Brava to unload and reload cargo. *Praia; Tel: 261.2564*

Cabo Verde Fast Ferry The operation of Cabo Verde Fast Ferry was projected to begin in the fall of 2009. Stocks have been sold since that date and there was at least one boat in production at the time of research, but directors now expect to begin in the spring of 2010. It would be best to verify this information before counting on the services of CV Fast Ferry. Head office is after the rotary on the way to Achada Santo António in Chã d' Area.
cvff.info@cvfastferry.com; www.cvfastferry.com

GETTING AROUND

From São Filipe it is possible to get to any spot on the island. That said, you can charter a taxi or some private Hiaces for a trip to the crater or a *volta ilha* (trip around the island). Taxis are easy to spot with their newly regulated yellow paint, but public cars can be a bit more mysterious. If you aren't pressed with a schedule and are feeling a bit adventurous, public transportation will save you a fair amount of money and provide an opportunity to be immersed in the lives of your fellow passengers. During the day, Hiaces and covered trucks line the streets by the markets and *praças*, alternately circling the streets. They may seem to be haphazardly strewn throughout the city, but each resting point is claimed by a different location and though there is no strict schedule, there is a flow.

To head to the lush northern side of the island (Campanas Baixo, Salinas, Ponta Verde) look for a vehicle in the *praça* outside of TACV. Though they generally run throughout the day, there is a lull during lunch hours.

Cars also run throughout the day for the more barren southern half. Cova Figueira, the newest Conselho (district) that claims dominion over Chã das Caldeiras peppers the road with small villages and farms fed with drip irrigation.

Hidden above the main road is a second tier of villages. Many cars stop in Curral Grande or Lomba, so ask drivers if they go all the way to Ribeira Filipe.

EXCURSIONS

There is a small kiosk in the *praça* in front of the *Câmara* in São Filipe that offers some tourist information and sells souvenirs. At the bottom of the *praça* you will find the headquarters for **Qualitur** (Tel: 281.1089; qualitur@cvtelecom.cv; www.qualitur.cv) that offers a variety of excursions around the island.

You can also speak to any number of drivers to organize a private tour around the island. **Vergilio Barbosa Amado** is highly recommended (Tel: 283.1711, m. 996.7018).

It is also possible to arrange smaller tours and hikes for yourself within Chã das Caldeiras at the information building. See contact information in the section on Chã das Caldeiras. Other tour companies include:

Chãtour Advertised throughout the islands celebrating the "wine and cheese" natural to Fogo, they are also willing to help arrange a customized visit to and around the island. *Tel: 282.1528; chatour@chatourfogo.com, www.chatourfogo.com*

 D'jar Fogo Will organize individualized tours for small groups in addition to a homestay experience (advanced notice required). See pg 214 for contact information.

Zebra Travel Relatively new to Fogo, but has grand ambition to organize tours, big game fishing and excursions to Brava. *Tel: 991.4566; info@zebratravel.net; www.zebratravel.net*

São Filipe

Whether arriving by boat or by plane, you will find yourself in the capital city of Fogo, São Filipe—commonly referred to as "Bila." Looking toward the crater, the residential area expands upwards and the commercial area lies below. The heart of the city sits perched over the black sand beach that seems to stretch for miles. Here you will find a range of *sobrados*, mansions left from the years of Portuguese colonialism characterized by large open quintals and porches lined with intricate woodwork, from deteriorating to well restored and preserved. In the past, Bila was notorious for its cleanliness and though this has declined a little in recent years, there is still a strong emphasis placed on beautification of the city. Painted murals and well planted *praças* abound, though you can be hard pressed for shade.

During the day, the city streets come alive as thousands of students are bused in from the surrounding rural areas and people come from all over the island to trade and *fazi compras*—do their shopping and take care of business. When the last of the students leave around 18:00, you can feel a hush come over the city. Despite being the fifth largest city in Cape Verde, São Filipe can be peacefully quiet at night and is generally safe.

IMPORTANT INFORMATION

Bank On Fogo, you will find BCA, BCN and Caixa Económica all within the immediate downtown area. All banks are open Monday-Friday from approximately 8:00-15:00.

Hospital There are actually two hospitals in São Filipe. The national hospital (Tel: 281.1130*)* is located on Rua do Hospital. *Cutelo d' Açúcar*, an Italian built and hospital with better facilities, is located at the eastern end of the city beyond the high school.

Pharmacy *Farmácia Santo António* On the corner up from the *praça* between the hospital and Minimercado Mimosa.

Post Office *Correios* Open Monday-Friday, across from the Sucupira open market at the top of town (*zona* Santa Filomena).

Police *Polícia* Also at the top of the town heading down toward the *liceu* (high school). Tel: 281.1152

TACV Fogo Impossible to miss in the main *praça*, the office is open from 8:00-13:00, 15:00-17:00. Tel: 281.1340

WIFI WiFi is available in the *praça* by the *Câmara*.

Fogo

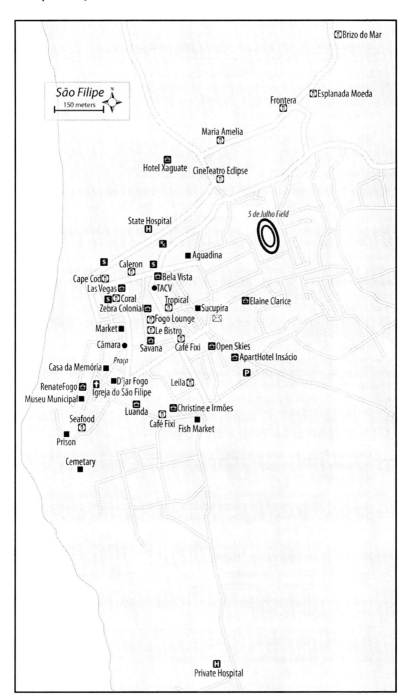

São Filipe
N
150 meters

Brizo do Mar

Esplanada Moeda
Frontera
Maria Amelia

Hotel Xaguate
CineTeatro Eclipse

5 de Julho Field

State Hospital

Aguadina

Caleron
Cape Cod
Bela Vista
Las Vegas
TACV
Coral
Zebra Colonial
Tropical
Elaine Clarice
Sucupira
Fogo Lounge
Le Bistro
Market
Savana
Cámara
Café Fixi
Open Skies
ApartHotel Insácio
Praça
Casa da Memória
D'jar Fogo
Leila
RenateFogo
Igreja do São Filipe
Museu Municipal
Luanda
Christine e Irmões
Seafood
Café Fixi
Fish Market
Prison

Cemetary

Private Hospital

STAYING IN TOUCH

There are a growing number of internet cafés scattered throughout the city and wireless is now available in the *praça by the Câmara Municipal.* Recommended internet cafés are the **Terra Nova** internet café above Cintia Market (across from the bottom of the Municipal Market) and **Ca' Jose** below Cape Cod Restaurant across from the *praça.*

WHAT TO DO

Though the city limits extend upwards, the commercial/historical area of Bila is fairly small and contained. Coupled with the mid-day sun, a hike around hilly São Filipe can be a bit strenuous, but in the morning or early evening it is possible to cover the entire area and get a feel for the ebb and flow of business. Because the city is built on a steep slope, it is recommended that you begin at the top and work your way down. There are a multitude of bars, restaurants and internet cafés scattered throughout the city as well as shops and beautifully planted *praças.*

Pé de Campo (Foot of the Field)

This area is named for proximity to the newly turfed *5 de Julho* soccer field. There is generally a game to catch on the weekends and around the time of the city's festival the weeks prior are filled with men's and women's tournaments, races and other activities held at the field.

Aguadina

This large orange building is a public water facility that sits atop the city. It is also a good place to find some shade. In the gardens you will find a statue of João de Figueiredo, former governor of Cape Verde, and generally a group of taxi drivers huddling in the shade.

Sucupira (Clothing Market)

Diagonally across from the *correios* is Fogo's version of *Sucupira.* Though many of the products are similar, prices are inflated for the cost of shipping to this more remote island—relatively expensive and more for tourists rather than locals.

The next cross street down is filled with shops, businesses and restaurants and decorated with various murals. Heading toward the center, you will eventually hit the TACV *praça* where you can take a break in the shade and watch women from all over as they try to sell fruit, clothing and furniture while fighting over spots under the trees.

Zig-zag back across the city and you will pass a series of restaurants most notably Le Bistro and Fogo Lounge. Stop in at Le Bistro for an excellent view of Brava and the best cup of coffee in town.

After Hotel Savana, the road drops dramatically. Turn right here and admire the copper relief mural on the edge of the road that chronicles the history and culture of Fogo. Straight ahead is the *Câmara Municipal.* Turn right before the *Câmara* to take a stroll around the market. This whole area is strictly reserved for *negoçias*—selling, trading and buying. In the morning, it can be impossible to weave your way between the women selling the day's catch, the hundreds of people that have come from

Fogo

outside the city and the cars that brought them and, during fruit season, the excess of ripe fruit. You will hear the cries of *"bem negoçia"* or *"negocia ku mi!"* ("Make business with me!" or better yet,"Buy my wares!") as the women beg you for your business. Inside the market, fruits and vegetables are piled on the counters and you can wind through the narrow passages on a quest for famous Fogo goat cheese.

Casa da Memória

This restored *sobrado* houses photos and artifacts of the many European and African influences that converged to create Fogo and Cape Verde. It is run and has been compiled by Monique who has spent over 20 years in Cape Verde. In the back, there is a small library with Portuguese, English and French books. Don't miss the small binder that contains written and visual accounts of the 1995 eruption. Monique also occasionally shows films in the *quintal* (open patio), a tradition restored here from years past. *Tel: 281.2765; moniquewidmer@yahoo.com.br; www.casadamemoria.com.cv; Open Wednesday-Friday 10:00-12:00 or by appointment; Cost 300-500*

D'jar Fogo

Certainly the most unique place on this unique island, this intimate shop is run by Agnelo. Originally from Fogo, he lived in Portugal for many years, but returned to Fogo to embrace, enliven and educate about the history and culture of rural life on Fogo. In the office/center/café located in São Filipe, it is possible to purchase books (a rarity on Fogo), witness the process of roasting coffee (including sampling the fresh product), and engage in some of the most informed conversation about the history of Fogo. Agnelo offers specialized tours for small groups (max 4) ranging from a circuit of the island in a private car (6000$+) to overnight stays in his family's house, Quinta das Saudades, outside of the city (minimum of 2 days, please provide advance notice). The house has been maintained for historical integrity (no electricity or running water) with minor conversions to accommodate tourists. He speaks Portuguese, Kriolu, English and French and offers a familial and historical perspective while maintaining traditional integrity. Every Thursday he hosts a cultural event at the shop. It is essential to communicate what you would like for your experience and he will be more than willing to provide and establish a price based on the request. *Rua Dr. Costa; Tel: 281.2879, m. 991.9713 agnelo@djarfogo.net; www.djarfogo.net*

Museu Municipal de São Filipe

The Fogo Ethnographic Museum is located at the bottom of the city is a new addition to the sites of São Filipe. The rooms showcase the traditional *sobrado* house while displaying artifacts and historical information. Though some displays are a bit sparse, overall, the museum does a nice job telling the story of Fogo. *Tel: 281.1295; camaramunicipalalsf@yahoo.com.br*

Igreja do São Filipe

The recently restored and beautifully painted twin peaked church is visible throughout the city. Mass is held on Sundays and becomes packed for saint's days and is a popular place for weddings.

Prison and Cemetery

On opposite cliffs, these two remnants of times past look across at one another with an air of abandon. The prison has been closed for many years and the cemetery is a remnant of colonial time where only Portuguese settlers were buried. Below, there is an expanse of black sand beach that is often filled in the early morning and early evening with crowds playing soccer and practicing *capoeira* (Brazilian style martial arts). You can also watch as fishermen drag in the days catch. The sides of the path are littered with trash from visitors and, though the water may be tempting in the hot sun, the tide is strong and it can be quite dangerous to swim. Beware if travelling alone as the path down is long and isolated and you may become an easy target.

WHERE TO EAT

 Le Bistro May change ownership, but the food here is excellent and the outdoors veranda is even nicer. On a clear day you can sit at the cheerfully painted chairs and upturned barrels and look out over the city, the Atlantic and wonder at Brava. Great for a hearty breakfast. Closes in the afternoon between 15:00-17:00. $$-$$$

Café Fixi There are actually two cafés Fixi in São Filipe. One located higher up in the town on the way to the *correios* and one located on the way to the church in the lower side of town. Both are intimate and you will get more than what you pay for. $

Restaurant Seafood The veranda looks out over the cemetery, the path to the beach and a patch of black sand constantly battered with waves. Window panes have recently been added which may or may not keep out the bugs, but definitely destroyed some of the appeal. Lunch and dinner here is pricy, but a traditional breakfast of refried *cachupa*, bread, cheese and coffee is relatively inexpensive and will keep you full through dinner. $$$ *Tel: 283.1045*

Bar/Restaurant Leila From the outside, it doesn't seem anything special, but walk in and head down the stairs to the right and you will find nicely painted murals and some of the best fish in São Filipe. $$ *Tel: 281.1214*

Brizo do Mar Across from Super Rodrigo on the northern exit of the city, here you will find a variety of dishes influenced by the owner's time living outside of Cape Verde. $$-$$$ *Tel: 281.3409*

Maria Amelia In three years, this restaurant has moved three times. It may undoubtedly move again, but it will likely remain a fixture. Mystique and rumor surround Maria Amelia and you may find some interesting clientele, but the food is good and if you're looking to live on the edge. $$ *Tel: 281.2327*

Bar/Restaurant Frontera Frontera is frequented by expats and deportees. You may encounter an interesting group in the evening, but you can certainly find the standard dishes. $$ *Tel: 281.2534*

Fogo

Esplanada Moeda Great for a quick bite on the way in or out of the city, the round blue building offers a cheap plate of the day. Women traveling alone should be aware of unwanted attention. $ *m. 9979936*

 Fogo Lounge A new addition to the Fogo restaurant family, Fogo Lounge has been an immediate success. The outdoor patio area is covered to protect the cushioned wicker furniture and those that occupy the seat. The menu offers everything from simple snacks to elaborate meals. $$-$$$ *Tel: 991.4566*

Tropical Worth going just to sit under the lighted tree. On a cool evening, it is a great place to relax and unwind. The food is fairly expensive, but service is excellent and reliable. A good place for mixed drinks, try the *banana sujo* (dirty banana). $$$ *Tel: 281.1188 / 281.2161*

 Caleron Another great place to get a *prato de dia*. There is almost always *bife de atun* (tuna steak) or *bife de serra* (wahoo steak) and it is absolutely delicious. Prices can be a little more upscale, but one plate is more than enough for two. $$-$$$ *Tel: 281.3296*

Cape Cod Restaurant Some of the best *cachupa* in town, Cape Cod is popular with locals. You can rely on a plate of the day, but the dish varies greatly depending on availability. The staff is happy to oblige, when they have the ingredients required. $$

CineTeatro Eclipse More popularly known as *Casa Cinema* here you will find an under-utilized open air cinema area and a bar/restaurant with an amazing view. Breakfast is readily available for 250$, but for dinner and a sunset, you must order from the menu. Great for a sundowner. $$ *Tel: 281.4155*

 Coral The front room is fairly dismal, but if you enter there is a rather large and nicely planted sitting area. Coral is very popular for lunch and with good reason. The food is excellent, plentiful and inexpensive. $$ *Tel: 281.3136*

 Xaguate The restaurant in the hotel of the same name is open to the public during meal times with the most expensive *prato de dia* on Fogo. If you feel like splurging, the view is fabulous and the food is even better. The poolside bar is open to the public. $$$-$$$$

WHERE TO STAY

Hotel Xaguate There are 39 rooms, some with verandas and some with a view of the ocean (for an additional price). There is a pool and fitness room and all the amenities would expect of an established hotel. Breakfast is included and there is an option to include other meals as well. $$$$ *Tel: 281.5000 / 281.1222; www.hotelxaguate.com*

 Savana Savana opened in 2009, so the entire building is newly renovated. It is a converted *sobrado* with a small pool in the center. The rooms have high ceilings and beautiful wood floors with private bathrooms, hot and cold water and air conditioning. Breakfast is included, no restaurant for lunch/dinner. $$$. *Tel: 281.1490; reservasavana@yahoo.com; www.hotelsavanafogo.com*

Luanda Owned by the same proprietor as Savana but in a different, older building. The prices here are lower, but guests are given access to the pool in Savana. Contact Hotel Savana for reservations. $$

Pousada Bela Vista Located at the central *praça*, from here you have easy access to the entire city. Despite the somewhat bland outside, the rooms and building are beautiful and well maintained. There are 11 rooms and one apartment with three bedrooms. A/C is available at an additional cost and Internet is available on request. $$-$$$ *Tel: 281.1734*

Zebra Colonial Bed & Breakfast Expected to open in October, this project began in 2007 and is developing into a single handed tour operation. The proprietors have taken over use of Pensão Fatima as well as a massive *sobrado* in the center of town. When completed, there will be nine spacious rooms with access to a central pool and spa area. $$$

Rooms in the former Pensão Fatima (located at the bottom of the city on the way to the beach) are much less expensive ($), with access to the main building. Through Zebra, it will be possible to rent a car, arrange fishing trips, charter a boat to Brava and plan guided tours of Fogo and Brava. *Tel: 991.4566; info@zebratravel.net; www.zebratravel.net*

ApartHotel Inácio Located above a supermarket in the upper reaches of the city, Aparthotel is quiet and clean. You may have to climb a few stairs to reach your room. One thing lacking is a central reception area and a place to sit. Price start from $$. *Tel: 281.2746*

 Pensão Elaine Clarice Hidden in the upper reaches of Santa Filomena above the *correios*, the rooms here are simple and quaint and the halls are beautifully painted. The view from the roof is marvelous and well worth the climb. Julinho, the proprietor claims to speak English, Portuguese, French and Spanish... and of course Kriolu. Prices vary depending on number of people and amenities. Breakfast is included. $$ *Tel: 281.2181, m. 992.2996*

Pensão Christine e Irmões Located on a side road toward the bottom of the city across from the fish market, it is probably more well-known for its inexpensive lunches (300$). The rooms seem more frequented by traveling Cape Verdeans than tourists, but there is certainly no opposition to expanding business. There is one double room and a shared room with 3 beds. Breakfast is included. $ *Tel: 281.1572*

Pensão Las Vegas A large orange building below the main *praça*. The rooms have a decent view and the location is good for centrality. Single, double and triple rooms are available. Breakfast is included and a *prato de dia* (plate of the day) is available for lunch and dinner at 350$. $-$$ *Tel: 281.2223*

RenateFogo In the process of changing hands. LeBistro, currently owned jointly with the rooms (located separately) is one of the best foreign owned/run restaurants. Try the breakfast, a full spread for 500$ that includes an egg of your liking, bread, jam, goat cheese, papaya or banana and a good, strong cup of coffee or tea. $$$ *Tel: 281.2518; www.cabo-verde.ch*

Pensão Open Skies The easiest place to spot in São Filipe. Open Skies is extremely tall and extremely purple. When you enter, the rooms are much more quietly decorated and though a little old, are clean and well kept. There are eight rooms, 4 single and 4 double (price varies on use of air conditioning). $-$$ *Tel: 281.2726 / 281.2012*

Tortuga Resort Just east of Cutelo de Açúcar, these bungalows are nestled into the cliffside along the expanse of black sand beach. The eccentric owner can be spotted throughout the day cruising around São Filipe on his quad, picking up food for the guests. Contact Qualitur for contact information and prices. $$$$

Around Fogo

A popular activity, even with locals, is a *volta da ilha* (trip around the island). There is one road that wraps along the coast, making it possible to get a feel for the diverse landscape and scarce population. Heading southeast from São Filipe is recommended for better views.

When you leave Bila and head southeast, you will pass through dry, barren stretches marked by bursts of green, a product of *gota-gota* (drip irrigation). You will find stretches of banana plantation, sugar cane and corn creating a sharp contrast to the dry, rocky soil. Along the way, you will pass through Patim and Luzia Nunes. In Luzia Nunes you can bear right and head down toward to the coast to the lonely *Igreja de Nossa Senhora de Soccoro*. You will not find a large crowd unless you visit on August 4 for the massive festival, drawing crowds from across the island.

There is a large soccer field in Patin, but not much else. If you pass through at lunch, you may be hard pressed to find someplace to eat. There are, however, a number of small shops where you can grab a cold drink.

Before you reach Cova Figueira, the seat of the municipality of Santa Catarina, you will pass through Salto. On the left, you will see a sign pointing to the *Parque Natural de Fogo*. Bear left here to begin the ascent to the park. While climbing, you will pass through Achada Furna, a town of identical houses that were built in 1957 to house the dislocated residents of Chã das Caldeiras. Another area similar to this exists in Monte Larga—a fifteen minute drive along the top road west. Many of the houses have since been abandoned as families have returned to the crater to live. Other houses are occupied by those who chose to stay and yet more are filled with the second and third families of some more affluent men of Chã.

Rough Roads

If coming from Praia, keep in mind that the projects paving roads have not yet made it to Fogo. Transportation can be poorly planned and executed and cobblestone roads have either just being completed or are in desperate need of repair.

Chã das Caldeiras

Inside the crater of the volcano is a small village of about 1,000 that truly defies expectations. Split into two equally tiny towns of Portela (the upper zone) and Bangaeira (the lower zone), the residents have lived for generations through multiple eruptions to take advantage of two yearly cycles of harvest that yield corn and beans for subsistence and a multitude of fruits no longer existent in the increasingly arid archipelago. The most notable of these products are the famous Fogo coffee beans and the rich grapes that are used to produce wine. To visit Fogo and not visit Chã das Caldeiras would be a mistake, and hidden below the crater are endless opportunities for relaxation, excitement and a taste of the island of fire.

Though each island is of volcanic origin, Fogo is unique in that it is the only currently active volcano. The cone of Fogo rises up from the ocean, culminating at Pico de Fogo. The most recent volcanic activity occurred on April 2, 1995 causing major destruction, but no fatalities. Outside of the lava fields from this and other more recent eruptions, the soil of Chã is rich in minerals and the area itself receives more precipitation than other parts of the island and archipelago. The residents of Chã take full advantage of this fact, growing an array of fruits that includes apples, figs, pomegranates, peaches, quince and grapes used largely for production of wine.

Possibly one of the most mystifying places in the world, the road to this remote village climbs to impossible heights, passing through a few scattered villages. In a public car, it takes almost three hours to make the climb with all the various stops and errands on the way. Once you pass through Achada Furna, you have seen the last of the houses for 30 minute switchback climb through the barren lava flows. Aside from the occasional goats and agricultural workers, the varying landscape is all there is to keep you company. Peaks and valleys of different geologic make-up are a stunning companion for the ascent.

When you think the summit could not possibly end, there is a sudden temperature drop and the soil around the road changes from windswept weeds to dark rich soil. A few houses and various plants and trees are scattered along the road. The car will take a turn and Pico de Fogo appears as if out of nowhere. It is here that the enchantment begins, but the journey is not over. Once you enter the crater, there is close to 2 miles (approximately 3 km) of road to cover before reaching the village of 1,000 that exists 5,345 feet (1,629 m) above sea level.

The plain of craters has been formed over the past few hundred years. Since the late 1700s, eruptions have created a cluster of smaller peaks and overlapping lava flows within Chã das Caldeiras. Over the past few years the road has been repaired, fixing the damage that was caused by the 1995 eruption. It now passes smoothly through the most recent lava flows that destroyed a large percentage of the arable land. Miraculously, no one was killed in this most recent eruption. The houses are clustered on the northwest side of the *caldeira* and are watched over by the looming Pico do Fogo.

GETTING THERE

Cars for Chã das Caldeiras and Mosteiros tend to circle the public market or park behind the newly restored Cintia II in São Filipe. As they only make one morning run, start asking around before 11:00 to guarantee a spot. Public cars should cost 300-500. Alternately, it is possible to charter a taxi or car to take you to the crater. 5000$

WHAT TO DO

For a tiny village with no electricity, there is also no shortage of activities in Chã das Caldeiras. The most immediate option is climbing the almost 4,000 feet (1,200m) to the peak of the volcano, but there are a number of other hikes as well. If you aren't up to the challenge of the peak, the *volcanzinho* ("little volcano" associated with the 1995 eruption) on the southwest side of the peak is less taxing, incredibly peaceful and has pockets of sulfur vents—a reminder of the living earth below. The park also recently installed permanent steps to climb into the gaping crater. Chã das Caldeiras is a peaceful area, so a walk around the village and out into the fields of fruit will be relaxing and "other-worldly." There are a number of well trained guides available for the various hikes. Inquire at the information center.

Forty-two Children?

Nearly as famous as the volcano in Chã das Caldeiras is Senhor Fatinho. At 45 years old, he is the father of almost as many children as he has years. Each of his four wives has a separate house and the 42 children are distributed throughout. His children range in age from 27 to 18 months and the women will jokingly ask if you would like to take a child with you as you walk by. The cluster of houses that shelter his massive family is impossible to miss as you walk through Bangaeira. You will know you've reached it by the mural painted on the front house and the cluster of youth that perpetually stream about the area.

The information center is located in a *funco*—the traditional round houses built out of volcanic rock and variably thatched or cemented peaked roofs—across the street from the *Associação* and down the hill a little ways. You will find Carmen there seven days a week between 9.00-13.00 and 15:00-18:30. From here, it is possible to arrange a tour guide to any of the available treks. If you intend to climb to the peak, it is necessary to spend at least two full days in Chã das Caldeiras as cars do not arrive in the crater until mid-day/afternoon and you should begin the hike in the early morning. The ascent takes 3-5 hours (depending on pace) and the descent is rapid. Loose volcanic rock covers the side of the volcano and it is possible to literally run/slide down in less than 45 minutes. It's possible to hike down into the crater and spend the night under the stars. Beyond hiking the peak, there are number of walks, hikes and excursions within the crater including the *bordeira*—the ridge that stands over Chã das Caldeiras (a two day excursion), Monte Pretu—an older peak with verdant surroundings and hidden caves and hikes down from the crater to villages below—Mosteiros, Estâncio Roque, Achada Grande.

Wine Harvest

During the grape harvests—end of July through September—the entire crater is a bustle of activity. Grapes are collected during the day and brought to the *Associação das Agriculturas de Chã* for wine production. Work continues throughout the night until the next day's harvest is brought in. It is possible to go and watch if you visit during the time of harvest. If not, you can still tour the building where the wine is aged and kept chilled without electricity through the use of drip irrigation and cool blankets.

Cooperativa

Where the road turns to connect Portela to Bangaeira is also where the magic happens after the sun sets. Under a blanket of stars, the inside lit only by a few candles, the cooperativa hosts an almost nightly celebration of music, wine and dancing. The walls reek of *manecon* (the home brewed, thick, rich and strong wine popular with locals) and cigarette smoke, but the number of people that can be squeezed into the tiny area is incredible—especially when they pull you up to dance.

Available Guided Hikes
Price will vary by hike and by number of people

Pico de Fogo (3-5 hours) The (mildly) grueling climb to the summit of 2,829m

Volcanzinho-Pico 2 de Abril (1.5 hours) A gentle climb to the point of the most recent eruption (aka "little volcano.").

Mosteiros (4-5 hours) Descent from the crater to the coastal village of Mosteiros

Ribeira Filipe (4-5 hours) Descent to the remote village of Ribeira Filipe (arrange transportation in advance as there is nowhere to stay and irregular transportation)

Pé de Bordeira (2-3 hours) Trek along the *bordeira* that stands over 2/3 of the crater.

Bordeira hike (2 days) High above the crater, a hike along the top of the border.

Monte Preto caves (3 hours) Hidden caves surrounding the distant Monte Preto.

Manecon

Chã' is famous for a wine called *manecon*. It's a traditional homemade wine that residents make for personal consumption (although there is now a budding commercial enterprise around *manecon* due to its popularity). This local favorite can be red or white, sweet or dry. The sweet variety, however, is the most popular.

WHERE TO EAT

Pedra Brabo (The Wild Rock) Originally opened by a French man, the meals take traditional Cape Verdean ingredients with an infusion of foreign techniques and flavors. If it is in your budget, take the opportunity to eat here, peruse the book selection and enjoy the well maintained terrace. $$$ *Tel: 282.1521/2*

Casa Marisa Next to the *pensão* of the same name, there is now a bar and restaurant that serves breakfast, lunch and dinner for guests at the hotel and the general public. Plates vary on availability, but the food is reliably good. $$ *Tel: 282.1662, m. 989.6036*

Antares In front of the new Bed & Breakfast (Sirio), Antares is run by the same cooperation—COSPE. The Italian influence comes out in the pasta and pizza dishes, but all the plates are delicious. If you are not a fan of pizza with local goat cheese (a favorite), try the *atum com natas* (tuna in cream sauce). Local dishes of *djagacida, feijoada, cachupa* are also available. $$$ *Tel: 282.1528*

Bar/Grill There is an orange building with arches next to the Adventist Church. Though it has been there for over a year, the woman who owns the shop has yet to put a name. She does grill chicken and *pinchu* (pork skewers), but not regularly. If you see her cooking, it is worth stopping by. $-$$

WHERE TO STAY

Pedra Brabo (The Wild Rock) The most upscale hotel available in Chã das Caldeiras. Has 12 rooms with 2 single beds in each. 3 shared bathrooms. The lodging here is nothing spectacular, especially considering the price. Benefits include transportation from Sao Filipe, arguably the best food in Cape Verde and a beautiful terrace. $$$ *Tel: 282.1521/2*

Chã das Caldeiras Homestays

In addition to traditional lodging, many residents are willing to open their houses to tourists for a more affordable price. Some may offer breakfast. Additional meals can often be arranged if given enough advance notice. A few are listed here and more are listed at the information center in Chã das Caldeiras. Please note that prices and availability may change. It's best to call ahead to confirm.

Casa Madjer (at the Posto de Vigilância) – Portela; Tel: 282.2542, www.chatour.com; Six rooms available for single 1500$, double 2500$

Casa Leopoldo – Portela; Tel: 996.4293
Seven rooms available for 1500$.

Casa Matilde – Bangaeira; Tel: 282.1571, m. 9896036
Two rooms available for 1500$ Author Recommended.

Casa Mecilde – Bangaeira; m. 9989242
Two rooms available for 1500$.

Fogo

Casa Marisa Opened in 2007, Casa Marisa has gained popularity and expanded in the past year to include a separate bar/restaurant. Owned and run by Marisa, you can be sure that your money will be well circulated in Chã. The lodging is quaint and well maintained with single, double and triple rooms. Prices vary depending on number of guests. Shared bathrooms. $$ *Tel: 282.1662, m. 989.6036*

Sirio The restaurant and *pensão* are recent additions to Chã. Developed by COSPE, the Italian cooperation, much effort is placed on hiring locally and using local products. You can assure quality service. Single, double and triple available. $$ *Tel: 282.1568; chatour@chatourfogo.com; www.chatourfogo.com*

 Casa Fernando What originated as the occasional rented room has developed into a full-fledged family run guest house. Fernando and his wife have transformed their house into a welcoming place of rest. Business has gone well and they have expanded to a separate building with six bedrooms and 2 shared bathrooms. Single $, double $$ *Tel: 282.1531*

Casa Audelia Located up a *caminho* (path) behind the school, Audelia and family have also renovated their house to accommodate guests. The rooms are a little cramped, but are well-kept and bright. There are currently 3 single rooms and one double, but in April of 2009 had three more rooms almost completed. Single $, double $$. *Tel: 282.1569*

Cova Figueira

From the turn to Chã das Caldeiras, it is not long until you reach Cova Figueira. It is almost unexpected and sneaks up on you, but is gone just a quick. Cova Figueira only recently reached the status of a city, receiving a *Câmara Municipal* and jurisdiction over the new *conselho* of Santa Catarina, separated from São Filipe in 2005. In addition to the *Câmara*, the former primary school is in the process of expanding to accommodate high school students.

Despite the newly acquired status, Cova Figueira is still in the process of developing its tourist appeal. This smaller and relatively quiet village remains fairly unknown. It is trumped by Chã in the same *conselho*, but does offer a good time for the municipal festival throughout the month of November, generally culminating at the end of the month with a three day music festival.

MOVING ON

You pass through the city limits of Cova Figueira almost as you enter. Houses become more and more sparse as the landscape turns from semi-lush to semi-prehistoric. As the road winds along at incredible heights looking out over the ocean below, there is a stopping point at a bend that offers the most remarkable view of the volcano outside of the crater. During the rainy season, lush green is torn by strips of black of varying shades and ages. A cloudy day will block the magnificent view, but the village of Tinteira is always visible along the road with small houses gripping onto volcanic remnants. The work of the few dwellers is evident by the round corrals and gardens encircled with the stone pulled away in order to access the land.

You can almost hear the wind whispering through what seems to be a ghost town, the first along the lower section of road. Leaving the *coneselho* of Santa Catarina, the landscape becomes increasingly dramatic. Bridges pass over chutes of lava flows, frozen permanently and enduring generations.

Mosteiros

Before reaching the coastal villages of Mosteiros, the road passes through Relva. Though the images and reality of life here are difficult to describe, this village built entirely on and of volcanic devastation will not quickly leave your mind.

The *conselho* of Mosteiros radiates out from the small cluster of coastal homes and businesses. Igreja, the commercial center of the city, is small and quiet, especially after business hours. Most places listed for eating or staying are located within Igreja. Despite being small and fairly self contained, there is something almost depressing about the humid, cloud covered village with its rows of houses crushed between the sea and cliffs.

This coastal village in the north of the island has a feel much different from the rest of Fogo. Home to the only other full high school outside of São Filipe, there is a substantial population, between 7,000-8,000, spread across the coast and hidden in the cliffs over the city. A high population of deportees gives a roughness to city. There is no immediate threat of violence or crime toward tourists, but women in particular may find it uncomfortable to venture into Quemada Guincho and Fajãzinho as they will receive very forward and sometimes threatening attention. Walking at night may not be a problem, but is not recommended.

If you travel to Mosteiros by car, you may find it small and insular, but be sure to get out of the city into the higher reaches. It is possible to climb up Feijoal in 15 minutes on a steep path beginning to the left of the *Câmara*. When you arrive, you will find an entirely different community, lush, humid and much cooler from a near constant cover of clouds. The turn off the road to Pai António and the *Miradouro* ("view of gold" lookout point) leads up to the foot of one of the few forests in Cape Verde, *Floresta de Monte Velha* (Forest of Monte Velha) where you will find coffee plantations and be able to spot a few endemic plants.

If you take the four hour hike down from Chã, you will pass through the *Floresta de Monte Velha* and experience the variety of micro-climates that exist on Fogo. The hike begins in the hot sun across the barren volcanic rock of the crater. After about 45 minutes, you will find yourself walking on a path bordered by trees imported from all over the world in an effort at reforestation. The descent begins above the clouds in a semi-lush forest with man-made steps that give the knees a bit of respite and make the loose soil more manageable. Keep your eyes open for *dragoeira* trees as you walk through the mist and enter coffee and banana plantations with scattered houses and a few cows tied off the path.

IMPORTANT INFORMATION

Bank In Mosteiros, you will find BCA and Caixa Económica within Igreja. All banks are open Monday-Friday from approximately 8:00-15:00.

Health Post *Posto Sanitário* There is a hospital being built between Quemada Guincho and Fajãzinho that is not yet complete. The health post is located in Igreja. Tel: 283.1034

Post Office *Correios* Open Monday-Friday, in the main *praça* across from the police station.

Police *Polícia*: Down from the *Câmara* at the top of the main *praça*.

TACV Mosteiros Impossible to miss in the main *praça*, the office is open from 8:00-12:00, 14:00-16:00. Tel: 283.1033

WIFI: WiFi is available in the *praça* by the police station.

Myguy Internet Café

Started with the help of U.S. Peace Corps volunteer Dave Trainer, MyGuy internet café, named after the quirky head of business, made affordable internet and international calls possible for the population of Queimada Guincho and surrounding zones. Tel: 972.3007

WHAT TO DO

Wine Sampling

If you drive in from Cova Figueira, you will pass through Achada Grande and Mosteiros Tras. These are more rural areas of Mosteiros with cooler air and a quieter feel. In Achada Grande, you can try to stop by **Ca' Eduino** (Eduino's House). A former resident of Chã, Eduino will, on occasion, serve up samples of his homemade wine and will always welcome the sale of any surplus. Call ahead for a guaranteed visit. *Tel: 283.2793*

The Wild Atlantic

While it is sometimes possible to swim in a few quiet coves, be sure to watch the current before venturing in. The ocean around Fogo is particularly notorious for strong currents and dangerous tides. If you cannot swim, the ocean is still a treat. Be sure to sit on the wall on the stretch of road that connects Igreja with Quimada Guincho beyond the Shell station. Here, the waves crash on the rocky coast and the sound of the water rushing back out through the gaps in the rocks is something quite wonderful.

Beyond Fajãzinho, along a winding path you will find **Praia de Baleia**— Whale Beach. Sometimes good for swimming, it is the cliffside hike that will take your breath away. Be warned that there are sometimes falling rocks.

Artesanato 🖐

Ask around for Tony or call him at Tel: 995.0836. This energetic young man has been working to develop an art education program at the CEJ (local youth center). There is a studio of sorts set up, but without funding, they do what they can with what they have. It is difficult in many places to get art or souvenirs that are genuine to Cape Verde, but Tony makes a variety of crafts, including wood carvings, paintings and some recycled artifacts that he is willing to sell.

WHERE TO EAT

In addition the restaurants at the *pensões*, there are a few good places to get something to eat. A plate of the day is generally available at the smaller restaurants. It is always a safe bet and fairly regulated in regards to price. If that doesn't appeal to you, you may find yourself forced to eat in one of the hotels as they have a tendency to have more supplies readily available.

In the evening, head to the kiosk looking out over the ocean on the Queimada Guincho side of town. You can look out over the ocean and enjoy the moist air or, if you are lucky, there might be music playing a little bit of a crowd milling about. Simple snacks are available and plate of the day style meals.

In Igreja, around the corner from the *Posto Sanitário* (health post) is **Restaurant Beleza**. It is unmarked and off the beaten path, so ask around. Here you will find lunch and dinner for 200$ a plate if you're willing to eat what is provided. **Fogo Food** offers similar options around the corner from the pharmacy, but the food tends to be a little better at Beleza.

WHERE TO STAY

Tchon de Café Across from the Shell, it's one of the few established *pensões*. All amenities are available though there is variation between new and older rooms. Treat yourself to a coffee from beans grown on the land of the family. Prices vary depending on number of guests and use of hot water. $-$$ *Tel: 283.110; m. 992.7262*

Pensão/Restaurant Christine This large *pensão* is located across from the *Câmara*, but there is also an apartment style room available down the street and around the corner by the ocean. You will find a variety of rooms here, including basic rooms with shared bathroom and no A/C. As amenities increase, so does the price. The daughter, Vanessa, speaks excellent English and Portuguese and a bit of French. $-$$ *Tel: 283.1045*

Piramide There are four simple rooms here, but they are well maintained and have excellent light. The food here is excellent. It is rumored to be the best place for a 200$ plate of *cachupa*, and *prato-de-dia* plates are served in heaping portions. $-$$ *Tel: 283.1395, m. 992.6584*

MOVING ON

On the way out of town, you will pass the abandoned airstrip and a hospital project that has been years in the making. For those walking, the climb out is steep and doesn't really level at all until you pass through Atalaia and return to the *conselho* of São Filipe in Campana Baixo, a cluster of houses along the descending road that fills up once a year in February for one of the largest community festivals on Fogo. From here the road winds in and out and up and down along agave lined cliffs. It can become disorienting, giving the impression that the car is not making progress but actually backtracking.

Salinas

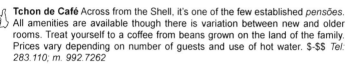

In the dip between São Jorge and Galinheiro is a turn toward the coast that will take you to Salinas. If you are looking for a place to get in the water, Salinas might be one of your only options. Don't come expecting a sandy paradise, but rather a dark, beautiful cove. A large grotto extends over half of the inlet and guards a small pool. At times, the water is fairly calm in this protected cove. There are some visible rocks, but caution will prevent any unavoidable scrapes.

Salinas is mainly used by fishermen from the surrounding villages as a launching point, but it can also be popular during the weekends and summer as a spot for group trips. The festival at Salinas is May 19th and is

Fogo

full of music, drinking and dancing. At least one fatality occurs every year as the someone in the crowd drinks a bit too much and dares to swim. If you choose to attend, use caution as the way out is long and steep.

The Second Tier

In addition to the road that wraps around the island, there is a second tier of road running along the southwestern half of the island at a higher elevation. The houses and communities existing above are frequently out of sight of the road below.

SÃO LOURENÇO

It is difficult to say if this small village is more popular for the large church or for the large soccer field. There is a constant influx of people on the weekends for either religion, but not much happening otherwise. On August 10, however, the village celebrates its festival drawing crowds from throughout the island.

CHÃ DO MONTE

Here you will find one of the oldest Baobab trees on the island of Fogo, located right before the road forks leading toward Chã to the right and Curral Grande to the left. If you bear left at the fork, you pass through a series of towns gradually increasing in elevation. The road itself ends in Monte Preto, but there is a path that continues down through a *ribeira* and leads to Campanas de Cima. High above Campana Baixo, this "twin city" exists, almost completely cut off from the rest of the world. From here it is possible to hike up to Chã das Caldeiras and vice versa.

Festivals on Fogo

January 20 – São Sebastião

February 17-19 – in Campana Baixo

April 2 – Festival commemorating 1995 eruption in Chã das Caldeiras

April 27-May 1 – Festa de Nhô São Filipe in São Filipe

June 24 – São João (various locations) Many fesitvals throughout the month

June 29 – São Pedro

Second Sunday in July – Santa Rainha de Cabo Verde in Chã das Caldeiras

August 5 – Nossa Senhora do Socorro at the Igreja de Nossa Senhora do Soccoro

August 10 – in São Lourenço

August 15 – Assunção (Assumption of Mary) in Mosteiros

November 1 – All Saint's Day (various locations)

November 24 – Santa Catarina in Cova Figueira

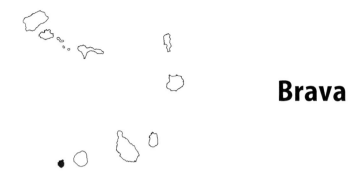

Brava

Looking out from the southern half of the neighboring volcanic island of Fogo, Brava is almost always visible, standing alone and keeping watch toward the western waters. It is said that Brava is the bride of Fogo because on most days, a thick veil of clouds cover the mountainous ridges of Brava. On a clear day it is possible to see houses that litter the mountainside of Brava and at night a string of lights serves as a reminder that there is a small world that exists on the otherwise mysterious rock.

Brava, like all the other islands, possesses a style entirely its own. As they would say in Cape Verde, *Brava é dificil* (Brava is difficult), but what makes it difficult to get to is also what gives this remote island its charm. Hidden and removed from the everyday bustle, life seems to happen here entirely removed from the rest of the world. If you are looking for excitement, Brava is not the place to look—the exception being the festivities for São João in June. If, however, you are looking to take a step back from the stress and chaos that seeps into your daily routine and savor the moments of life, living slowly for a bit, Brava is the island for you.

GEOGRAPHY

Brava is more than just the bride of Fogo, this smaller, slightly older island is separated by a channel only a few hundred meters deep. Some of the oldest rocks on Fogo are found on the western side of the island facing Brava where very similar rocks have been found. Though there have not been recent eruptions on Brava, residents occasionally experience mild tremors and the most recent volcanic cones only date back roughly 10,000 years. This could explain the small size of this 64 sq km island.

HISTORY

Brava was discovered on June 24, 1462—the saint's day for São João Baptista, for whom the island was originally named. The name was later changed to *Brava*, Portuguese for brave, or in Kriolu, *Brabo* for wild.

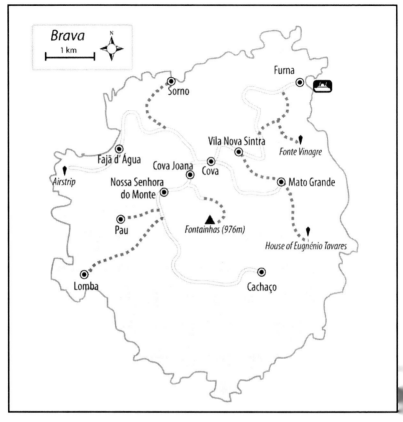

Like most of the other islands, Brava was not populated until many years after its discovery. There is a legend that Brava was first inhabited by a young Portuguese aristocrat and his peasant lover. There is also proof that some of the first settlers were fishermen from the Azores and Madeira as early as 1578. Fajã d' Água was used as a port, but most settlers opted to live high in the plentiful mountains.

Even during the early years, Brava was overlooked. It was virtually untouched by the slave trade and though Brava was touched by the greedy hands of Sir Francis Drake, it was immediately released when he failed to find the few settlers living up in the mountains.

It wasn't until the late 1600s that the population began to swell in establishing towns. When Fogo erupted in 1680, many fled the fiery island by the boatload and less returned. Despite this influx, life on Brava remained quiet and contained with a population of less than 3,000 until well into the 1700s.

Though it remained overlooked by much of the Cape Verdean economy, Brava began building its own interests elsewhere. Whaling ships from New England began stopping on this tiny island to rest and restock. It wasn't long before the seaworthy men of Brava were recruited to help in this trans-Atlantic enterprise.

In 1843, an American consul was established and a secondary school was added to the local infrastructure a few years later. This began the development of the Cape Verdean diaspora in the United States and established what has been a long time relationship between the two lands. The once overlooked island became more appealing and the population began once again to grow. Despite lack of much work on the island, the economy grew as well from the increasing amounts of immigrants who had settled and begun working in the U.S. and elsewhere.

Brava is still considered a pleasant place, but has returned to being fairly overlooked by the rest of the country. As the depression took hold of the US in the 1930s, many immigrants returned to the then fruitful island. Tragedy struck when the land began to dry along with remittances. When drought hit Cape Verde in the 1940s, famine claimed the lives of many of those who had returned. Though the population had reached a peak of close to 10,000 in the 1900s, it dropped dramatically and now hovers between 6,000 and 7,000.

LOGISTICS

Though there was once an airport nestled in Fajã d' Água, service was stopped years ago due to unpredictable and treacherous crosswinds. Currently, it is only possible to get to Brava by boat from São Filipe and sometimes from Praia. The schedule varies and can be affected by weather, availability of boats and a variety of other factors. Like other ferry service on Cape Verde, all schedules are subject to change, so flexibility and patience is key when choosing this route. "Vomidrine" is also recommended as the rough waters and long boat ride can cause nausea and all around discomfort. The motion sickness pills are readily available at any pharmacy and are highly recommended.

From Praia

Cape Verde Navalis "The Marina Princess" has been running since late 2009 and makes the Praia-Fogo-Brava circuit four days a week. Slightly faster than the older the older boats, the trip from Praia to Fogo takes just over four hours and from Praia to Brava just under five. The agency is located on the corner across the street from Sucupira. *Tel: 262.1023*

Agentur S.T.M. (Praia) S.T.M. is the main agency in Praia, but the office has been moved off of Plateau. This agency sells tickets for the *Praia Aguada,* which runs the Praia-Brava-Fogo circuit twice a week. Not to be confused with the *Praia D'Agua* which strictly runs between Fogo and Brava. *Tel: 261.2564*

From Fogo

Agenmar Located in the Rodrigo/TACV *praça* (square) next to the ice cream shop, do not expect special or even necessarily helpful treatment. The men that work there can be a bit rough around the edges.. They will sell you a ticket to Brava, but you will need to purchase your return ticket while in Brava, making it impossible to plan an itinerary. However, tickets are 500$ and the trip itself is less than an hour. *Tel: 281.1012, m. 991.4706; open 8:00-12:00, 14:30-17:00*

From Brava

Agência Brava Located off the main street in the vicinity of the *Mastro*, Senhor Pedro is responsible for the sale of tickets. He is a little easier to deal with than the men in Fogo, but once again, do not expect priority seating or special treatment. The hours are fairly consistent, but doors close when the boat is arriving or leaving to head down to the pier. *Tel: 285.1270, m. 993.3958; open 8:00-12:00, 14:30-17:00*

ARRIVING IN BRAVA: FURNA

The port town of Furna is not immediately visible while approaching and it is hard to imagine where the boat will land until the little port town creeps into view. This sleepy town of less than 1,000 is nestled between dramatic crags that drop straight into the ocean and its limits are clearly defined by steep rock faces only a few hundred meters back from the water.

When the boat comes in, Furna comes to life. Cars from all over the island come down carrying departing passengers and cargo. For a short while, the streets fill up with people with fish to sell and families reuniting on the pier. Then the boat is left at dock to unload, passengers in transit head into the small town in search of stable ground and a bite to eat. The restaurant looking out over the water fills up and the many *lojas* (general stores) quickly sell their bread, cheese, beer, juice and water. Once the cars begin to leave, you can feel the blanket of quiet closing in around you.

If you intend to walk to Vila or try to arrange a place to stay in Furna, you can relax and enjoy the peaceful atmosphere of a slow coastal town. However, if you still need to arrange a room in Vila or are in a rush to arrive, be sure to arrange a car when you first get off the boat to ensure that you make it. A ride to Vila in a public car should only cost 200-250. If you aren't careful or would like to charter a car, it will be upwards of 500$.

EXCURSIONS

If you head to Brava from Fogo, it is possible to arrange a guided excursion around the island with **Agnelo** from D'jar Fogo or through **Zebra Tours** (see pg 210). Currently, there are no guides or tours available on the island of Brava, though there are a number of people that speak English who would happily show you around for a small fee. Ask around at your hotel or arrange a guide on your own. Drivers are also happy to take you around, though they may or may not be able to communicate. Keep an eye out for the driver **Pepe** (m. 999.9764), as he's recommended.

Vila Nova Sintra

Leaving Furna, you come face to face with the sheer mountainside. The road to Vila Nova Sintra is long, steep and, though it is easy to lose count, it is rumored to have 98 curves. Secure yourself well in the back of the truck as you will be rolled from side to side as the truck weaves around the curves. Just when you think you will never arrive, you round a bend and some houses come into view. The road splits off in three directions and gives an immediate feel of a much larger place, but as you begin to explore, it quickly becomes clear that your feelings have been misled.

Vila Nova Sintra, named for the historic borough of Sintra in Portugal, is the central town on Brava. It is beautifully designed, well maintained, charming and quaint. Everyone is friendly and welcoming and you will likely hear English peppered in various conversations. You can expect to encounter open curiosity about your presence as a *strangeiro* (foreigner).

In the center of town there is a large *praça* from which the main roads disperse like the points on a compass. It makes it impossible to drive straight through town, but because it is so small, there is no need to get directly from one end to the other. If anything, the *praça* filled with planted flowers, plenty of benches and a scale model of the island is a welcomed detour. It is possible to get a bit disoriented walking around Vila, but impossible to get lost. The roads leading out of town are marked, and the rest of the roads lead back to the *praça*. The planted streets give Brava a refreshing atmosphere and offer an opportunity to glimpse the rare *Dragoeiro* tree.

During the day, the streets are often filled with people going about their business and more people watching people going about their business. Hanging around and sitting on the wall or a bench is a large part of the culture in Cape Verde, and that is no different in Brava. Women travelling alone or with other women will notice that they are given extra attention. In most cases, attention comes in the form of direct stares and hissing that sounds offensive, but is as much a part of the culture as *cachupa* and the "thumbs-up." To avoid unwanted attention, the best thing to do is just ignore the source of the attention. This may be difficult when you are approached, and especially on Brava as you may be approached and spoken to in English.

Eugénio Tavares (1867-1930)

Eugénio Tavares is an important figure not only to Brava, but to Cape Verde as well. He used his education and words to take a musical style unique to Cape Verde, *morna,* and capture an essence that is so deeply founded in the culture—*sodadi (saudade)* a word and idea that is difficult to translate. The literal meaning is homesickness or longing, but it is a word that can only be understood by people forced to leave their families and homes in search of a better future. Tavares is most famous for his *morna* "Hora di Bai" (time to go) about preparing to leave knowing the pain that would stay. He also wrote about the power of love in "Força de Cretcheu," literally meaning, the power of love.

Ca tem nada na es bida	There is nothing in this life
Mas grande que amor	Greater than love
Se Deus ca tem medida	Even if God is immeasurable
Amor inda é maior.	Love is less so.
Maior que mar, que céu	Greater than the ocean, the sky
Mas, entre tudo cretcheu	But among all great loves
De meu inda é maior	My love is yet more grand

- *Learn and see more at www.eugeniotavares.org*

Brava

IMPORTANT INFORMATION

Bank BCA, Open Monday-Friday

Health Post *Posto Sanitário* There are no facilities for serious health issues, but the post can provide bandages or other small services. Tel: 285.1130

Pharmacy *Farmácia Irene* Located right off the main *praça*. Tel: 285.1223

Post Office *Correios*: Open Monday-Friday

Police Polícia: Tel: 285.1132

TACV Brava The TACV "office" is up by the Residencial Nazare. You will not be booking flights to or from Brava, but you might need to change a flight if you end up stuck there. Tel: 285.1192

STAYING IN TOUCH

MC Multichoice Local *papelaria* (paper store), also offers internet service and advertises tourist information. Tel: 285.2287

Biblioteca (library) Offers internet for 150$/hour amongst other services.

WHAT TO DO

Beyond spending time in the *praça*, there is not much really to *do* in Vila. The house of **Eugénio Tavares** is located up by Residencial Nazare and marked by a worn and fading statue. There have been plans to open a museum and according to some sources, it is already open (see website: www.eugeniotavares.org).

If you visit during the months of June and July, there is no shortage of festivals. The festival of São João is almost larger than the island as it commemorates not only the saint's day, but the discovery of this tiny island. The *maestro* (mast or may pole) is across from the boat agency and stands watch above the village of Horta. The rest of the year, it is a lonely, forgotten relic, but during the festival it is brightly decorated with flowers and food. Adults and children alike attempt to climb the pole to reach the riches and at the right time, it is cut and becomes free-for-all. There is music, dancing and food for all during the time of the festival.

WALK ABOUT

There are many places near Vila that are easily accessible by foot and make interesting destinations. There is a path that leads to **Fonte Vinagre**, a natural water source that has a high mineral content and acidity, giving it the taste of vinegar. *Bravenses* (people of Brava) believe the water to have medicinal properties, likely attributed to the high mineral content.

There are a number of *Miradouros* (lookout points) in various higher points of the island that, when there are no clouds, give a stunning view of Fogo or off into the Atlantic. From these spots (while ignoring the modern graffiti) it is possible to imagine what it must have been like for the wife or child of an immigrant or member of the whaling crew to watch out over the vast expanse of ocean, wondering what the future would hold.

You can also walk to the house that Eugnénio Tavares built to the far East of Vila through Mato Grande and Baleia. The path can be rough in areas, so it is best to bring water and verify the trail as you go.

Ilha das Flores - The Island of Flowers

Despite the drought that plagues this West African nation, Brava is still known as the island of flowers. The veil of fog that seems to permanently cap the smallest inhabited island keeps the soil more moist than other windswept islands. The roads in Vila are lined with planted gardens, bougainvillea, plumeira, jasmine, hibiscus and rescued dragoeiro trees.

WHERE TO EAT

Because of the low level of tourism and lack of culture of eating out at restaurants, literally everywhere operates on an "advance notice" basis. The plates are typical to Cape Verde (rice, meat/fish, beans or cucumber/tomato salad and french fries) unless you request something special (which may or may not be available). As you wander the streets during the day, be sure to stop in, ask what there is and place an order. You can try to walk in at mealtime, but you will likely wait upwards of an hour for food. It is also generally possible to arrange food where you are staying. Brava, like much of Cape Verde, is known for fresh fish as many make their living on the plentiful ocean and may be your best option. Reservations are highly recommended for all restaurants.

> **Pensão Paulo** Known more for simple meals and good breakfast, Paulo will be willing to prepare what you request-pending availability. Can be less expensive and more readily available than other places. $$ *Tel: 2851312*
>
> **O Sossego** Located a little out of the center of town off the main road, there is a quiet, laid back atmosphere. The meal may be lacking in ingenuity, but makes up for it in quantity. $$ *Tel: 285.1484, m.995.3436*
>
> **O Poeta** O Poeta is possibly the most appealing option with an outdoor sitting area and open ambience. If you forget to order in advance, the time will likely pass more quickly while sitting out among the planted gardens watching the movement in the streets. Has been known to have live music in the evening on occasion, swing by on the weekends or ask around. $$ *Tel: 285.2640*
>
> **Bar Veronica** Bar Veronica may or may not have meals. It was closed during research because the owner was in the United States. This may be an occasional problem with any of the bars/restaurants and possibly *pensãos* so be sure to check in advance and have a back-up plan. $ *Tel: 285.1666*

Casa Mansa

There are a multitude of buildings with this written above the doorway. Mansa came from West Africa with a fortune and prospered in Brava. He marked his patrimony with his name. The blue building in the *praça* serves food and drinks in a typical Cape Verdean fashion—heaping piles of rice and beans with a small side of meat for a reasonable price ($$).

WHERE TO STAY

As is the way with many things in Cape Verde, price is negotiable. If you know someone or have the ability to arrange a room in advance, chances are you will pay less. Realize that it is a small place and the proprietors, in the end, are more interested in the business than sticking with an estab-

Brava

lished price. Ask around in Fogo before leaving to see if someone will help you out (taxi drivers or hotel proprietors). You can go through a travel agency in Fogo (see pg 210), but that may or may not work in your favor. Be sure to agree on a price for the duration before you begin your stay.

Residencial Nazare Located across from the weather worn statue of Eugenio Tavares, Nazare is locally proclaimed the "nicest place" to stay in Vila. Well established, clean and professional. There are five rooms and a suite style area for larger groups, breakfast included. $$ *Tel: 285.1375, 285.1547, 993.1162*

Pousada Vivi's Place Formerly the Pousada Municipal, the building has been renovated and modernized. Vivi lives alternately in Cape Verde and the U.S. and speaks English, Portuguese and Kriolu. There is a large veranda where meals are served and a small sitting area. Rooms are clean and welcoming. Price vary depending on number of guests, breakfast included. $$ *Tel: 285.2562, m. 994.4033; pousadavivisplace@hotmail.com*

Pensão Paulo Paulo's place has gained notoriety for a variety of reasons. The eight rooms are handsomely furnished with an odd collection of old furniture. It is an old building and an established *pensão*, but in need of some revitalizing. Paulo will literally fight for your business, so if you are looking to bargain, this may be your best bet. Not all guests, however, have left happy. $$. *Tel: 285.1312*

Around Brava

Brava is small, so it is possible to visit everything by car in less than a day. There is public transportation to and from Vila once a day to most areas. Look around the *praça* for cars or ask the proprietor where you are staying. Either way, a good bet is to get an early start. Cars will drive up and down around the *praça*. The best way to explore Brava, however, is probably by foot. It is possible to spend many days walking through the more remote areas of Brava, but even the most remote trips can be fit in a day. The walk from Vila to Fajã D' Água can be done in less than three hours as it is largely downhill. All the villages are within walking distance, though the trip may be a bit grueling with steep gradients and uneven cobblestone.

FAJÃ D' ÁGUA

It is possible to rent a car to visit Fajã d' Água for approximately 1000$ each way from Vila or take public transportation for approximately 200-250. It would be wise to begin looking a little after 7:00, though the car may not leave with any sense of rush. If you do not intend to spend the night, inform the driver that you want to return with him and find out when.

Alternatively, it is also possible to walk to Fajã d' Água. The road leaves from the top of Vila. When you pass through Cova, there is a brief detour to the left, but continue on and beyond Cova, you want to bear right at the fork and continue to the coast (approximately 4 km).

Fajã di Água is famous for the role it has played in the history of Brava, but it has gained notoriety as one of the most beautiful bays in Cape Verde. This hidden cove is arguably one of the most stunning secrets of the archipelago; it offers a perpetually green oasis and a leisurely day of fishing, hiking or exploring the "ruins" of the former airstrip. The infamous *grogue* is also locally produced in Fajã d' Água (indulge at your own risk).

Where to Stay & Eat

Food is available at both of the hotels, Pensão Sol na Baia is more expensive, but is made with ingenuity.

Motel Fajã d' Água (Pensão Burgos) The clear choice for a traveler with a budget. Located along the coastal road, the simple rooms all have access to the balcony with a spectacular view of the open ocean. $$ *Tel: 285.1321*

Pensão Sol na Baia Foreign owned and operated. Offers the comforts and convenience expected of a more expensive option. The four double rooms are more expensive than Motel Fajã d' Água, but full board is available. $$$ *Tel: 285.2070; pensao_sol_na_baia@hotmail.com*

THE LEFT FORK

If you choose to bear left at the fork beyond Cova, you will enter the heart of the island and pass a series of small villages, some worthy of note.

Located about 5 km from Nova Sintra, the small village of **Nossa Senhora do Monte** offers further removal from the happenings of daily life. During the rainy season, the island transforms into a lush garden, and the semi-deserted (due to emigration) country-side becomes almost enchanted. It is possible to stay in nearby Cova Joana at **Pensão José/Casa da Isabel** ($-$$, Tel: 285.1081), a small homestyle Bed & Breakfast run by a Cape Verdean couple that lived in the U.S. for a number of years. A nice, quiet place to stay.

The highest point on little Brava, **Fontainhas** is easily attainable and, on a clear day, offers a spectacular view of the island as well as Fogo off in the distance.

One of few villages with access to the water, a large percentage of the island's fishing is focused in the charming, but evidently impoverished village of **Lomba**. Located inland, there is a path descending to the ocean where a small bay shelters the boats of the fishermen.

The end of the road from Vila, **Cachaço** is reliant on farming and a living example of the failure of agriculture to adequately support the needs of Cape Verdeans. Despite the rich soil, the hunger and poverty here is evident.

Festivals on Brava

January 6 – Twelfth Night, celebrated most everywhere

June 13 – Santo António; the start of festivals leading up to São João.

June 24 – São João; largely celebrated in Vila

July – There are festivals throughout the month of July. Ask around to find out where/when.

August – Nossa Senhora do Monte; Furna hosts a large festival the second weekend

August 15 – Nossa Senhora da Graça

Kriolu Survival Guide

As a Lusophone country, Portuguese, Spanish or any romantic language base will help you get around, but it is Kriolu that is widely spoken and understood. Written Portuguese can be easily deciphered by English speakers as many words share similar roots and the number of English speakers is slowly growing as Cape Verde makes an effort to open itself to visitors. A small Portuguese dictionary can be helpful.

Kriolu di Kabu Verde

The Kriolu of Cape Verde grew from the mixture of Portuguese with various African dialects. It was not until recently (proposed in 1994) that initiative was taken to standardize an alphabet and written form of the language and it is still debated and modified today.

Special thanks to **Lanuage Link**, a professional language consultancy and training firm based in Cape Verde, for their contribution to this language guide. You may find more information about language link at www.languagelinkcv.com, or by contacting them directly: languagelinkcv@gmail.com, Tel: 238.262.5101

Due to the geographic separation of islands, pronunciation, form and vocabulary varies from island to island and often from one isolated town to another.

The Kriolu of the Barlavento islands differs sharply from that of the Sotavento, leading to a debate over the merit of two standard languages. In the northern islands, words tend to be shortened and more abrupt, while on southern islands great emphasis is placed on pronouncing the word in full and, particularly on Fogo, accenting it by extension and variation in tone.

Kriolu guide

PRONUNCIATION KEY/ALUPEC

ALUPEC (Alfabeto Unificado para a Escrita do Cabo-Verdiano)
The alphabet created from Kriolu is a phonetically based language. The
majority of words are pronounced as they are written, with variations in
local pronunciation.

A/a B/b D/d Dj/dj E/e F/f G/g H/h I/i J/j K/k L/l Lh/lh
M/m N/n Nh/nh O/o P/p R/r S/s T/t Tx/tx U/u V/v X/x Z/z

Most consonants have a similar sound to that of their English counterparts,
but there are a few variations listed below.

Consonants	Example	Sounds like...
Dj	A**dj**uda – help	J – **j**ump
Lh	I**lh**a – island	l-y – cal**l-y**ou
Nh	**Nh**a – my/Senhora	n-y – ca**n-y**ou
Tx	**Tx**uba - rain	Ch – **ch**erry
X	**X**ingua – chewing gum	Sh – **sh**ort

Vowels	Example	Sounds like...
á	k**á**la – close/glue	Ah - sof**a**
a	Pra**i**a – capital / beach	Uh - b**a**r
é	kan**é**ta - pen	Eh - b**e**t
e	M**e**du - fear	A - b**ai**t
ê	**Ê** posivel – it's possible	Ey – h**ey**
i	M**i**dju - corn	Ee - m**ee**t
ó	B**ó**ka - mouth	Oh - b**oa**t
o	B**o**m - good	O - ad**o**re
ão	P**ão** (with nasal ending) - bread	Ow/aw - ab**ou**t
u	M**u**da - move/change	Oo - b**oo**t

PERSONAL PRONOUNS

Nominative/Objective	Possessive
I/me- N/Ami	My – nha/ d'mi

You – Bô/Bu, (informal)
    Nhô (m)/Nha (f) (formal)
	Your – di bo
	    Di Nhô/Di Nha

He/Him /She/Her It – Ael/Ela	His/Hers – d'ele/d'ela
We/Us – Nôs	Our – d'nôs
You – Nhôs (South) Bizots (North)	Your – d'nhôs
They/Them – Aes/Eles	Their – ses / d'eles

COMMON TERMINOLOGY AND PHRASES
Courteous Expressions

Good morning!	Bon dia!
Good afternoon!	Bo tardi!
Good evening!	Bo noiti!
Good night!	Bo noiti!
See you later/	Ti maz tardi/
tomorrow/soon!	manhan/ Maz un poku
Hello, goodbye.	Oi, Txau
Welcome!	Benvindu
Have a good day!	Bon dia pa bo
Yes, thank you.	Sin, obrigadu
No, thank you.	Nau, obrigadu
Let me introduce you to...	Txan prezentau na...
Nice to meet you!	Prazer.
How are you?	Modi ki bu/ nhô/ nha sta?
How are you(plural)?	Modi ki nhôs sta?
What's your name?	Modi ki bu /nhô/ nha txoma?
How old are you?	Kantu anu ki bu /nhô/ nha ten?
Very well.	Bon
Thank you, and you?	Obrigadu e bo/ nhô/ nha
My name is...	N' txoma ...
Please?	Favor
Thank you.	Obrigadu
You're Welcome.	Nada
It's okay.	Ka ta fazi nada
Forget it.	Skesi
Excuse me.	Kon lisensa.
Pardon.	
I'm sorry.	Diskulpan.

Numbers

One	um	seventeen	dezasete
Two	dois	eighteen	dezoito
Three	três	nineteen	dezanove
Four	quarto	twenty	vente

Five	cinco	twenty-one	vente e um
Six	seis	twenty-two	vente e dois...
Seven	sete	thirty	trinta
Eight	oito	forty	quarenta
Nine	nove	fifty	cinquenta
Ten	dez	sixty	sessenta
eleven	onze	seventy	setenta
twelve	doze	eighty	oitenta
thirteen	treze	ninety	noventa
fourteen	catorze	one hundred	cem
fifteen	quinze	one thousand	mil
sixteen	dezaseis	2,500	dois mil e quinentos

Directions

Right	direta
Left	eskera
Up	pa riba
Down	pa baixo
Straight ahead	pa frente
Behind	pa tras
Next to	djunto di/ ao lado de
Near by	perto di
Far from	lonji di
Before	antes di
After	depois di
A lot	txeu
A little	um poku

Days

Day	dia
Week	semana
Month	mês
Year	ano
Morning	di manhan
Afternoon	di tarde
Night	di noite
Monday	segunda-feira
Tuesday	terça-feira
Wednesday	quarta-feira
Thursday	quinta-feira
Friday	sexta-feira
Saturday	sabado
Sunday	domingo

Months

January	janeiro
February	fevreiro
March	março
April	abril
May	maio
June	junho
July	julho
August	agosto
September	setembro
October	outubro
November	novembro
December	dezembro

General Phrases

Yes/no/never/sometimes.	Sin, Ayan/Nau/nunka/az bes
I don't know.	N' ka sabi.

Impossible.	Inposivel/ Ka ta da.
It's possible.	Ë posivel.
A lot/ a little/ nothing	Txeu/ poku/ nada
Can you help me please?	Bu/ Nhô/ Nha podi djudan favor?
Can you tell me please?	Bu/ Nhô/ Nha podi flan favor?
Can you show me please?	Bu/ Nhô/ Nha podi mostran favor?
Do you speak English/	Bu/ Nhô/ Nha ta papia
French/ Italian/ German/	Ingles/ Franses/ Italianu
Spanish/ Portuguese/	Alimon/ Spanhol/ Portugês
Creole?	Kriolu?
Where are you from?	Bo/ Nhô/ Nha ê di undi?
I am from America/	Ami ê di Merka/ Inglatera/
England/ Spain/ France/	Spanha/ Fransa/ Itália/ Alimanha/
Italy/ Germany/ Cape Verde.	Kabu Verdi.
Can you give me...?	Bu/ Nhô/ Nha podi dan?
What would you like?	Kuze ki bu/ nhô/ nha krê?
Do you need any help?	Bu/ Nhô/ Nha mesti djuda?
I need help.	N mesti djuda.
What does this mean?	Kuze ki ke li ta signifika?
Are you sure?	Bu/ Nhô/ Nha ten serteza?
Call me on the telephone.	Tilifonan.
It's important.	Ê inportanti.
Please wait a moment.	Spera un kuzinha favor.
Do you understand?	Bu/ Nhô/ Nha ntendi?
Yes, I understand.	Sin, n'sta ntendi.
No, I don't understand.	Nau, n' ka sta ntendi.
Please speak slowly.	Papia divagár favor.
I'm lost, how can I get	N' sta perdedu, modi ki n' podi
to...?	bai pa...?
Listen.	Obi li.
I'm listening.	N' sa ta obi.

Kriolu guide

Hurry up!	Faxi.
Urgent!	Urgenti.
Help!	Nhôs djudan.
Call a taxi.	Txoman un táxi.
I would like to make a formal complaint against...	N' kria daba kexa di ...
I have been robbed!	Es dan kasu bódi!
	Es furtan.
	Es asaltan.
Call the police!	Txoma pulicia!
Come with me.	Ben.
I would like...	N' kria...
We would like...	Nu kria...
What a pity!	Forti pena!
How ugly/beautiful!	Forti feiu/bointu/a!
How interesting!	Forti intresanti!
How lucky!	Forti sorti!
Stop!	Pára!
I'm very happy/sad.	N' sta rei di contenti/tristi.

Relationships and Family

Have you met my friends/girlfriend/boyfriend?	Bu/ Nhô/ Nha dja konxi nhas amigus/ nha pikéna/namorado?
How is your wife/husband?	Modi ki bu mudjer/maridu sta?
	Modi ki mudjer/maridu di nhô/nha sta?
Are you married or single?	Bu/ Nhu ê kazadu o solteru?
I'm married.	Ami ê kazadu.
I'm single.	Ami ê solteru.
My father, mother, and grandparents live with me.	Nha pai, mai, i nhas avoz ta vivi ku mi.
How many children do you have?	Kantu fidju ki bu/ nhô/ nha ten?
I have two sons and one daughter.	N' ten dos fidju mátxu i un fémia.

Would you like to have Dinner with me?	Bu/ Nhô/ Nha krê janta ku mi?
No, I can't.	Nau, n' ka podi.
Do you mind if I sit here?	N' podi xinta li?
Where can we meet?	Undi kin u podi encontra?
This is my cousin.	Ke li ê nha primu/a.
My parents are in Praia.	Nhas paiz sta na Praia.
My aunt went to the beach.	Nha tia ba mar.

Travel Expressions

I would like to make a reservation for two plane tickets for São Vicente.	N' krê fazi un rezerva pa dos bilheti di avion pa Son Vicenti.
How much is the fare per person?	Kantu ê presu pa un alguen
How do I pay?	Modi ki n' podi pága?
I would like you to make a reservation in a hotel of three or four stars.	N' ta gostaba di fazi un rezerva na un otel di tres o kuatu strela.
We would like to confirm/ cancel my flight reservation to Fogo.	Nos ta gostaba di konfirma/kansela nha rezerva pa Fogu.
Do you have any pamphlets, Maps, guides?	Nhôs ten algun panfletu, mápa, guias?

Car Rentals

Automobiles	Karus
Rent a car	Rent a kar
I would like to rent a car, with a driver/ without a driver.	N'ta gostaba di luga un karu, ku kondutor/ sen kondutor.
What cars do you have available?	Ki karus ki Nhu, Nha, Bu, Nhôs ten?
How much is the car rental per day or per kilometer?	Kantu ki ê aluguer pa dia o pa kilómtru?
And for a weekend?	I pa fin di simána?

Is the insurance included?	Siguru sta inkluídu?
When can I pick it up?	Kandê ki N'podi ben buskal?
Do I need to leave a deposit?	N'mesti dexa algun dipózitu?
Is the documentation in the car?	Dukumentus di karu sta dentu del?
Do you have a branch in the city...?	Ten algun reprezentanti di nhôs rent a kar na sidadi...?
Could I leave the car there when I get there?	N'podi dexa karu la hóras kin txiga la?

Vocabulary

Cancellation	Kanselamento
Confirmation	Konfirmason
Vacation/Holidays	Féria
Tour guide	Guia
Translator	Tradutor
Itinerary I	tenirario
Tourist Office	Postu di turizmu
Travel Insurance	Siguru di viagi
Visas	Visto
Customs	Alfândega
Exchange	Kambio
Change to	Troka
Travellers' Checks	Cheques di viagem
Money	Dinhero
Airport	Aeroporto
Airplane	Avião
Bus	Autocarro
Taxi	Taxi
Public car	Hiace/Aluguer
Luggage	Bagagi
Driver's license	Karta di konduson
Taxes	Taxaz
Nationality	Nasionalidadi
Name and last name	Nomi i apilidu
Police	Pulisia
Passport	Pasaporti
Road	strada
Path	kaminho
Beach	praia (di mar)
Square	praça
Market	mercado

Town	zona
City	cidade
Mountain	montanha
Valley	ribeira
That man	Kel homi
This woman	Ke li mudjer
Those girl(s)	Kes menina(s)
These boy(s)	Kes rapaz(es) li
Eat	komi
Hungry	ten fome
I'm full	N'sta fartu
Drink	bebi
Have breakfast	toma kafé (breakfast – pequeno almoço)
Lunch	almosu
Dinner	djanta
Beer	cerveja
Wine	vinhu
Water	agua
Bottle	garafa

Menus

Tuna/Wahoo steak	Bife di atum/serra
Rice and shellfish dish	Arroz mariscos
Squid	Lula
Octopus	Polvo
Lobster	Lagosta
Moray eel	Moreia
Cod	Bacalhau
Garopa	Grouper fish
Chicken	Galinha/Frango
Beef steak	Carne di vaca
Pork	Carne di porku
Sausage	Linguiça
Turkey	Peru
Vegetables	Legumes
Onion	Cebola
Cheese	Queijo
Beans	Feijão
Egg	Ovo
Fried	Fritado
Baked	Cozido
Grilled	Grelhado
Sauce	Molho
Dessert	Sobremesa

Kriolu guide